Making It Count

Making It Count

The Improvement of Social Research
and Theory

Stanley Lieberson

UNIVERSITY OF CALIFORNIA PRESS
Berkeley • *Los Angeles* • *London*

University of California Press
Berkeley and Los Angeles, California

University of California Press, Ltd.
London, England

Library of Congress Cataloging in Publication Data

Lieberson, Stanley, 1933–
  Making it count.

  Bibliography: p. 245
  Includes index.
  1. Sociology—Research—Methodology. 2. Social
sciences—Research—Methodology. I. Title.
HM48.L49 1985   301'.072   84-25285
ISBN 0-520-05350-8

Printed in the United States of America

1 2 3 4 5 6 7 8 9

In Memory of My Parents
JACK ZYTNIK LIEBERSON
IDA COHEN LIEBERSON

Contents

Preface

This volume deals with the methodology underlying modern empirical social research. It reviews the inherent nature of such research—its logic, procedures, assumptions, limits, and potential functions. Neither the critical review of present practices nor the proposals for change are fully compatible with any existing school of thought in social science. To minimize needless controversy and misunderstanding, it is important at the outset to trace the origins of the book, what it seeks to accomplish, and what it does not attempt. I am fully sympathetic with the empirical research goals found in much of contemporary American sociology, with its emphasis on rigor and quantification. However, for reasons that will become clearer to the patient reader, I have reluctantly reached the conclusion that many of the procedures and assumptions in this enterprise are of no more merit than a quest for a perpetual-motion machine. Even worse, whereas the latter search is innocuous, some of the normal current practices in empirical social research are actually counterproductive. Good social research, as we now define it, involves criteria and thought processes that are harmful because incorrect empirical conclusions are drawn that lead us to reject good ideas and accept false ones.

Fortunately, it is not necessary to abandon the enterprise and turn to activities that give up on rigorous empirical social research, as some schools would have us believe. Rather, it is necessary to

reconsider the analogies drawn from the natural sciences that under-
lie much of our social research. For these analogies are inappropriate, leading us to pursue impossible models. By reconsidering
these matters, we can approach the potential and limits of social
research in a more fruitful way. This volume is written, then, not in
the spirit of abandonment or bitterness but in an attempt to rethink
the fundamentals underlying the methodology of empirical social
research. In doing this, I believe we will discover a wide array of
empirical research opportunities, avoid traps, and place new
demands on the theories that both drive our research and must
respond to our results.

These conclusions, and the proposals for alternative ways of
thinking about empirical social research, were not reached easily or
lightly. In a sense, I first started to think about the nature of social
research over thirty years ago when, as a college sophomore, I read
Chicago: An Experiment in Social Science Research (T. V. Smith and
Leonard D. White, eds., 1929). The book, then nearly twenty-five
years old, impressed me deeply. Its collection of papers, written by
social scientists at the University of Chicago with a strong sociological bent, waxed enthusiastic about a variety of empirical social
research projects. If the controlled experiments of the natural scientists could not be duplicated in the social world, then the next best
thing would be the many simulated experiments possible in the real
world in which the influence of all significant factors would be
determined and measured. The book's index includes numerous
references to such terms as "laboratories," "measurements," and
"data." Here was a collectivity of scholars doing empirical research
on various facets of society. They were not content to speculate on or
debate the issues but instead approximated natural science procedures to answer the questions. It made good sense to me.

Later, while attending graduate school at Chicago in the mid-
fifties, I experienced my first reservations about these under-
pinnings of social science during a course with the late J. S. Slotkin
on that topic. One of the books assigned to us was the Morris R.
Cohen and Ernest Nagel classic first published in 1934, *An Introduction to Logic and Scientific Method*. It occurred to me even then that
probably very few of the articles I had seen in the research literature

would have received passing marks from Cohen and Nagel, at least as judged by the rigorous scientific procedures expounded in their book. *Why was this the case?*

In 1958, the *American Sociological Review* published a report by the Committee on Research of the American Sociological Society on a three-year project to evaluate research publications. The methods used in seventeen articles published in the two leading journals of the discipline received an average rating' from the Committee almost midway between the categories of "substandard" and "standard"; the yield from the average article likewise fell midway between these two categories, which meant more than "useful hints or suggestions toward solution of problem" but less than a "tentative solution of problem."

It was, of course, very clear to many that empirical research and theory rarely went together in an integral way. Robert K. Merton had contrasted, with much success, the major European theorists who contribute without much empirical basis or rigor with the relatively hard-nosed but piddling contributions from many American sociologists (1957: 439—454). Was there no solution? Why were theory and research so often divorced such that rarely did one seriously affect the other? If empirical research often did not come very close to the ideals of the scientific model and if it did not interact too closely with theory, these were not issues to upset for very long an energetic Ph.D. who was off to do research and obtain answers as best he could. Several years later, as it turned out, Kuhn in 1962 would present a convincing case for the hard sciences that the simple crucial empirical study rarely existed and that these sciences did not really advance in such a simple manner anyway. But that, for the moment, is beside the point.

In recent years, I have come to reflect more and more on the research enterprise and have gradually reached the conclusion that something is "off" somewhere in the system that we follow. Discussions with various colleagues and scholars at other institutions have led me to recognize that I was not alone in this feeling and that others were equally unsure as to the source (albeit there were many who did not share this intuition). An important step for me involved the secondhand comments of a Nobel Prize-winning biologist who, although admiring a specific sociological monograph that he had read, nevertheless wondered why it and most sociological research were confined to explaining away the variance in the observed dependent variable, employing a variety of independent variables of the standard sort. Both the recipient of this query and I puzzled over that one—what could be an alternative approach? The more I thought about it the more I realized how this style was so deeply ingrained in standard empirical social research. If something was wrong about the basic premises of this approach, it was so much a part of our thinking that few would critically examine it. Perhaps, unbeknownst to us, we were following assumptions and procedures that were leading to dead ends.

Pursuit of this clue led me, a number of years later, to new conclusions about the failures and shortcomings of social research. It is not enough that there be more people doing better research—as "better" is currently defined—or that we have scholars who give greater thought to making their rigorous work relevant to important theoretical issues. Likewise, it is not enough to have theorists who dirty their hands with data or even think about the data with which others might work. Rather, there is a radically different interpretation as to why research and theory rarely go together in a very strong way, or why policies based on empirical research evidence seem to backfire as often as they work, or why the results of empirical research so often appear inconclusive. Namely, as presently conceived, it is impossible for empirical research to accomplish what we expect simply because it is based on an analogy with natural science experiments which cannot work.

The aim of this volume, however, is not to justify theory without research (indeed, much of the criticism of empirical social research is equally applicable to the logic underlying many theories). Nor is this a plea for a radical style of sociology in which statistics and quantification are tossed out. Likewise, I abhor arguments for a propositional formalization, as if the difference between sociology and physics would disappear if we were only careful to distinguish our corollaries from theorems, and our theorems from our propositions. Alas, none of the above is my goal. Rather, this book is written with appreciation for the desirability of empirical social research but recognition that a radical reformation is desperately needed in the way we approach it. The aim of this volume is therefore to improve upon the existing logic underlying non-experimental empirical research in sociology. Indeed, it is my contention that some of the present practices are radically off the mark to the point that the logic behind our work is often actually counterproductive.

Since the primary goal is to advance social research and the relevant theories, there are two otherwise attractive tasks that would only be distractions if pursued here. First, no attempt need be made to determine in any formal sense exactly what natural scientists do. One is happy to gain clues and ideas by learning from them, but thoughtless mimicry is bound to be sterile. Second, the interest that philosophers of science might have in the methodological issues is secondary to my concern for those engaged in social research. Again, there is no hard and fast resistance to the use of philosophy's conceptual apparatus when it is helpful. Finally, the response of several very thoughtful scholars to my description of this under-taking merits a special comment. Although prepared to admit that our empirical research procedures may be based on some very shaky assumptions, they saw no point in saying much about this unless superior alternatives are presented. I understand this concern; after all, what do you do today if yesterday's rules are no longer accept-able? Wherever possible, I have proposed new solutions and new perspectives. Nevertheless, a hard look at the skeletons in the closet is beneficial, especially when there is a propensity to keep the door locked. Nothing is gained by avoiding that which the discipline must face up to sooner or later. If a current procedure appears to be patently wrong, I have not hesitated to indicate this, even if the alternatives remain to be developed.

My first concentrated effort at dealing with this problem occurred during an enjoyable year spent as the Claude Bissell Distinguished Visiting Professor at the University of Toronto. Raymond Breton, Robert Brym, Bonnie Erickson, W. W. Isajiw, Robert MacKay, Harry Makler, Jeffrey Reitz, and Gail Sarginson were kind enough to discuss the issues with me. Special thanks are due Barry Well-man, who encouraged me to move this project off the back burner.

Former colleagues at the University of Arizona, present colleagues at the University of California in Berkeley, and others who were generous in their time for discussions include: Howard Becker, J. T. Borhek, the late Donna K. Carter, Bernard P. Cohen, Richard F. Curtis, Ray P. Cuzzort, Otis Dudley Duncan, Claude S. Fischer, Neil D. Fligstein, Glenn V. Fuguitt, Andrew M. Greeley, Travis Hirschi, Michael Hout, Gary F. Jensen, Leonard V. Kuhi, Keith E. Lehrer, Robert C. Leonard, Rebecca Lieberson, Roland J. Liebert, Patricia MacCorquodale, James McCann, William Mason, Jerry L. L. Miller, Albert J. Reiss, Jr., Peter H. Rossi, Merrilee Salmon, Martin Sanchez-Jankowski, Lawrence Santi, Karl F. Schuessler, William H. Sewell, Michael E. Sobel, James A. Wiley, and James J. Zuiches.

Paul Rosenblatt, then Dean at the University of Arizona, was both understanding and supportive of this project in ways that went beyond the normal duties associated with his position. Pamela Anstine, Mark Scarbecz, and Mary C. Waters assisted in various bibliographical and research facets of the project. Jo Migliara typed several of the chapters. In a variety of ways, Jean Margolis has helped get this manuscript ready for publication. A modest grant from the National Science Foundation (SES-8207346) was greatly appreciated, as was the support received from the Survey Research Center, University of California, Berkeley. Both Allen D. Grimshaw and Donald Treiman provided detailed comments and suggestions that were very helpful.

For the most part, I have avoided zeroing in on the work of specific writers. My comments deal with more general issues. In those cases where some specific study seemed especially appropriate for discussion, I hope the authors realize that these are done out of respect and admiration for the clarity of the way in which their studies were shaped and developed.

Stanley Lieberson

Grand Lake District
Oakland, California

PART ONE

Current Practices

CHAPTER ONE

Introduction

There were many failures before humans successfully learned to fly. After watching birds flap their wings, bold and adventurous individuals built huge winglike structures, leaped off cliffs, flapped their wings vigorously, and broke their necks. There are principles of flight to be learned from watching the birds all right, but the wrong analogy had been drawn. In similar fashion, our empirical approach to social behavior is based on an analogy. The natural sciences are incredibly appealing, the physical and biological sciences have been generating counterintuitive and esthetically elegant ideas for centuries. No wonder scholars thought: "Why not a science of society, too? Just find out what the natural sciences do and then apply the same procedures to social events. That is what has to be done." We have attempted, I believe, to apply science to society in as crude and inappropriate a way as when mankind modeled human flight after the behavior of birds. The issue is not how to get as close as possible to the natural sciences in terms of quantification, verification, formalization, and the like—not that any of these is undesirable. The problem is more fundamental, namely the goal itself is based on an ill-conceived analogy. This argument, which will be developed in this volume, does not lead to the conclusion that we should forget the whole business of pursuing a scientific approach to society. Rather, it will lead to a different way of thinking about the rigorous study of society implied by the phrase "science of society."

Most sociological research is nonexperimental. This is an understandable situation, given the inevitable and proper limits imposed by society. We are not about to assign identical twins randomly at birth to different family units; nor can we suddenly double the income of some third world countries and halve the income of others. Moreover, it is by no means certain in many cases that actual experiments could duplicate adequately events that would change, by their very nature, if strict experimental procedures were used. This is not a debate that we need enter here, however. For good or bad, most empirical social research is based on nonexperimental situations, even though one recognizes the desirability of experiments whenever possible.

Surprisingly, although most sociological research is based on nonexperimental data, the experimental approach does not occupy a secondary position in the development of research procedures. To the contrary, nonexperimental data—the normal source of empirical information—are treated as far as possible *as if they were truly experimental data*. The data are sliced, chopped, beaten, molded, baked, and finally artificially colored until the researcher is able to serve us proudly with a plateful of mock experiment. A great deal of attention is paid, of course, to approximating the experimental model, but little to the distinctive features of nonexperimental social research. Texts in sociological methodology—at least the ones I have looked at—give far more attention to the pure experimental model than to the nonexperimental simulation so frequently employed in sociological research (see, e.g., Galtung 1967; Kaplan 1964; Lazarsfeld, Pasanella, and Rosenberg 1972; Nowak 1977; Sellitz, Wrightsman, and Cook 1976; Smith 1981). Discussing the influence of John Stuart Mill on contemporary sociology, Costner (1971: ix-x) observes that his "basic ideas . . . still dominate methodological thinking, even though these basic ideas have been elaborated in ways that Mill did not foresee." In effect, we are still totally oriented to the experimental model.

What is this experimental model that sociologists have in mind? How appropriate is it for societal data generally and nonexperimental results in particular? Note that there is no point in asking about what it is that natural scientists really do. First, natural scientists do lots of different things; astronomy, nuclear physics, and plant ecology are not the same. But, more to the point, it does not matter for the purposes at hand what these scientists do—what does matter is the notion of science driving the actual work being done in social research. And it is the simple—deceptively simple—experiment that was and is the model used.

> There is at least one important difference between the laboratory of the physical scientist and that of the social scientist. In chemistry, physics, and even biology the subjects of study can be brought into the laboratory and studied under controlled conditions. This as yet, except on a small scale as with institutes of child research, is not feasible in the social sciences. The objects of social science research, as persons, groups, and institutions, must be studied if at all in the laboratory of community life.
>
> Yet it is quite as necessary in the social as in the physical sciences to make observations and comparisons of behavior under controlled conditions. One method of obtaining control in the social science laboratory is, first, to determine the significant factors, or variables, which influence behavior, and then to find out for each its quantitative value in extent or degree. In this way, where it is possible, the social sciences obtain what is an approximation of the controlled experiment in the method of the physical sciences. (Burgess 1929: 47)

Boyle's law epitomizes the model implicit in much of the sociological research, both in terms of the kind of data analysis that would be ideal and the linkage between empirical research and theory. In a nutshell, the law posits a certain constant relationship between the pressure (P) and volume (V) of a gas when held at a given temperature, such that $PV = K$. Thus, as pressure goes up or down, the volume of gas declines or expands accordingly. Empirically, one can visualize a leakproof container with a pistonlike top holding a certain quantity of gas, in which the pressure on the top is increased and then decreased over and over again with the same consequences for the volume of gas in each case. The pressure is doubled and the volume of gas goes down by half; the pressure is then halved and the volume of gas doubles; ad nauseum.[1]

One can visualize this experiment being performed in a rather different manner. Instead of shifting the pressure on one piston to determine changes in gas volume, we could use a set of containers that are identical except for the weight (pressure) on their piston tops. If an equivalent weight of the same gas is introduced through a valve at the bottom of each container, one should find that the volume varies between containers in accordance with the pressures of their tops in the same way as occurred earlier in the single piston. The difference here is that the conclusion is now based on a *cross-sectional* analysis, whereas in the earlier experiment the conclusions were drawn from *longitudinal* approach in which the pressure in one container was manipulated in various directions to determine the consequences this had for the volume of gas. In the case of Boyle's law, this difference seems to be much ado about nothing. However, since much of the data in sociological research are of necessity cross-sectional rather than longitudinal, there will be much ado about this later.

This simple experiment, performed in either of two ways, represents the model of natural science research that is implicit in most sociological research based on nonexperimental data. Researchers, automatically and without thought, attempt to manipulate their analysis of nonexperimental data so as to approximate, as closely as possible, the kind of experiment that would be used to examine Boyle's law. To do so, it will be shown, they are obliged to make impossible assumptions—assumptions that appear to be matters of convenience but in reality generate analyses that are completely off the mark. What are these analogies? How and why does the application to nonexperimental social research take us so far afield? If these criticisms are correct, what alternative exists that would not abandon efforts at rigorous empirical social research?

THE UNDOABLE

Before addressing these questions, first consider the possibility of removing a horrible constraint that burdens the thinking of most sociologists. Namely, some of the tasks that social researchers undertake are simply undoable in the way that they are presently conceived. Natural scientists, to my knowledge, intentionally avoid certain issues in both their theories and their empirical research. Divine entities or other supernatural powers do not usually occupy a place as either a causal force or as a topic whose existence they can test with their normal methods (Grüner 1977: 150—151; Barbour 1968: 5—6). The science of society likewise excludes deities as either plausible causal forces or as a potentially verifiable empirical truth. Otherwise, if the event in question is observable or if the theory under consideration has observable consequences, then the empirically oriented social scientist reasons that this is a matter for social research. There is no notion of the *undoable* if observation and measurement are possible. To be sure, the problem may not be solvable in practice because of practical considerations, such as: the number of cases is too small; the probable contribution of the variable is so slight that measurement errors will swamp the hypothesized influence; sampling problems; enumeration errors; absence of suitable indicators or quantitative measures; sticky statistical problems that are difficult to manage, and the like.

The early giants in the natural sciences, in order to construct simple mathematical theories, intentionally ignored a large number of features and factors that could be observed in their data (see the distinction between primary and secondary qualities appearing throughout Burtt 1954). To be sure, we are not bound by what they did—after all, thoughtless modeling will get us as far as our ancestors did by flapping mechanical wings. But it is of interest to compare that situation with contemporary social research. At present, we do not think of questions that are purely and simply unknowable, regardless of the quality of the data, or if potentially knowable, that are unanswerable at present because basic underlying knowledge would be required before the questions could be approached. Because research reports so often conclude with one or another variation of the famous theme, "Further Research Is Called For," we have to ask ourselves if there is a special reason for this. Is it simply the quality of the data, or the need for more data, or the need to repeat research over and over again before the conclusion can be nailed down? The typical project involves working with data sets that are far from ideal. Because of this, perhaps we are apt to avoid the issue of whether *some* questions are simply not answerable with the tools of empirical social science even if the available data are of exceptionally high quality. If current research does not appear to

answer the question it addresses, one must also consider whether it
is really a researchable problem. (This ignores the issue of whether
the theory driving the research is adequate, since that is what the
research results will presumably help the investigator decide.)

This, then, is one of the fundamental issues to be addressed in
this volume: Are there questions currently studied that are basically
unanswerable even if the investigator had ideal nonexperimental
data? If so, what are the alternative questions that can be dealt with
successfully by empirical social research, and how should they be
approached? In the chapters ahead, it will be important to keep in
mind this doctrine of the undoable. Of course, one cannot simply
mutter "undoable" when a difficult obstacle is encountered, turn off
the computer, and look in the want ads for a new job—or at least a
new task. Instead, it means considering if there is some inherent
logical reason or sociological force that makes certain empirical
questions unanswerable. There are four types of undoable questions
to consider: those that are *inherently* impossible; those that are
premature; those that are *overly complicated*; and those that empirical
and theoretical knowledge have *nullified*.

The first undoable refers to issues that are inherently no more
answerable with the techniques of social science than are questions
about the existence of a deity resolvable by the astronomer. In
addition to supernatural forces and issues, one can include here
many of the questions addressed by poets, novelists, humanists, and
others. There should be no conflict between the different practitioners since each field has its own tasks and problems occur only
when they are confused. But here I would also include as undoable
those questions that simply cannot be addressed through the usual
nonexperimental social research. After all, experiments seem to
imply *control*: the researcher sets conditions that allow certain
hypothesized consequences to follow. Or the investigator simply
wants to see what will occur under some specific combination of
circumstances. Naturally occurring events are therefore ersatz data
for an experimental model; under *some* conditions the results may
represent inherently undoable research. It is vital that one determine this more precisely since the experimental analogy appears to
be either applied without reservation or rejected flatly and totally by

its critics. This reexamination of the experimental analogy is a task that will commence in the next chapter.

Another type of undoable is the premature question—that is, a question that cannot be approached until a more fundamental base of knowledge exists. It would be as if one tried to build a locomotive before the wheel was discovered, or tried to change a base metal into gold with the knowledge available to alchemists. This does not mean that a premature problem will take a book with ten or even twenty-five chapters to answer fully, rather than a journal article or two. Rather, it means that basic unanswered questions require considerable work before the query can be approached. It is valuable simply to recognize this possibility, because when one does see an issue raised in the sociological literature as empirically undoable, it is usually with respect to the quality of the data or the statistical issues, and so on. Rarely is an empirical question viewed as premature simply because underlying knowledge is not yet available before the specific problem can be approached. It would be nice, of course, to have a way of determining at least some of the time when a problem is premature without having to wait for the benefit of hindsight.

There are empirical research questions that are undoable simply because they are too complicated. Visualize a lengthy chain of events to be analyzed. At some or many of the junctures, there are a variety of forces influencing the outcome and some of these are not totally understood. Under such circumstances, even though considerable knowledge is available about the outcome at each juncture, the chain is so long and complicated that a model is helpless to deal with the final outcome. This would be no different than asking economists to generate a theory of interest rates that would enable them to predict what the rates will be a year from now, or asking meterologists to determine the weather in a specific place one year from now. In each instance, there are so many forces operating, and they are so complicated, that the outcome is in doubt even though knowledge is very good for each point in the chain.

Karl Popper, in his battle with historicism, puts it well:

> The crucial point is this: although we may assume that any actual succession of phenomena proceeds according to the laws of nature, it is important to realize

that practically *no sequence of, say, three or more causally connected concrete events proceeds according to any single law of nature.* If the wind shakes a tree and Newton's apple falls to the ground, nobody will deny that these events can be described in terms of causal laws. But there is no single law, such as that of gravity, nor even a single definite set of laws, to describe the actual or concrete succession of causally connected events; apart from gravity, we should have to consider the laws explaining wind pressure; the jerking movements of the branch; the tension in the apple's stalk; the bruise suffered by the apple on impact; all of which is succeeded by chemical processes resulting from the bruise, etc. The idea that any concrete sequence or succession of events (apart from such examples as the movement of a pendulum or a solar system) can be described or explained by any one law, or by any one definite set of laws, is simply mistaken. There are neither laws of succession, nor laws of evolution. (1964: 115)

Finally, there are questions that at first glance appear to be reasonable and answerable but are undoable simply because available empirical and theoretical knowledge has nullified them. When John F. Kennedy was assassinated in Dallas, among the questions a shocked nation asked was, "Why Dallas?" On the surface, this would appear to be a reasonable question; after all, the president was assassinated and it was in Dallas. Reflection on the matter will show that it is a nullified question, voided because existing empirical and theoretical knowledge shows that it is without meaning. Let us assume that there are people throughout the nation with a propensity or disposition to assassinate the president. Let us assume that this disposition fluctuates with the mood of the time, the mood in their local place of residence, and the characteristics of the president. If there are such people everywhere (albeit their relative frequency may vary from place to place), and if there is a small probability that on any given day an assassination attempt will be made, and if there is in turn a small probability that such an attempt will prove successful, then its occurrence at any given place is indeterminate. To be sure, its probability will be raised if the president spends much time in the city; hence, in that respect, the probability is higher in Washington, D.C., than in Dallas. However, the exposure to risk will obviously be greater in public settings than in controlled and restricted situations. In that regard, an open vehicle in Dallas is of greater risk than a reception in the White House. If there are proportionately more people in Dallas than in the rest of the nation with such impulses toward Kennedy—and that is an open empirical question—then a day's exposure in Dallas has a greater risk than a day's exposure elsewhere (assuming people never leave their city of residence in order to attempt the assassination). But it is without meaning to ask why it happened in Dallas if, in that sense, is meant an event that could have happened only in Dallas. For to ask such a question is to ask a question that has been nullified by the available empirical evidence coupled with a certain theoretical approach to the event. All one can ask is whether the chances for such an event occurring in Dallas were greater than for another place, but it is without meaning to ask why it occurred in Dallas.[2]

Observe that the question is nullified, and hence undoable, because of the joint influence of theory and empirical data. If the disposition to assassinate occurred only in Dallas, or if the social conditions leading people with such dispositions to act out their impulses were only found in Dallas, then it would be a doable question. The intriguing feature here is that the question on the surface appears so reasonable and yet it is not—given certain knowledge. The nondeterministic statistical explanation need not involve a high probability of an event's occurring and can be applied to events that are "intrinsically improbable, even though they sometimes occur," and would otherwise, "defy all explanation" (Salmon 1971: 9). Observe a simple fact that will be worth returning to later: a complete explanation, in the sense of accounting for all of the variance, under specified conditions can be a nullified task. Evaluating research in terms of variance explained may be as invalid as demanding social research to determine whether or not there is a deity or to determine accurately the world's population a hundred years from now. This argument will be developed in chapter 5.

This is not an effort to generate an exhaustive list of all possible undoables. But the four just discussed—the inherently undoable, those that are premature, the overly complicated, and the nullified question—are sufficient to help the reader see that undoables exist. Moreover, this raises very different issues about empirical research from the ones generated by those who complain that empirical social research attempts to do too little. Rather, the existence of undoables means that empirical social research can get itself into a hole because, in some respects, it is too ambitious and seeks to tackle questions that cannot be answered. In critically examining the methods underlying social research, we are therefore free to recognize that there may be some goals and procedures that are totally inappropriate, that involve efforts to do the undoable.

FREEDOM AND CHALLENGE

Some of the most bothersome features of social research need not be problems if it turns out that our initial concerns were generated by a simplistic and inappropriate effort to apply the experimental science model. If this model is not an appropriate one for the subject matter of society, then we are free to shed these concerns and go on to empirical problems and theoretical issues that are appropriate to a science of society. For example, in worrying about sampling problems over time and space, we often compare with envy the situation faced by the natural scientist who takes some oxygen from one place and time with no concern about this matter. Indeed, we should envy the natural scientist if we are trying to work with the same methods as the natural scientist. But if we carry the time and space sample problem to its ultimate end, then we are defeated anyway. There are samples that cannot be taken no matter what the researcher does—to wit, samples of the future are unavailable. For all purposes, there are samples of the past that are unavailable, at least with the data that one wants. Indeed, for most problems, there are samples of the present that are not available either.

What does one do? There are really only a few outcomes thus far. One of increasing popularity is to abandon any serious and rigorous empirical effort altogether. This, to my way of thinking, means throwing the baby out with the bathwater. For empirical research and observation is an absolute must—I say this not to persuade the unpersuadable, but rather to leave no doubt what the starting point is. As Kaplan observes:

> If science is to tell us anything about the world, if it is to be of any use in our dealings with the world, it must somewhere contain empirical elements (or, like mathematics, be used in conjunction with such elements). For it is by experience alone that information about the world is received. . . .

It is in the empirical component that science is differentiated from fantasy. An inner coherence, even strict self-consistency, may mark a delusional system as well as a scientific one. Paraphrasing Archimedes we may each of us declare, "Give me a premise to stand on and I will deduce a world!" But it will be a fantasy world except in so far as the premise gives it a measure of reality. And it is experience alone that gives us realistic premises. (1964: 34−35)

The mystique and prestige associated with science are not important. What does seem eminently reasonable is the notion of using evidence to provide feedback on the theories and propositions developed about society. Hence, a conclusion to throw it all out appears unreasonable.

However, it also seems unreasonable to ignore the possibility that the simulated experimental model followed by most empirical social researchers incorporates indefensible and illogical procedures accompanied by a certain scientific ritualism. Again, we can turn to Kaplan:

There are behavioral scientists who, in their desperate search for scientific status, give the impression that they don't much care what they do if only they do it right: substance gives way to form. And here a vicious circle is engendered; when the outcome is seen to be empty, this is taken as pointing all the more to the need for a better methodology. The work of the behavioral scientist might well become methodologically sounder if only he did not try so hard to be so scientific! (1964: 406)

It is therefore a plague on both houses: those who would give up on any effort at rigorous empirical social research and those who contend that the imitation of hard sciences is the answer. Given this reasoning, it seems natural to reexamine and reconsider the model of empirical research underlying most empirical work. The goal is neither a whitewash nor capital punishment, but rather it is to reform and mold empirical research into an activity that contributes as much as possible to a rigorous understanding of society. Without worrying about defining science or even determining the essence of the scientific enterprise, the goal is one that pools together logical thinking and empirically determined information.

CHAPTER TWO

Selectivity

A key feature of the experimental approach is that the subjects (whether they be individuals, groups, organizations, nations, or what have you) are randomly assigned to the conditions under study. If the assignment process is not random, then the investigator must be fully satisfied that it has no bearing on the likely outcome. In the social sciences, however, we are continuously dealing with situations in which the subjects have not been randomly assigned to the different conditions; rather, some selective process is operating which itself may be influencing the outcomes observed in the conditions under study. The ensuing simulation of a true random assignment experiment is what is called a *quasi-experiment*

experiments that have treatments, outcome measures, and experimental units, but do not use random assignment to create the comparisons from which treatment-caused change is inferred. Instead, the comparisons depend on non-equivalent groups that differ from each other in many ways other than the presence of a treatment whose effects are being tested. (Cook and Campbell, 1979: 6)

There is not much that can be done about avoiding this situation because, as noted earlier, there are many situations where true experiments are either socially unacceptable or, if acceptable, would certainly not duplicate the actual events occurring in a "natural" setting (Nagel 1961: 451).

The absence of random assignment causes enormous difficulties if there is reason to believe that the subjects thereby placed in each condition differ in other ways that themselves have a bearing on the outcome of interest to the researcher. Cook and Campbell (1979: 6) go on to describe the special problem that occurs in quasi-experimental work:

The task confronting persons who try to interpret the results from quasi-experiments is basically one of separating the effects of a treatment from those due to the initial noncomparability between the average units in each treatment group; only the effects of the treatment are of research interest. To achieve this separation of effects, the researcher has to explicate the specific threats to valid causal inference that random assignment rules out and then in some way deal with these threats. In a sense, quasi-experiments require making explicit the irrelevant causal forces hidden within the *ceteris paribus* of random assignment.

Accordingly, the researcher has the special problem of not knowing whether the observed outcome reflects the forces under consideration, pure and simple, or whether to some unknown degree it is reflecting unmeasured differences between the initial populations experiencing each condition. (The difficulties are compounded if we consider the possibility of interactions between selective assignment to a condition and subjects' responses to that condition.)

Some examples are in order. Suppose one wishes to determine the influence of military service on civilian earnings years later. The initial tendency will be to compare the incomes of those experiencing military service with those who did not. However, there would be every reason to believe that military service is not a random event, whether this be in a period where there is a draft or only voluntary service. Rather, the subjects are sorted in some manner such that draftees, volunteers, and those never serving will differ from one another on dimensions that in turn have a bearing on one's life chances later on. Griliches and Mason (1973: 289), for example, after analyzing a 1964 sample of post–World War II veterans, concluded that those at the extremes of either ability or socioeconomic position were less likely to serve. (For a number of specific background comparisons, see Mason 1970: 18–20.) In the model for the social sciences suggested by the simple physical science experiment, this type of selectivity is usually not an issue. In the experiment with Boyle's law discussed in the previous chapter, we saw that the cross-sectional study can reasonably assume that the gas molecules are identical in each vial. Hence one is reasonably confident that there is no sorting of subjects (in this case, molecules) in some manner that is related to the conditions under investigation. This analogue would not hold in the military service issue and is relevant insofar as selectivity affects variables or attributes that in turn influence the outcome (also to be called the "dependent variable" or the "explanandum").

Selectivity is an obvious issue in the case of military service, but it is by no means an unusual or unique example. The output of any institution has to be considered not only in terms of its impact on the social processes but also the initial qualities of those entering the institution.[1] To be sure, it is standard sociology to assume that an institution has an impact on those entering it—and this is an assumption with which I am generally comfortable. However, it is an empirical matter to separate that impact—if it does in fact occur—from those due to the initial selective sorting process. If one wishes to compare the impact on students of elite private colleges with the impact of large state universities, for example, it would be foolhardy to assume that the students themselves are identical before starting college. The very finest social researchers are obliged over and over again to turn to data sets in which this issue of selectivity in the initial sorting process raises its ugly head. If one considers, for example, how blacks in racially mixed schools compare with blacks in essentially all-black schools on various performance criteria, it is reasonable to assume that more than random forces determined the type of school blacks attend (an issue in the landmark school segregation study by Coleman, et al. 1966). Likewise, an analogous assumption would operate when comparing whites in all-white schools with whites in mixed schools. In the school situation, nonrandom allocation or assignment processes almost certainly are selective of factors that in turn influence school performance.

Bear in mind that selectivity is not a problem if the factors do not affect the dependent variable under consideration. A quasi-experimental situation is a good approximation to the purely experimental case if selectivity involves only characteristics that have no bearing on the outcome. As a general rule, however, the quasi-experimental situation encounters selective assignment processes that make it difficult to gauge the influence of a given condition on the dependent variable of interest. It can be especially complicated when the selective processes are themselves a variant. In the case of school integration, for example, there is no reason to assume that the same selective forces are operating on black children as on white children such that they have similar net consequences. An excellent review by Smith (1972) of the "Coleman Report" cited earlier illustrates a number of these selectivity issues. He points to two kinds of selectivity processes: student self-selectivity in terms of the schools that they attend, and selective school assignment practices (232). The latter occurs because students "are selected to attend particular schools on the basis of their past achievement" (274). There is no reason to assume that the groups are similarly affected by these selective processes. The closer association between achievement and student-body characteristics for blacks than for whites is explained by Smith exactly in these terms. "I question whether this difference in association is caused by characteristics of the student body. The data instead suggest that student selection and school assignment policies cause the association between the student-body characteristics and achievement" (280). This is not the place to rehash the detailed criticisms found in either Smith's paper or the volume in which it appears (Mosteller and Moynihan, 1972), but it ought to be clear that unmeasured selective processes are probably operating in most nonexperimental social research settings and that their effects, if unmeasured, may massively influence the results observed. Moreover, the selective process is not necessarily of the same nature or magnitude for each group. Also note that there is more than one type of nonrandom process: there is self-selectivity, in which the population units (or institutions, or what have you) sort themselves out by choice; there is selective assignment by the independent variable itself, which determines, say, what members of the population are exposed to specific levels of the independent variable; and there is also selectivity due to forces exogenous to variables under consideration at the time.

THE CONTROL VARIABLE APPROACH

The selectivity problem posed above has led to the "control variable approach," in one form or another, as a possible solution. The argument is very simple: If two or more populations differ in their initial characteristics in ways that may affect the outcome attributed to the test variable, then one takes into account these differences in order to determine what the linkage is between the explanandum and the specific force under consideration. This is perhaps the most commonly found step in quasi-experimental social research, reported over and over again. Indeed, in the standard quasi-experimental situation, the researcher would be subject to severe criticism for failing to take into account all of the controls that may influence the dependent variable under consideration. Imagine the embarrassment that a researcher on occupational mobility would face if age or parental education or some such factor was not "controlled" or otherwise "taken into account."

Thus most social researchers recognize the special problems involved in working with existing data sets that were not generated through experimental means, and they attempt to resolve the problem as best they can. There are a variety of statistical possibilities available to them, including: log-linear analysis, path coefficients, multivariate regression techniques, demographic forms of standardization, and various cross-tabulating measures. All are commonly used by researchers to gauge the consequences that test conditions have for some dependent variable, net of the influence due to a variety of other characteristics. The results observed with these statistical techniques are interpreted as if a true experiment had occurred, with the net pattern seen as approximating what would have occurred had an experiment been used. In effect, the test and control populations are matched up as closely as possible through statistical controls of the ways in which they initially differ (ways that would not have occurred if random assignment procedures had been possible—except, of course, for those differences due to random errors). I believe that most practitioners, if confronted with the matter, would begrudgingly admit that such procedures are not quite the same as a true experiment. For the most part, however, such statistical manipulations would be seen as a "reasonable" approximation to the ideal—*reasonable* insofar as all plausible controls have been taken into account.

The populations are matched up as closely as possible through statistical manipulation. In the military case, for example, if those drafted differ in parental backgrounds from men who were not, then the argument runs that parental background differences should be taken into account in order to determine what the income gaps between drafted and nondrafted men are net of this factor. It is as if the two sets of men were to be matched as far as possible on every conceivable characteristic that might have a bearing on income. This is the heart of the procedure: Nonrandom assignment is virtually assured in actual real-life situations; in turn, there is a strong chance that the populations in each test condition differ on other attributes that affect the explanandum; therefore, it is necessary that the researcher somehow cope with this sharp difference from the true experiment. This is done by using various statistical techniques to nullify or minimize the impact of selective processes. For example, comparisons between blacks attending racially mixed and racially segregated schools will take into account differences between the children themselves and their parents.

Unmeasured Selectivity

What is wrong with this procedure? If there is any feature of social life about which a high degree of confidence exists, it would be this simple principle: social processes are *selective* processes. As a consequence, the reason for taking into account the differences found between the populations is also the very same reason for doubting whether such efforts can be successful very often. For selective processes are probably operating within the control variables themselves. If Coleman, Hoffer, and Kilgore (1982*a*) find that children from wealthier families are more likely than poorer children to attend private school, then comparisons between private and public schools should obviously take this into account—insofar as family background itself plays a role in affecting the explanandum (test performance).[2] So far, so good. But it is probably not a random event that determines whether children within a given socioeconomic background class attend one or the other type of school. Difficult questions remain unless it is by chance that some children of wealthy parents go to private schools and other children go to public schools. One can ask analogous questions about children in other income classes as well—and separately by race and sex and a variety of other attributes. Moreover, it is by no means certain that the level of selectivity is the same for each of the subsets.

Consequently, if there is reason to believe that nonrandom sorting operates within each control variable *and* the sorting involves factors that affect the dependent variable, then the controlling procedure is incomplete. There is still unmeasured and uncontrolled selectivity operating and, to an unknown degree, the responses attributed to the independent variables under consideration are actually due to the allocation process. In other words, to the degree that there is unmeasured and unadjusted selectivity, to that degree the experimental analogue breaks down. In the public-private school example, parental and child's attitudes toward school and achievement might help account for divisions *within* each economic category in terms of the type of school attended. Nevertheless, unless we are confident that such controls (or cross-tabulations, or what have you) fully account for the sorting processes such that some children go to one type of school and others go to another type, our conclusions are not secure. For one would still have the right to ask whether those children attending public schools of a given economic level X and a given personality attribute Y and whose parents have characteristics Z differ only by chance from other X-Y-Z children who attend private school. The researcher has reached an experimental analogue only if one can assume that it is chance that determined which members of the population with a given combination of control characteristics were assigned to each test condition *or* that the nonrandom factors affecting such assignments have no bearing on the dependent variable.

Control procedures are more complicated and difficult than would appear from the casual fashion with which they are applied in contemporary social research. For the issue remains: is it just chance factors operating within each control that determines if the subjects (whether they be individuals, or groups, or societies) are in one or another of the test conditions under study? If the answer is no, then are the sorting factors themselves affecting the outcome? An account from the popular literature, which describes a private high school in which many of the children have lower income parents, illustrates this point rather nicely. "Many parents struggle to scrape up the tuition, which averages $1,000; a few endorse welfare checks to pay part of the fees" (Harris 1981: 94). To be sure, the policies of the schools no doubt make a contribution. "The campus is closed to outsiders, and students who cut classes, talk back to teachers, violate the dress code or vandalize school property must appear on Saturdays to do work around the school" (Harris 1981: 94). The point, then, is that it is difficult to disentangle the independent variable of interest—in this case, school type—from the selective forces operating to begin with. When controlling for income, say, we would still face the enormous unmeasured differences between parents on welfare who send their children to such a school and those who do not. Presumably one could use controls that take into account possible differences between parents of a given income level and so forth. But still this issue would operate within those controls unless we reach a point where further differences are unrelated to the dependent variable or are simply random events.

APPLICATION OF CONTROLS WHEN THERE IS UNMEASURED SELECTIVITY

The comments made about unmeasured selectivity should not be startling for most social researchers, although most seem to prefer to ignore the matter as far as possible.[3] Clearly, this is a fundamental way in which the application of controls in quasi-experimental research differs from true experimental situations. The issue remains, however, of whether we are still better off proceeding in this way under less than ideal conditions rather than giving up entirely on a simulation of the experiment. Even if less than ideal, one may argue, surely it is beneficial to control for as many variables as possible that might be masking or affecting the true influence of the independent variable of interest. It is safe to say that most researchers act as if application of controls—even if there is unmeasured selectivity within each of these controls with respect to both the dependent and independent variables—is either beneficial (in the sense that the net results are closer to the truth than would occur otherwise without such controls) or is at least harmless. Hence, although willing to acknowledge the shortfall when compared with the experimental situation involving random assignment, most researchers are prepared to go ahead with the quasi-experimental situation even if some selective forces are not taken into account.

Alas, a careful examination indicates that the controlling procedure has consequences that are quite contrary to the standard assumptions in social research. Under some conditions, the application of controls generates results that are actually farther removed from the truth than would occur if no controls were applied whatsoever. Under other conditions of unmeasured selectivity, the application of controls generates results that are closer to the truth than would occur otherwise, but which still either underestimate or overestimate the influence of the independent variable under consideration. There are circumstances when the application of controls does indeed generate "correct" conclusions, but under other conditions, unmeasured selectivity can also cause controlling procedures to generate results in the opposite direction from the true relationship.

For the sake of illustration, suppose that we wish to examine the influence that type of school (private vs. public) has on test performance among students. Let T represent the "true" influence of school type, with the superscript designating the direction of this true influence. By "true" relationship, at the moment one can say it is the test score results that would occur if children were randomly assigned between private and public schools. (This corresponds quite well to the implicit meaning most social researchers would have in mind since they are indeed simulating an experiment.) Thus T^+ means that the dependent variable, test performance, is higher among those attending private schools; T^- means that it is higher among public schools; and T^0 means that there is no relationship between school and performance. In chart 2.1, it is assumed that T^+ holds.

Let us further assume that a control variable, C, is introduced which represents a socioeconomic background variable (SES) of the sort that are virtually ubiquitous in contemporary social research. In this hypothetical case, it will be assumed that the private school children are of higher SES background than those attending public school. At times, it will be assumed that the association between SES and test performance is positive (C^+); at other times, that it is negative, such that lower SES children get higher scores (C^-); and at times, that there is no association between SES background and test score results (C^0). Finally, with respect to selectivity, S, at times we will assume that its direction favors T^+; in other words, that within each SES category those inclined to do well on the tests are more likely to attend private schools (S^+). At other times, we will assume that there is no selectivity operating with the control variable (S^0). Finally, we will also consider the operation of a selectivity factor in which those children of a given class especially likely to do well go to public schools (hence S^-).

Obviously, the situation would be more complicated in a real-life research situation, with a number of controls expected and the opportunity to consider all sorts of interesting interaction effects, but this hypothetical case gives us a chance to examine calmly the implications of control variable analysis when searching for the truth in the quasi-experimental situation with unknown selectivity operating. At any rate, here is a brief review of the assumptions before we begin:

1. The true relationship between school-type and test performance is T^+, meaning that if children were randomly assigned to private and public schools, we would have found that the average test scores (the dependent variable) would have been higher in private schools.

2. The SES distribution of children in the private schools is higher than in the public schools.

3. The influence of SES on test performance will vary in the examples: in some cases, higher SES students do better (C^+); in

some cases, lower SES do better (C^-); and in some cases, SES has no bearing on test performance (C^0).

4. Similarly, selectivity within SES will vary such that within each SES the students especially likely to do well may concentrate in private schools (S^+), in public schools (S^-), or be randomly distributed between school types (S^0).

S^0

There are nine different combinations of control and selectivity influences to consider (chart 2.1). Let us dispense with the simplest of these first, Situation I. If there is no SES influence on test performance (C^0) and if there is no selectivity within socioeconomic classes in terms of those being especially likely to perform well on the tests going to private or public schools (S^0), then the controlling procedure is a benign affair. The true relationship is found even without control—since SES has no bearing on test performance—and nothing would be altered after applying controls.[4]

The application of controls is a most productive procedure when Situations II or III are encountered. In Situation II, the control variable (SES) generates a bias favoring the true relationship; in Situation III, the control generates a bias in the opposite direction from the true relationship. Thus, the influence of school on test performance is overestimated in Situation II before controls are applied because SES is also operating to favor higher test scores in the private schools. The opposite holds in Situation III, where the true influence of schooling on test performance is either underestimated (if $|C^-| < |T^+|$) or actually hidden (if $|C^-| > |T^+|$). In either case, since there is no selectivity within these control factors in terms of who experiences the test or the control condition, the net effect of taking SES into account is ideal. Application of the control leads to results that correspond exactly with the true relationship between schooling and test performance.

In short, in all three cases where there is no selectivity within the control variable, application of the control helps us simulate the results that would have been obtained under random assignment conditions—as would occur in a true experiment. To be sure, this

CHART 2.1
INFLUENCE OF DIFFERENT SELECTIVITY AND CONTROL VARIABLE COMBINATIONS ON RELATIONSHIP OBSERVED BETWEEN AN INDEPENDENT AND DEPENDENT VARIABLE

Situation	Direction of control (C)	Direction of selectivity (S)	Relationship observed	
			Before control is applied	After control is applied
I	0	0	Exactly correct.	Exactly correct.
II	+	0	In direction of T$^+$, but overestimates relationship.	Exactly correct.
III	−	0	Could be in either correct or incorrect direction. If former, then T$^+$ is underestimated.	Exactly correct.
IV	+	+	In direction of T$^+$, but overestimates relationship.	In direction of T$^+$ and overestimated, but less severely.
V	−	+	UNCERTAIN (see chart 2.2)	
VI	0	+	In direction of T$^+$, but overestimates relationship.	No change; in direction of T$^+$, but overestimates relationship.
VII	−	−	In opposite direction from T$^+$.	Still in opposite direction from T$^+$, but less severely.
VIII	0	−	In opposite direction from T$^+$.	No change; still in opposite direction from T$^+$.
IX	+	−	UNCERTAIN (see chart 2.2)	

NOTE: True relationship between the independent and dependent variable is positive in above examples (T$^+$). Column 2 indicates whether association between the control and dependent variable is in direction of true relationship (+), in opposite direction (−), or unrelated (0). Column 3 indicates whether the selectivity operating within the control variable tends to favor the true relationship (+), or is in opposite direction (−), or that there is no selectivity (0).

would not deal with the impact of a random assignment process, but that is another matter.

S^+

For Situations IV, V, and VI, selectivity within control categories (S^+) is in the same direction as in the true relationship (T^+), but the situations differ in the influence of the SES control variable, which is C^+, C^-, and C^0 respectively. Hence, in all three situations, application of the controls still leaves an untapped and unmeasured selectivity operating in the direction of the true relationship and hence leads to results that overestimate the magnitude of T^+.

Situation IV, in which selectivity is in the same direction as C and T (here all are $+$), is probably a fairly common pattern. Suppose, for example, that private school education generates the best test scores. Accordingly, wealthier parents are better able to pay for their children's private schooling and hence are especially likely to send them to such institutions. In addition, however, within each economic category those parents especially concerned about their children's education have a higher probability of sending their children to private schools. As a consequence, taking C into account moves the results toward the true value of T^+ (assuming in Situation IV that there is a positive association between SES and test performance), but there remains an overestimation of this effect because of selectivity within the categories. Controlling the C^+ has no bearing on the direction of the conclusion (which is correct both before and afterward), but it does reduce the magnitude of the apparent influence and makes it closer to the truth. Nevertheless, the operation of selectivity within classes in this direction (S^+) means that the true influence is still overestimated after a control is applied because of unmeasured selective forces operating within the control variable.

The same basic pattern also emerges in Situations V and VI; after controls are applied, there is an unmeasured selectivity that keeps the researcher from determining the true pattern. Since this has rather complicated potential consequences in the Type V Situation, its analysis is postponed briefly. Situation VI leads to post-control conclusions that are identical to those found before controls are applied. This is because the control variable has no impact on test performance (C^0). Hence the magnitude of the school situation on the dependent variable is in the correct direction in both instances and, likewise, in both instances it is overstated because of unmeasured selectivity. In all of these S^+ situations (including Type V), the direction of the conclusion is correct after controls are applied, but because unmeasured selectivity is operating in the direction of the true relationship, there is an overstatement of the magnitude of the independent variable's impact.

S^-

There is also an unmeasured selectivity operating in Situations VII, VIII, and IX, but in these cases it is S^- rather than S^+. Selectivity in these cases means that among children of a given SES background, those going to public schools are especially likely to do well on tests. Hence the selective pull remaining after controls are applied (S^-) will either minimize the magnitude of the true relationship, T^+, or actually generate the opposite net effect. At the very least, the magnitude of the true relationship will be understated because of the counterpull generated by selectivity in the opposite direction. It is even possible in these Situations for the actual direction of the relationship to be determined incorrectly— that is, for the relationship observed between school type and test performance to appear to favor public schools once SES is taken into account. This will occur when the strength of the true relationship is weaker than the selective forces operating in the opposite direction (T^+ and S^- respectively). To be sure, the application of controls in Situation VII will at least move the answer closer to the truth since the added negative pull of SES will have been eliminated. In Situation VIII, the application of the control will have no effect on the biased results because the SES control variable is unrelated to the dependent variable. Nevertheless, because selectivity pulls in the opposite direction from the true relationship in all three of these Situations, there is no avoiding the fact that conclusions drawn after controls are applied will either underestimate the magnitude of the true relationship or actually generate conclusions that are in the opposite direction from it.

Counterproductive Controls

In Situations V and IX, the pulls of the control variable and selectivity are in opposite directions. In the former, the variable to be controlled is operating in the opposite direction from T^+, and selectivity within is operating in the same direction as T^+ (C^- and S^+ respectively); the opposite holds in Situation IX, with C^+ and S^-. In some circumstances, the results are further from the truth *after* controls are applied; indeed, the application of controls could lead to an actual reversal of the direction of the association from a correct one (here, presumably, in which private schools do better to one in which the researcher will conclude that public schools have a more favorable effect).

Chart 2.2 elaborates on the three subtypes found in each of these two Situations. In the first of these, Va, we see that the zero order relationship corresponds precisely to T^+ because the S^+ and C^- forces counterbalance each other exactly. Application of the control variable in that circumstance would, of course, eliminate one part of the counterbalancing influence but not eliminate the unmeasured selectivity (S^+). As a consequence, the net results after controls are applied would overstate the true relationship and move the conclusion further from the truth than what was observed in the zero order circumstance. However, the conclusion would still at least remain in the correct direction. In Situation IXa, the analogous circumstance in which S and C counterbalance each other exactly, but their signs are in opposite directions, will also mean that the application of controls will lead to a conclusion that is further from the truth (in this case, underestimating the magnitude of T). Indeed, in this circumstance, the conclusions obtained after controls are applied may actually be in the wrong direction (if $|S^-|>|T^+|$).

Returning to Situation V, the zero order results will be overstating the truth if $|S^+|>|C^-|$. Under that combination, Vb, the truth will be overstated even more when the control variable is taken into account. Under Situations Vc, IXb, and IXc, the consequences are by no means simple. In Vc, since $|C^-|>|S^+|$, the zero order results will either understate T^+ or even be in the wrong direction [the latter if $C^->|(T^+ + S^+)|$]. Regardless, in this situation, the application of controls will ensure that at least the direction is

CHART 2.2

INFLUENCE OF DIFFERENT SELECTIVITY AND CONTROL VARIABLE COMBINATIONS ON RELATIONSHIP OBSERVED BETWEEN AN INDEPENDENT AND DEPENDENT VARIABLE, SUBSETS OF SITUATIONS V AND IX

Situation	Direction of control (C)	Direction of selectivity (S)	Relationship observed	
			Before control is applied	After control is applied
Va $(|C^-| = |S^+|)$	−	+	Exactly correct; the opposite pulls of C^- and S^+ counterbalance each other.	Now overestimates the relationship, in direction of T^+.
Vb $(C^- < S^+)$	−	+	In direction of T^+, but overestimates relationship.	Remains in direction of T^+, but overestimates the relationship even more.
Vc $(C^- > S^+)$	−	+	Consequences uncertain; could be in opposite direction of T^+ but could be in correct direction of T^+, but underestimated. See text.	Now in correct direction of T^+, but overestimates the relationship.
IXa $(|C^+| = |S^-|)$	+	−	Exactly correct; the opposite pulls of C^- and S^+ counterbalance each other.	Now reports the relationship in opposite direction from T^+.

CHART 2.2 (Continued)

Situation	Direction of control (C)	Direction of selectivity (S)	Relationship observed	
			Before control is applied	After control is applied
IXb $(C^+ > S^-)$	+	−	In direction of T^+, but over-estimates relationship.	Consequences uncertain. Could show T^+, but move further or closer to true value of T^+; could show results in opposite direction from T^+. See text.
IXc $(C^+ < S^-)$	+	−	T^+ will either show up but underestimated, or results could be in opposite direction.	Results uncertain, but T^+ less likely to show up or more likely to be underestimated. In absolute sense, however, results could be closer to true value of T^+. See text.

NOTE: Direction of true relationship and meaning of all columns same as in Chart 2.1.

correct afterward. The conclusion, however, will overestimate the magnitude of T^+ since the bias in that direction of S^+ will no longer be counterbalanced by C^-. The true magnitude of T^+ will not be found either before or after controls are applied in this circumstance; but the zero order observation could be closer to that truth than the conclusion based on controlling (if $|2S^+| > |C^-|$).

In Situation IXb, where $|S^-| < |C^+|$, the zero order observations will overstate the magnitude of T^+. Taking into account C^+ will in all cases lead to an underestimation of the magnitude of T^+. In some circumstances, however, it will be a closer approximation to the magnitude of T^+ than would occur without controls (if $|2S^-| < |C^+|$). However, if $|2S^-| > |C^+|$, the zero order results are a closer approximation to T^+ than occurs when the control variable is taken into account. In Situation IXc, where $|S^-| > |C^+|$, the zero order results will understate T^+. The results will be even further from the truth after controlling for C, with an even greater under-estimation of T^+. Indeed, if $|S^-| > |T^+|$, the erroneous conclusion will be made that the public schools have a more favorable net effect on test performance (in other words, as if T^- were correct rather than T^+).

Conclusion

It takes little effort to visualize a more complicated set of events in which there are more than two populations—a test and a control—and where more than one variable is taken into account, with selectivity of an undetermined magnitude and direction operating in each of the controls. But the results are sufficient to suggest that the normal control procedures will only rarely determine what the "true" relationships would have been between the independent and dependent variable had there been random assignment conditions under an actual experiment. This is because it is almost inevitable that selectivity will be operating within each of the control categories. In many cases, albeit not all, there is nonrandom assignment within the attributes being controlled. For the most part, research-ers have operated as if the application of controls still moves one closer to the truth—or at worst is a benign procedure. However, the results shown suggest not merely that the true relationship is certain to be underestimated or overestimated when unknown selective forces are operating, but that the true relationship in some circumstances is more closely approximated *before* controls are applied rather than *afterward*.

Bear in mind that all of these conclusions would be equally true if T were negative rather than positive—it is just that much of our discussion would have to be reversed. Note also that certain standard ideals in social research are largely inappropriate for coping with this problem— for example, the repetition of research findings through follow-up studies. Moreover, none of these problems generated by unmeasured selectivity is unique to a specific statistical procedure. In different contexts and/or times, there are probably different levels and magnitudes of selectivity operating to generate the observed relationships. But it is almost certain that the buildup of a set of consistent research findings will not resolve this issue.

INFLUENCE OF SELECTIVITY WHEN THE HYPOTHESIZED CAUSAL FACTOR DOES NOT OPERATE

What is the impact of selectivity when the causal force under consideration has no influence on the dependent variable? The consequences are disastrous, with unmeasured selective processes showing up as an apparent test effect. (Again the reader is reminded that the selective processes are relevant insofar as they have an impact on the dependent variable. Selective processes that have no impact on the dependent variable will have no bearing on the conclusions reached when control variables are applied.) In the Type I, II, and III Situations shown in Chart 2.3, where no selectivity is operating, the T^0 conclusion will be correctly reached after controls are applied. (Indeed, in the Type I Situation, the absence of any linkage between the independent variable under consideration and the dependent variable will be observed in the zero order situation since no controls are relevant either.) But in all other cases, an erroneous conclusion will be reached in which either T^+ or T^- will appear to be true. In Situations VI and VIII, where in effect the control variable alters nothing, the same incorrect conclusion about

T would exist after applying the control as before. As a matter of fact, the researcher is apt to feel especially encouraged since the initial results appear to be unaltered by the controls. In Type IV and VII Situations, an erroneous conclusion would be drawn that T is $+$ and $-$ respectively, but at least the magnitude of the error would be reduced in each circumstance after controlling. In Situations V and IX, however, not only will the researcher erroneously conclude, respectively, that T^+ and T^- are true, but also the magnitude of the error in some cases will be larger after controls are applied rather than before. In circumstances where the control and selectivity forces are operating in opposite directions, the uncontrolled value of T will be closer to T^0 than will the value of T after controls are applied when $|2S|>|C|$. For example, if $C^- = -20$ and $S^+ = +3$, then T will appear to be -17 before controls are applied $(-20 + 3)$, whereas it will appear to be $+3$ after controls. However, if $C^- = -20$ and $S^+ = +15$, then T without controls will be -5, whereas it will appear to be $+15$ after controls.

What does this mean for research situations where the independent variable under study would have no influence at all had there been ideal experimental conditions with random assignment of subjects? Unless there is reason to expect no selectivity within categories with respect to factors that influence the dependent variable, there are exceptionally strong chances that T^0 situations will appear to researchers to be either T^+ or T^-, depending on the direction of selectivity. Therefore, when T^0 is in fact correct, nonexperimental social research has a strong bias toward finding either a T^+ or T^- conclusion.

In the criminological area, there is evidence that certain non-null findings occur only when a less than adequate random assignment procedure is used. In other words, selectivity operates that is not adequately taken into account with the usual procedures. For example, Jensen and Rojek (1980: 379–380) observe that, "Prevention strategies that treat individuals, attempt to organize communities, or provide jobs or special education have not been found to reduce or prevent delinquency. . . . *Studies that have randomly assigned subjects to experimental or control groups have yielded the most discouraging results of all*" (italics mine). Likewise, Reid (1979: 760) concludes that, "the

CHART 2.3
Influence of Different Selectivity and Control Variable Combinations on Relationship Observed between an Unrelated Independent and Dependent Variable

Situation	Direction of control (C)	Direction of selectivity (S)	Relationship observed	
			Before control is applied	After control is applied
I	0	0	Exactly correct.	Exactly correct.
II	+	0	Appears to be a positive relationship.	Correct T^0 relationship is found.
III	−	0	Appears to be an inverse relationship.	Correct T^0 relationship is found.
IV	+	+	Appears to be a positive relationship.	Still appears to be a positive relationship, but less extreme.
V	−	+	UNCERTAIN (see Chart 2.2)	
VI	0	+	Appears to be a positive relationship.	No change; still appears to be a positive relationship.
VII	−	−	Appears to be an inverse relationship.	Still appears to be an inverse relationship, but less extreme.
VIII	0	−	Appears to be an inverse relationship.	No change; still appears to be an inverse relationship.
IX	+	−	UNCERTAIN (see Chart 2.2)	

NOTE: The independent and dependent variable are unrelated (T^0) in the above example. See Chart 2.1 for interpretation of columns 2 and 3.

more rigorous the research design, the higher the percentage report-
ing no change or detrimental effects from treatment."

PSEUDOCONTROLS

Elsewhere I have used the term "pseudocontrols" in referring to the
general problem that occurs when the control variables incorporate
unmeasured differences that in turn affect the dependent variable
under study (Lieberson 1978: 959—964). The analysis thus far has
dealt with the way selective forces can lead to this occurrence, such
as when students of comparable socioeconomic background are not
randomly distributed between private and public schools but rather
differ in terms of attributes that affect their academic performance.
However, the pseudocontrol problem is caused by more than simply
the operation of either self-selective or assignment processes, even if
they are important sources. There are often deep underlying structural forces that cause a variable with the same formal properties to
vary in its consequences because it masks differences on other
attributes.

Consider the situation that originally led to the notion of pseudocontrols (Lieberson 1978). A comparison was made in the North
between the incomes of two black groups: those born in the North
and those who had migrated to the North from the South. Obviously, there are serious issues about selectivity in migration to the
North as well as return migration, but these can be ignored for the
purposes at hand (see, however, Lieberson 1978: 947—959). Of
concern is the fact that the two birthplace groups differ in their
educational distributions, with the northern-born boasting higher
levels of formal attainment in each age group. Accordingly, it is
reasonable to ask what the income differences are between the
birthplace groups after educational levels are taken into account. So
far the procedure is identical to the private school matter discussed
earlier: the true linkage between the independent and dependent
variables (here birthplace and income respectively) may be confounded by the influence of some other causal factor (in this case,
education) on the dependent variable. As was the case for the

private-public school matter, here too there is an analogous issue of whether the control variable, educational attainment, has the same meaning in the two regions. The difference here stems, however, not from selectivity within a control between those going to private or public school. Rather, it stems from regional differences in educational opportunity and the attributes thereby associated with educational attainment.

First, consider the enormous educational gap between southern- and northern-born blacks of a given age and sex. Somewhat less than half of the southern-born black men 45−64 years of age in 1970 had achieved at least an eighth-grade education. By comparison, 78% of the northern-born black men had at least finished eighth grade. There are still pronounced birthplace differences among young adults in 1970; just under 7% of the northern-born blacks in the 25−34 year-old age group have less than an eighth-grade education whereas the figure is more than double for southern-born blacks, 15.2%. The gaps for women in the different ages tell essentially the same story. It is reasonable to assume that this pattern is largely due, directly or indirectly, to regional differences in the opportunity structure for blacks. . . .

If there is a more limited opportunity structure for black education in the South, one may assume that the personality traits and background characteristics required for southern blacks to reach a given educational level are not the same as those for northern blacks of the same age. Under such circumstances, the income gaps observed among blacks living in the North need not reflect regional differences in work-ethic distribution or other traits which affect income but may be due to birthplace differences in the association of a given personality characteristic with educational attainment. For example, being a grade school dropout is probably more negatively selective in the North of various traits affecting the ability to generate income than it is (or was) among southern blacks.

More generally, assume that two populations (in this case, northern- and southern-born blacks of a given age and sex) have the same distribution with respect to some characteristic, X_1 (here, work ethos or some other personality characteristics which affect earning ability). Let us assume that some other characteristic, X_2, also affects income (in this case, formal educational attainment) and, moreover, that a correlation of 1.0 exists within each population between X_1 and X_2. Only if the regression of X_1 on X_2 is identical within each population will it be proper to control for X_2 without controlling for X_1 when accounting for some dependent variable (in this case, income). If southern b_{x1x2} ≠ northern b_{x1x2}, then a different average value of X_1 is associated with a given level of X_2 in each subpopulation and X_2 cannot serve as a surrogate for X_1. Under such circumstances, controlling for X_2 does not take into account the influence of X_1 and generates a pseudocontrol. This can lead to a counterintuitive pattern in which the southern-born blacks at all education levels have higher incomes although the birthplace groups have identical distributions on all attributes that affect income except education. This would occur if the cumulative percentage of the southern-born population in each education category is greater than the northern-born figure in all but the highest educational category. In that case, the mean northern value of X_1 would be lower than the southern-born X_1 at each education level—including the very highest. In short, higher southern incomes may not be due to North-South differences in various achievement factors but could merely reflect birthplace differences in the association of educational achievement with these factors. (Lieberson 1978: 959–960)

This is a particularly important issue insofar as social research so often involves surrogate variables—that is, the characteristic we are interested in is measured only indirectly by the use of another attribute that is highly correlated with it. The problem here, as the preceding paragraph makes clear, is that the regression of the desired attribute on the surrogate variable may be different for the various populations and this will have a deep bearing in turn on the ability to use controls. Nonexperimental social research will encounter this facet of the pseudocontrol problem over and over again. Hence, not only will selectivity among the units being studied operate to warp the results in nonexperimental social research but there is also another feature that cannot be solved by applying controls—namely, the controls will differ in social contexts owing to the broader structural processes operating within and between societies.

IS THERE A SOLUTION?

One can visualize the hard-pressed scholar muttering, "Thanks a lot, author. From now on I will be more careful to control for selectivity within my variables and also watch out for the general pseudocontrol problem that you describe. Also, I will approach my conclusions with a touch more humility, recognizing that it is at least *possible* that I am all wet. But, after all, some rather eminent authorities have noted that they don't really control for everything in natural science experiments either (Popper 1964: Section 25; Blalock 1961: 21). And, most important of all, why can't I just control for the selectivity processes themselves or otherwise take them into account?" Sorry, hard-pressed scholar, but neither the control approach nor the existing special statistical designs are likely to provide generally satisfactory solutions.

Controls

Suppose one wishes to determine the influence of conditions A and B on a dependent variable. If the distribution of a variable, X_1, is different in population A than in B and there is reason to think that X_1 may be affecting the dependent variable, then it would appear eminently reasonable to match up comparable X_1 segments within A and B. (The language and procedure for doing this varies greatly, depending on the statistical techniques employed and the assumptions made, but they all share a common logic in seeking to determine the influence of A vs. B on the dependent variable, net of their differences in X_1.) From the point of view of selectivity, one is not content, however, with such a step. For it is also necessary to determine whether there is some nonrandom process that led populations A and B to have different distributions of X_1. If nonrandom, then it is reasonable to wonder if the units in A and B with comparable levels of X_1 differ on some additional attribute, X_2, which itself has a bearing on the dependent variable. Alas, the same sort of issue will exist if we cross-tab the units within A and within B on both of these attributes and then compare accordingly. For we will then face the issue of whether it was just by chance, say, that some units with low X_1 and high X_2 are in population A and other units with comparable levels of X_1 and X_2 are in population B? As you can readily imagine, there is no point running a three-way tabulation involving X_3—even if we think there might be selectivity on that attribute—because we will remain with an analogous question: Was it just chance that led some units with low X_1, high X_2, and medium X_3, for example, to be found in population A whereas others are in population B? Thanks to the earlier analysis in this chapter, we cannot rest on the assumption that these controls will at least put us closer to the "true" relationship than would have been found had a random assignment procedure been possible. For we have seen that the controlling procedures are not necessarily beneficial or at least innocuous—they can actually be pernicious, moving the partialed or controlled results further from T than before. Moreover, in most social research projects, we are apt to run out of variables sooner than we are likely to find all of the possible measures of selectivity.

It is almost certain that some of the assignments to one or another condition are generated by random factors that we need not worry about, as opposed to selective forces of either a structural or self-generated nature. But the investigator is normally unable to determine this. The simple and initially appealing procedure of taking into account or otherwise controlling for every possible cause of the dependent variable, in order to isolate the influence of some specific causal force of interest, is therefore most unlikely to hit the "truth" (that is, arrive at the same results as a true random assignment experiment). Such results are "successful" insofar as they meet present-day criteria and concerns about going as far as you can in taking all other relevant factors into account. The only problem is that the ultimate success is knowledge—and this is not the same as what is obtained when a deeply flawed approach is carried out as far as it can go. Further tests, follow-up studies, newer statistical procedures, exchanges in the journals, bigger samples, more controls, and the like, may or may not support the original conclusion, but it does not really matter if they are all based on the same underlying false premise. In this respect, one can see why experiments on communication generate results that are quite different from those obtained through quasi-experimental analyses of social surveys (Hovland 1972: 439—452). Moreover, it is by no means all that simple to make statistical adjustments for preexisting groups. Expanding on a paper by Lord (1969), Cohen and Cohen (1975) show how such a standard and durable procedure as the Analysis of Covariance can generate incredibly misleading conclusions (see their discussion of yield differences between varieties of corn when flowering height is taken into account, pp. 397—398).

One may properly argue that the use of a shotgun approach in accounting for some dependent variable is despicable, to be sure, but is still a far cry from the models that thoughtful investigators develop. After all, such investigators operate with some theory of the causal order and interrelationships between the various independent variables and the events or conditions to be understood. This is valid, but rarely does one see an investigation that seeks to trace back fully the selective processes underlying the linkages observed. Bear in mind that it is not enough to follow the Lazarsfeld-Hyman Columbia tradition of "elaboration" in order to avoid spurious relationships, but rather it is necessary to be certain that the final underlying variable assignments and distributions are fully understood and/or involve essentially random forces. I think it very much helps to evaluate these studies in terms of the ideal implicit in the logic behind such exercises, to wit, arriving at conclusions that would have occurred had a true experiment been undertaken.

There is, of course, a kind of discouraging negativism generated in this argument since one seems to be never satisfied that all of the significant selective forces have been taken into account. After all, one may reason, do we not have to start on faith or some untested assumptions somewhere? Fair enough, but the question is whether these are indeed the appropriate assumptions to make. Especially bothersome is the fact that the normal empirical study is based on assumptions that are almost certainly wrong. Later, I shall attempt to indicate the very limited specific conditions under which current practices are appropriate. When such conditions are not met, alternative procedures must be found.

Special Models

Finally, one should note that there have been important statistical and design developments in recent years which seek to provide solutions to the nonrandomization issue for at least some specific conditions. Noteworthy is the pioneering work of Campbell and Stanley (1966) and Cook and Campbell (1979) in which specific designs were criticized and certain designs proposed as possibly the best solutions to an imperfect situation that occurs whenever non-randomization is encountered. (A matter that merits further consideration is the fact that the cross-sectional, single survey—which is so common in social research—fares rather poorly in their evaluations.) There are a number of special problems that occur in even longitudinal studies when selective nonrandom forces operate. As a consequence, various statistical procedures have been proposed in recent years: Barnow, Cain, and Goldberger (1980); Barnow and Cain (1977); Goldberger (1972); Kenney and Cohen (1979); Campbell and Erlebacher (1970); and Cook et al. (1975). Although some of these are promising for certain specific conditions and under certain assumptions, it is safe to say that special statistical solutions do not presently exist for most of the deviations from the random assignment model. As Cook and Campbell (1979: 201) observe:

When it appears that all plausible biases have been taken into account and a treatment effect emerges in spite of them all, conclusions can be made with reasonable confidence. Typically, a large degree of uncertainty will remain regardless of how much data sifting, careful reasoning, and creativity goes into the analysis. The size and direction of some biases will probably still be largely unknown, and one or more of them may provide a reasonable alternative explanation for any alleged treatment effect. In social science research where randomization is not present, it is difficult to avoid such equivocalities.

CONCLUSION

Quasi-experimental research almost inevitably runs into a profound selectivity issue. There is selectivity even in terms of who is studied to begin with; witness, for example, the nonrandom underenumeration of the population in censuses (Ewbank 1981: 62–66). The subjects experiencing different levels or qualities of the independent variable (depending on whether it is continuous or discrete) have not been randomly assigned to such conditions. The chances are strong that they have been selected in various ways that represent forces that themselves have a bearing on the explanandum. It is necessary to take these forces into account in order to approximate the true experimental ideal that involves random assignment. One feature of this problem is widely appreciated: the populations differ on other attributes that themselves influence the dependent variable. Less widely appreciated is the likelihood that more subtle forces have operated within each of these characteristics to assign nonrandomly members to the different conditions of interest. In other words, if high SES people are more likely to experience one condition and low SES people are more likely to experience another condition, then taking into account such SES differences is a sufficient control only if there is reason to believe that within each SES there is no difference between those experiencing the different conditions. There are three key problems in the way this problem is normally approached.

First, the assumption is made that taking into account at least *some* of the extraneous differences between the populations experiencing different levels of the independent variable is at least a step in the right direction. This means that applying some of the relevant controls will generate a closer approximation of the true influence of the forces under study. Much of this chapter has been devoted to indicating that this can be a false assumption in many different situations. It can be false not simply because the remaining unmeasured selectivity leads to either overestimating or underestimating the independent variable's influence. In addition, the initial zero-order association may more closely approximate the true association under random assignment than does the association obtained through some controlling or cross-tabulating procedure in which not all of the selectivity is taken into account.

Second, it is often not possible to take into account all of the selective forces that are operating. There is a simple practical problem: researchers are likely to run out of variables because a typical research problem will involve incredibly complex layers of selectivity. In addition, there is a theoretical difficulty that stems from the usual need to keep pushing further and further back into the selectivity operating within each selective force, and so on. The researcher is forced to go back ad nauseam to try to understand why the populations differ in order to take these factors into account and thereby truly isolate the influence of the condition of interest. All of this makes sense only if the selective forces operating to generate these initial differences are fully accounted for *or if the researcher can safely conclude that such selective forces are irrelevant.* Researchers rarely worry about this problem. As a matter of fact, researchers normally have no conception of when it is appropriate to make such an attempt. The "when" issue will be considered in chapter eleven, at which point we will see that this is an appropriate step only under certain specific theoretical conditions.

Finally, there is the implicit assumption in all of this that simulating our image of the simple natural science experiment is, indeed, desirable. If we think about it, all of these statistical approaches to quasi-experimental data are efforts to generate such an approximation. Why, and under what circumstances, should such a simulation be attempted anyway? It is not yet time for this to be seriously considered, since we are in the midst of critically examining current efforts to make such a simulation. As we go further in the analysis of current procedures, it is hoped that the reader will become increasingly receptive to such a question.

CHAPTER THREE

Comparisons, Counterfactual Conditionals, and Contamination

Sociological research, in one form or another, is *comparative* research. If high values of X are thought to cause certain levels of Y to occur, then the truth is ascertained by comparing the Y outcome when X is at a medium or low level. Should one wish to determine if race or ethnic origin affects the judicial process, for example, it is not enough simply to examine the outcome for one particular group. Rather, the research must involve comparisons between groups who are matched as far as possible on all other attributes (witness the research on black-white differences reported in Kleck 1981 and Radelet 1981). Propositions about macrosocietal forces likewise generally imply comparisons, regardless of whether or not they are performed. In the world-systems approach, for example, one expects peripheral nations to differ from core nations on dependent variables of interest and/or to change as the nation moves out of the peripheral category. If you come along and show that core and periphery nations do not differ on some dependent variable of theoretical interest, then it is necessary to reexamine the theory even if the peripheral nations do have the characteristic in question.

Under some circumstances, the comparison is not with another event but with time. For example, the research may deal with changes in a dependent variable which are closely linked to some theoretically driven proposition about the temporal pattern. Still, except for those propositions that are meant to hold under all conditions and without exception, virtually all theories with empirical ramifications imply some form or another of comparison.

Why are these comparisons made? Basically, this is a simulation of the four experimental methods proposed by John Stuart Mill, all of which entail comparisons in one form or another (consider the four methods and five canons in Nagel 1950: 211–233). In the first simple example involving low and high levels of X, the researcher wants to know if the influence of high X on a dependent variable is indeed of a certain nature. The simplest way to accomplish this calls for the researcher to compare situations that are as similar as possible on all characteristics except for the level of X. If the ideal comparison is not readily found, then various statistical procedures are used to simulate such a condition. Ignoring the selectivity issue raised in the preceding chapter, our concern here is with the comparative process itself. Given the importance of the comparative step, obviously it is vital that the researcher be extremely careful about how and with what such comparisons are made. Yet, as we shall see in this and the next chapter, such comparisons are often made in a remarkably casual manner. Even more significant, the logic implicitly used turns out to have serious deficiencies that can generate misleading conclusions.

COUNTERFACTUAL CONDITIONALS

When conclusions are predicated on events that did not happen, philosophers call such statements "counterfactual conditionals." An example of a counterfactual conditional is the assertion that if Lincoln had not become president, blacks would still be slaves. Since it starts with an untrue condition, Lincoln not being president, any consequences from such a condition are essentially unknowable in a *certain* sense. After all, Lincoln was indeed president, and therefore how can one truly verify or falsify a conclusion predicated on an event that did not occur? Another example of a counterfactual conditional is the statement: "Had I driven slower, there would not have been an automobile accident." In point of fact, I did drive faster and hence the premise is false. From one perspective, my statement might just as well have been: "Had I driven slower, California would have had an earthquake." Both statements are based on the same untrue premise and hence the wild conclusion about California is no more provable or disprovable in a certain sense than the statement about my automobile accident.

To be sure, the reader will certainly be more willing to believe my statement about the automobile accident than my statement about the earthquake; especially if more is known about the nature of the accident. Some counterfactual conditional statements seem to be virtually equivalent to being statements of fact, others seem likely but not certain, yet others are very puzzling, and some appear to be absolutely false. For example, Ernest Adams has noted that the first of the two following conditionals is probably true whereas the second conditional statement could easily be false (cited in Lewis 1973: 3):

If Oswald did not kill Kennedy, then someone else did.
If Oswald had not killed Kennedy, then someone else would have.

For a long time, counterfactuals were held in disrepute by philosophers, but in recent years there has been a reconsideration of their role and utility (e.g., Stalnaker 1968; Lewis 1973; Pollock 1976; Nute 1980). This is not the place to review the debates among philosophers, other than to take what is useful for our consideration here of the experimental model.

For the most part, sociologists and other social researchers pay no attention to counterfactuals (exceptions that have come to my attention are Hope 1980, and an incidental mention by Rosenberg 1979: 247). Counterfactuals are unavoidable because, in my estimation, virtually all research (experimental or otherwise) is based on such propositions, albeit ones that the researcher tries to be sure are as *reasonable* as possible. By definition, counterfactual conditional statements share in common the same quality that they are, strictly speaking, not necessarily true. But they are not equal in terms of the probability that they will be undercut by inconsistent evidence, or evidence that requires an increasingly complicated and convoluted explanation. The greater the level of confidence we have in a counterfactual statement, the easier it is to make further advances. Insofar as statements about "what would have been" can be employed with reasonable confidence (albeit without total certainty), then to that degree it is easier to attribute a specific effect to a given condition. The less certain we are about a counterfactual, the shakier are our grounds for obtaining additional empirical evidence.

Strictly speaking, the conclusion of any statement based on a counterfactual condition is unknowable—pure and simple. I did drive fast and Lincoln was president. So we cannot talk with complete confidence about events that *might* have happened had some earlier event been different. There are degrees of likelihood associated with each counterfactual conditional statement based on relevant facts and theory. On the one hand, based on what we know about earthquakes, I can say that it is rather unlikely that an earthquake would be generated by slow driving. However, I would have to say that it is not knowable for sure since the precondition did not occur. On the other hand, the influence of my driving speed on the automobile accident is clearly more complicated since my *existing* knowledge tells me that speed of driving influences the chances of an accident. Ultimately, we are obliged to make counter-factual statements, but we also know that there are various levels of risk involved in them. To be sure, radically new knowledge may substantially revise our ability to make certain counterfactual assumptions, weakening some and strengthening others.

Ironically, then, the comparative procedures used in both experi-mental and quasi-experimental social research require the use of counterfactual statements even though one knows that ultimately they are neither provable nor irrefutable. *The comparative approach is inherently one that makes counterfactual conditional statements.* Let us return to the simple problem of determining the influence of X on Y. If two situations (A and B) are identical on all counts except for the level of X (high in A and low in B) and different values of Y occur, then most social researchers are content to draw conclusions about the influence of X on Y. Although unaware of it, in point of fact they are obliged to make a counterfactual conditional state-ment. Namely, they are saying that were situation B also to have a high level of X, then it would also have had a level of Y identical to that found in situation A. Or, to put it another way, they are saying that Y in situation A would have been exactly the same as Y in B if X were as low as it is in B. Both of these statements are clearly counterfactual because indeed the levels of X were different in the two situations. The issue would not be avoided if the matter were to be examined temporally. Suppose X fluctuates over time in a situation where nothing else changes. If one finds that Y likewise shifts up and down (with an appropriate lag), then most researchers are virtually certain to infer a causal linkage. Again, however, the researcher is doing so on the basis of an implied counterfactual conditional statement—to wit, had X not gone up (or down), then Y would not have changed. Since X did change, again this clearly means drawing a conclusion based on a condition that did not occur.

Like it or not, then, counterfactual conditionals are unavoidable. We are continuously drawing conclusions about the consequences of acts that did not occur. Experiments, actual and simulated, are based on counterfactual conditions; both estimate the causal influence of some factor on another through the use of comparisons. Counterfactuals are therefore a necessary part of life. But it is important to make the comparisons on as reasonable a basis as possible. This requires determination of the appropriate controls, that is, the forces affecting the dependent variable. Even in natural science experiments, it is not possible to control for *everything* (Popper 1964: 93—97). Recognition of forces that had previously not been known to affect the dependent variable may radically affect the counterfactual conditional statements that can be made. This would obviously also apply to the quasi-experimental situation typically confronted by social researchers. As a matter of fact, researchers are continuously searching for additional controls that might alter the relationship hitherto observed. All of this is important, of course, but such procedures are only as good as the comparison that is made. Insofar as the comparison is inappropriate, so too will the counterfactual conditional statement be certain to be even more risky than it need be. Yet, it turns out that such is the case, with totally unjustifiable comparisons being used in many social research projects.

COMPARISONS: WITH WHAT AND HOW?

The true experiment requires very careful determination of the comparisons to be made; these comparisons—whether they are overt or simply implied—are a fundamental part of the experimental procedure. At this point, it ought to be painfully clear how much more demanding the issue is for social research situations that must confront the added problems of simulating the experiment. Nevertheless, if these comparisons are an inescapable step in the reasoning process, we do not wish to make them any more shaky than is necessary to advance our knowledge. "Than is necessary" is the key phrase—a risky assumption is all right when called for, but we certainly will not want to go out of our way to make unnecessary ones and, regardless, we will want to be aware of what we are doing.

Comparisons in quasi-experimental social research are often irretrievably damaged by four current practices. These are: (1) the contamination problem and the error it may generate; (2) the assumption of symmetrical causality; (3) the level of analysis (or the fallacy of triangulation); and (4) the misuse of variance in deciding what variables will be studied and how they will be interpreted. The remainder of this chapter is devoted to the contamination issue; the two following chapters will deal with the problems of symmetry, level of analysis, and variance.

CONTAMINATION[1]

Suppose a chemist wants to determine the influence of some ingredient, X_1, on a liquid, Z. The chemist fills two test tubes with Z, making sure that everything has settled down, and then adds X_1 to one of the containers. He will not be too happy if the interaction between X_1 and Z in the test vial somehow affects the behavior of Z in the control vial. Suppose that there is so much heat given off in the tube containing X_1 that the heat spreads to the other tube. In that case, the influence of X_1 will be underestimated because the observed heat gap has been contaminated by the proximity of the tubes. Likewise, if the addition of X_1 gives off some gas which in turn affects the control tube, this will alter the gap observed between the control and experimental situation from what it would otherwise have been. In either of these examples, the chemist will probably separate the two vials so as to prevent such an interaction. This makes sense. (Whether indeed many chemists actually go about doing their work these days in this manner is of no great concern to us here. What is of interest is that virtually all empirical sociological research is conducted with this implicit model in mind. To wit, comparisons are made with the assumption that events in the test condition have not affected events in settings where the test condition is absent.)

The contamination problem of the sort faced in the natural sciences is rarely appreciated and dealt with in quasi-experimental social research. In the example just given, the proximity of X_1 may alter Y in situations where X_1 is absent. This occurs when the change in Y generated by the presence of X_1 in turn affects the level of Y in the control situation. As will be shown, such problems occur in the social as well as the natural sciences. This would be bad enough; but beyond that, there is an additional difficulty unique to the social world. Namely, regardless of what happens to Y in the setting where X_1 is found, the sheer existence of X_1 in *some* setting may affect Y in situations where X_1 is not even found. Thus contamination can be a terribly severe obstacle in social research. If comparisons are made in circumstances where the *contamination problem* is not recognized as such, the research analyst will commit a *contamination error*. Namely, if the impact of an independent variable is not confined to the situations where it is present, then its influence cannot be correctly determined through the comparative method. Insofar as comparisons are a central feature of empirical social research, the knowledge gained from contaminated comparisons is at least flawed—if not misleading or outright erroneous.

EXAMPLES OF THE CONTAMINATION PROBLEM

Swedish Fertility in World War II

Suppose one wishes to determine the effect of Norway's entrance into World War II on fertility in that nation. One might readily compare its fertility rates with those found in a comparable country that did not enter the war. What could be a more reasonable choice than neighboring Sweden? Such a choice may be "reasonable" but it is not correct. Thanks to a fine study of Sweden's fertility early in

World War II (Lysander 1941), we can see quite clearly how the contamination error might occur. Allowing for the appropriate lag following conception, Lysander found that births in Sweden dropped precipitously nine months after: Chamberlain abandoned part of Czechoslovakia to Hitler in September 1938; Germany invaded Poland in September 1939; Russia attacked Finland in November 1939; and Norway was invaded by Germany in April 1940. An example of this shift is shown in figure 3.1. Notice that Lysander compares actual fertility in Stockholm and Malmö in 1939 (at the time when the impact of the Munich appeasement would have taken effect) with the monthly fluctuations found in earlier years. The evidence is quite convincing, with the sharp drop in fertility running counter to the seasonal fluctuations normally found at that time. This brief study—which is undeservedly neglected— also found a sharp increase in Swedish fertility stimulated by the end of the Russo-Finnish War in March 1940.[2]

What lesson is to be learned from this? Clearly, the dependent variable in the Swedish situation is affected by an independent variable that occurs elsewhere, to wit, war-related political events in other countries. That, of course, is the point of the Lysander study.

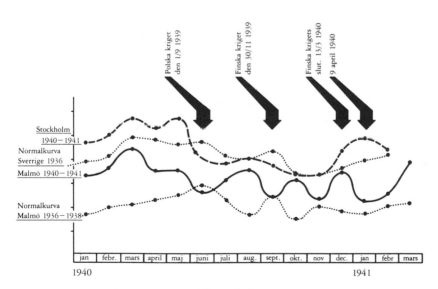

Figure 3.1

For the purposes at hand, however, observe how misleading a comparison would have been between events in Norway and events in Sweden if it were simply a matter of the presence or absence of war in the two nations.

It may be of interest to note here an analogous result obtained by Rindfuss, Reed, and St. John (1978). They found that the famous United States Supreme Court ruling of May 1954 declaring segregated public schools to be unconstitutional and the events that followed in that summer led to a temporary drop in Southern white fertility nine months later in 1955.

Contamination and Diffusion

Accompanied by considerable publicity, voters in California passed a proposition in June 1978 which placed severe limits on taxes in that state. According to one account at the time (*U.S. News and World Report*, 26 June 1978, p. 16): "From Oregon to Maryland and Massachusetts, taxpayers are organizing to amend state constitutions and local charters and otherwise slap tight limits on taxes. . . . Spending cuts suddenly have become popular." These comments proved to be true. Later in 1978, the Oregon Legislature offered voters a choice between a California type of proposition and a special legislative plan (*Taxes* 1978: 716); property tax relief was proposed by the governor of Utah in his budget in 1979 (*Taxes* 1979: 163); a California-style proposition was placed on the South Dakota ballot for November 1980 (*Taxes* 1980: 24); Arizona voters approved a constitutional amendment in a June 1980 election which placed limits on property taxes (*Taxes* 1980: 500). In turn, Massachusetts voters approved an initiative that limited property taxes, and Nevada voters approved initiatives that would lower their property taxes and eliminate the sales tax on food (*Taxes* 1981: 52). Later in 1981, New Mexico enacted a measure that reduced the rates on personal income and sales taxes (*Taxes* 1981: 250).

The foregoing are some of the details in what is obviously a general diffusion process. But these details also suggest that comparisons between states in their initiation of new taxes and in their spending records would be greatly complicated by this diffusion process. To wit, states without initiatives or constitutional changes were probably also affected by the events in surrounding states. After all, one significant feature of humans (and the institutions and groups to which they belong) is the ability to anticipate—or seek to anticipate—events. Accordingly, many of the state legislatures and governors no doubt attempted to head off such initiatives or other "taxpayer revolts" by voluntarily cutting back on taxes and limiting new increases in their budgets. All of this makes good sense, but visualize the impact this has on simple mechanical research designs. If state budget expenditures are visualized as the dependent variable, and the presence of a tax initiative is the independent variable, then surely the influence of the latter will be underestimated when the budgets of states without initiatives are compared with those of states that had such initiatives. The counterfactual conditional statement that would be used in such a comparison is extremely shaky here. It implicitly says, "Tax trends in the states that did not pass initiatives indicate what the trends would have otherwise been in those states that did pass initiatives."[3]

The existence of such tax initiatives, it is reasonable to assume, should have an impact for all of the states. Those not experiencing such initiatives would have dealt with the possibility anyway and hence may well have cut taxes or introduced only modest increases in order to forestall such moves. If social researchers ignore the Problem of Contamination and simply compare initiative states with those not having passed one, they are likely to underestimate the influence of the variable under study. This is, of course, not to question the impact of a tax initiative per se, but rather to suggest that its influence may be deeply underestimated by comparisons with states that were also affected even if no initiative was passed.[4]

SCHOOL DESEGREGATION: AN EXAMPLE OF THE CONTAMINATION ERROR

Suppose one wishes to examine the influence of court-ordered desegregation on white outmigration rates from central cities of metropolitan areas in the United States. Ignore for the moment the data that must be used and simply visualize a situation closer to the ideal than would actually be encountered. Suppose, through a random assignment process, that half of the cities are desegregated and half are not. Except for sampling errors, the two sets of cities are initially the same with respect to their distributions on all characteristics that might conceivably have a bearing on the dependent variable, white outmigration. Thus they are identical with respect to the initial levels of black-white residential segregation, population composition, absolute numbers of the groups, size of the cities, the relative numbers in the suburban rings and central cities, region, age of city, socioeconomic conditions in the cities, tax rates, quality of city schools, and any other factors that might influence white outmigration rates. Finally, let us assume that all of the desegregating cities are required to employ the same procedures, such as busing, magnet schools, and so on.

If the two sets of cities are compared, what might be learned about the influence of court-ordered desegregation on the movement of whites to the suburbs? Since the cities were randomly assigned, do we have reason to believe that differences in white outmigration rates for the two sets of cities will provide an answer to the question? Certainly the difficult selectivity issue raised in the previous chapter is not present in this context. If this were a classical experiment in the physical sciences, the answer would almost certainly be positive. But it is not, and the social analogue to this standard experimental model is by no means certain—and that is putting it mildly.

Suppose, for example, that the percentage decline among whites in desegregated cities during some specified period after the court decision is twice the average level experienced in other cities (say 12 and 6 percent respectively). It is reasonable to conclude that the effect of court-ordered desegregation is such that cities so ordered have a higher white exodus rate than do cities not so ordered. But one cannot conclude with any confidence that the effect of court-ordered desegregation is to raise white outmigration over what it would otherwise have been. It is one matter to observe that a certain difference exists (here a gap in outmigration rates between the sets of cities) and that it was caused by a certain condition (here the issuance of desegregation orders by the courts). But it is a radically different matter to conclude that the differences between the two conditions tell us what would have occurred had the test condition been absent. How can this be, given the difference between 12 and 6 percent in the average outmigration rate? The answer to this paradox is found by considering the severe impact of the contamination problem, even under these relatively ideal conditions, on the counterfactual propositions that can be made.

The key issue lies in the assumption most social researchers would make in such a situation, to wit, that the 6 percent outmigration rate of whites in the segregated cities is the rate that would have occurred in those cities regardless of the desegregation orders experienced in the other places. In turn, it is assumed that this 6 percent rate is also the rate that would have been experienced by the desegregated cities if they had not been ordered to desegregate. The heart of the issue is the assumption that events in one setting had no influence on events in settings with different conditions. In point of fact, for all one knows, the outmigration of whites would have been 12 percent in all of these cities during this period, but the segregated cities dropped to 6 percent because white residents guessed that their cities would not be picked for desegregation in the near future and hence any anticipatory incentive to leave declined.[5] At any rate, a plausible case could be made that the effect of court-ordered desegregation is to lower outmigration from the control cities and not to increase the outmigration in the experimental cities over what it would have otherwise been.

There is another way for this pattern to occur (in which desegregated cities have twice the outmigration rates of other cities) without its meaning that desegregation increases white outmigration. Such a gap could also occur if the outmigration rate from both sets of cities had been lowered from the level that "would have been" if no court-ordered desegregation had occurred anywhere. This outcome is possible if, say, it turns out that people in the desegregated cities discover that the actual situation is not as bad as they had feared it would be. Accordingly, their outmigration rate goes down to 12 percent from the 15 percent level it would have been had desegregation still been hanging over their heads. In the nondesegregated cities, in addition, white residents are not only aware of the fact that it is not disastrous in the experimental cities but also that they are less likely to be affected in the future. This might be owing to the desire to wait until results are obtained for the first set of cities or it could reflect a movement in the Congress and the administration to slow it down.

A third possibility is that the level of white outmigration—had there been no desegregation orders—would have been somewhere in between the levels actually observed in the two sets of cities. Suppose it is the case that 9 percent of the white residents on the average in either set of cities would have moved out if there had been no court-ordered desegregation. Under such circumstances, the effect of the order was both to raise the white outmigration rate in desegregated cities and lower it in the other cities. This would mean that the introduction of court-ordered desegregation did indeed cause white flight, but the magnitude of its influence is overstated by the degree to which the unaffected subjects (whites in cities without such orders) change in the opposite direction from what their level would have been. The existence of the test condition has caused the dependent variable in the control situation to change in the opposite direction. The influence of the test condition is over-stated if the Problem of Contamination is ignored under such circumstances.

There is yet another way in which such a pattern might be found—one that involves causes that are at least partially consistent with the initial interpretation. Suppose it was the case that outmigration in all of these cities would have been 3 percent if nothing had been done. The rate went up for both sets of cities, but more so for those experiencing desegregation. In that circumstance, a somewhat opposite error might be made. Namely, the comparison between the two subsets might lead to an underestimation of the effect of desegregation on white exodus since it accelerated the exodus in all cities, albeit more so in the ones experiencing the court order.

In summary, the *Problem* of Contamination occurs when the independent variable in one setting affects the dependent variable in other settings. The *Error* of Contamination occurs when this Problem is ignored and the social researcher operates as if the influence of an independent variable is restricted solely to settings where it is present. In terms of the example used here, the key question is whether the 6 percent white outmigration rate in the segregated cities would have been different in the absence of desegregation elsewhere. If so—and it is, strictly speaking, unknowable just as is the opposite assumption that the data are uncontaminated—then to that degree the conventional interpretation of the data is misleading and unwarranted.

Contamination is an especially widespread problem at present because of the intense communication within various social and spatial subunits of a society and, indeed, across nations. As a consequence, if X goes up in one society (or subunit within a nation) and generates certain changes in Y or nonchanges in Y, then the assumption cannot always be made that the linkage between X and Y in low X or unchanging X situations was not altered by these other events. Likewise, insofar as the social processes involve some form or another of anticipation or responsiveness to events occurring elsewhere, then the Problem of Contamination will also exist. We would not think much of a biological experiment where laboratory animals injected with some disease-causing virus were compared with control animals placed close enough to catch the disease through contagion. Yet, in point of fact, that is precisely the problem in many social research studies. To the degree that the absence of contamination is an incorrect assumption, then to that degree the application of the standard experimental simulation to real social events commits what is called here the Error of Contamination.

Needless to say, observation of the opposite pattern could be just as misleading. Suppose that 6 percent of whites leave the central cities that have been desegregated, compared with 12 percent of those in segregated cities. It is entirely possible that the outmigration rate would have averaged 3 percent in all of these cities if no court orders had been issued. Instead, outmigration increased to 6 percent in the integrated cities because of white distaste for integration but went to 12 percent in the other cities because of white panic over their being next and their distorted picture of the consequences of integration (perhaps helped by a few unappealing incidents in the mass media, and so on). In such a case, desegregation would have raised the overall level of white exodus in all cities from what would have occurred, but comparisons between the two sets would lead one to conclude that desegregation lowered the rate.

Using Past Trends to Determine What "Would Have Been"

The real difficulty with the Problem of Contamination, assuming success in getting social researchers to recognize and appreciate the issue, is in determining a workable solution. More about that later in Part II of this volume. It is appropriate here to consider why one simple solution—what might be called "the trajectory approach"—is unlikely to be of help. Namely, if we knew the course of events prior to the occurrence of a change in the independent variable in which we were interested, could we determine what would have happened if the change in the independent variable had not occurred? By examining the actual changes in the dependent variable, we would then simply determine the influence of the independent variable in question. In terms of the school desegregation problem, for example, a potentially attractive solution would exist if it were possible to determine with reasonable confidence what would have been the white outmigration rates in these cities if no desegregation orders had existed during the period under study.

It would be especially nice if there were a purely stable state in which nothing was changing before the independent variable changed—in this case, before half of the cities were desegregated. Alas, dependent variables are usually not constant over a long enough period prior to the changes in the independent variable. In this case, it is unlikely that there would have been any semblance of stability in the white outmigration rate from central cities over time. Hence the investigator could not estimate what Y would have looked like if X had remained unchanged. Moreover, as a general rule, it is not very satisfactory to abstract the existing set of changes before X changes (in this case, desegregation) to project or otherwise fit a curve to decide what the future would have been. It is one thing to project a set of current changes in order to demonstrate their consequences if they continued unaltered into the future—for example, what the population of the world would be one hundred years from now if the world grew at such-and-such a rate. But it is another matter to take such projections seriously as if they tell us what will occur in the future.

The situation is radically different in many natural science experiments because there are solid grounds for making counterfactual statements. (To be sure, their counterfactuals are also unknowable, strictly speaking; moreover, a major intellectual development occurs when an existing counterfactual assumption becomes questionable.) The old saw about the rich getting richer and the poor getting poorer is borne out by the difference between the natural sciences and the social sciences in their ability to make counterfactuals with reasonable confidence. The existence of a reasonably well developed body of knowledge makes it easier to generate counterfactual conditional statements. In turn, because this helps one determine what would have been the case in situations that are now of interest, it is possible to learn more and thereby make additional counterfactual statements and/or have greater confidence in existing ones. In social research, for example, if we really had a strong body of information about the outmigration processes in metropolitan areas, then it would be easier to determine the consequences of school desegregation. This is because the observed post-desegregation pattern could be compared with some expectation of what "would have been" had desegregation not occurred. This would not eliminate the contamination process, since it is a *social* process, but at least it would give the researcher some conception of what had occurred in the control situation (cities that remained segregated in the current example) as a consequence of changes introduced elsewhere. In turn, it would also permit the researcher to determine the effect of the test variable (here, desegregation) without comparing results with conditions that themselves have been altered through the contamination process.

Research on School Desegregation

It is not my intention to deal with the controversy raised by Coleman, Kelly, and Moore (1975) and Coleman (1976, 1977) regarding the causal link between racial desegregation in the schools

and "white flight." Any effort to determine the influence of school
desegregation on white flight, using real data and actual conditions,
will run into considerable difficulties since there is the added
problem of selectivity as well as the contamination issue. Recall that
the preceding discussion assumed the random assignment of cities
to one or the other condition. In reality, since cities are not randomly assigned, there is the added selectivity issue. Incidentally, a
thoughtful reviewer of the white flight question, Reynolds Farley,
found no significant relationship between flight and school integration in either 125 school districts of the North and South or in
the largest cities (1976: 16—17). Of particular interest here, however, is his linkage of the Problem of Contamination to the selectivity issue:

> It is possible that whites anticipate school desegregation and move away from a
> city before the schools are actually integrated. If this occurs, it is probably related
> to the racial composition of a district. That is, if the proportion of Blacks in a city
> is low, an integration order—even if it entails busing—will likely involve few
> students and the integrated schools will be predominantly white. However, if the
> proportion of Blacks is high, many children will have to be shifted out of their
> neighborhood schools and white students may be a minority in the integrated
> schools. Where this occurs whites may leave the public schools prior to
> integration. . . .
>
> These data are consistent with the hypothesis that whites fear integrated
> schools with large Black enrollments and withdraw their children from public
> schools prior to integration. (Farley 1976: 17)

CONCLUSION

The Problem of Contamination occurs when the influence of an
independent variable is not restricted exclusively to those settings
where the variable is found. Under that condition, the Error of
Contamination will be committed if the social researcher attempts
to approximate or simulate the model derived from early natural
science experiments. In social research, one cannot blithely assume
that the occurrence of change in an independent variable affects the
dependent variable under study *only* in those settings where the
independent variable has changed. To the degree that there is
information or some other impact crossing between the settings in

which X varies (whether they be communities, societies, social organizations, structures, individuals, subcultures, etc.), the linkage between X and Y is altered along the entire range of X. The assumption of separation or isolation, when in fact it is not operating, leads to the Error of Contamination.

Unless a change in X has instant consequences for the dependent variable, Y, it is rather likely that a contamination will occur such as to affect the dependent variable in those settings where X has not changed or has moved to a different level. Calculation of the expected levels of some dependent variable based on the levels found prior to a change in the independent variable of interest is also hampered by yet another factor, to wit, changes that occur in anticipation of the forthcoming change in the independent variable. For example, migration to the United States increased substantially right before World War I.[6] The increase probably represented a rush to get in before the war to avoid the anticipated obstacles to migration, the demands of military service in Europe, and the general hardship of war. Here then is an example of a dependent variable that is responding to events that have not even taken place.

The projection, as it were, of past events into the future is nearly always an exceptionally risky business in the social sciences. If it were possible to make a confident statement about what the dependent variable would have been in the period under study—based on the trajectory of changes prior to the events in question—then one could compare the actual changes observed with what would have otherwise occurred. (This involves a counterfactual conditional statement since one does not really know what would have been. The Swedish fertility study cited earlier succeeds precisely because there are such strong grounds for making a counterfactual conclusion about what "would have been" Swedish fertility in the absence of these international political events.) I believe it is fair to say that such an approach is usually not possible with even a modicum of confidence. Over and over again, social researchers have found some of the simplest of projections to be weak predictors of forthcoming events. Hence it is rather unlikely that one could come up with a counterfactual conditional about which there would be sufficient confidence. Moreover, the simple fact that the independent variable has changed (in the case discussed in this chapter, desegregation was introduced) should, in itself, alert the researcher to the strong probability that social conditions are different and that any form of projection is questionable.

The issue presented in this chapter involves something more than the usual run-of-the-mill argument that some alternative interpretation of the data is possible. Rather, the objection here is due to a deep problem encountered in social research, the Problem of Contamination, and the special error it can generate. In the school desegregation example, it is almost certain that the "control" cities were influenced by events in the experimental cities—indeed, by the existence of the experiment itself—and also by the response to events in the test cities. To ignore the contamination issue here and in many other social research settings would mean subjecting the conclusions to exceptionally dangerous and profound errors.

CHAPTER FOUR

Asymmetrical
Forms
of Causation

Some social researchers employ a probabilistic approach to causality; others use a deterministic approach. In either case, rarely is symmetric (or bidirectional) causality distinguished from asymmetric (or undirectional) causes. This is a different matter from the distinction between recursive and nonrecursive relationships, the former referring to models where "all the causal linkages run 'one way,' that is, if no two variables are reciprocally related in such a way that each affects and depends on the other, and no variable 'feeds back' upon itself through any indirect concatenation of causal linkages, however circuitous" (Duncan 1975: 25). The symmetric/asymmetric distinction is, however, an equally fundamental dimension to any relationship—despite the fact that most of us are completely insensitive to it. In examining the causal influence of X_1 on Y, for example, one has also to consider whether shifts to a given value of X_1 from either direction have the same consequences for Y. If this appears to be a rather odd question, it is because most empirical studies operate with the assumption that social relations are symmetrical; in other words, as if it does not matter whether X_1 had increased or decreased to reach its present level. Rarely does a researcher consider whether the upward movement of X_1 from, say, 10 to 20 will lead to a different value of Y than would a downward movement of X_1 from 30 to 20 (a possibility that is perfectly plausible if the causal linkage is asymmetrical). In other words, most research and theory implicitly assume symmetry such that a given value of X_1 will have the same impact on Y regardless of the direction from which it was generated. As we shall see, this distinction between symmetric and asymmetric forms of causality has significant consequences for theory, research, and applied issues. The issue exists, moreover, regardless of whether "causes" are explicitly discussed or the scholar prefers to think in terms of "relations" or "associations."[1]

SYMMETRICAL AND ASYMMETRICAL CAUSES

If the causal relationship between X_1 and Y is symmetrical or truly reversible, then the effect on Y of an increase in X_1 will disappear if X_1 shifts back to its earlier level (assuming that all other conditions are constant). Such a relationship is illustrated in chart 4.1, column 1. Between time 1 and 2, an increase in X_1 from 4 to 5 causes Y to move from 3 to 6. A return of X_1 to 4 at a later time leads Y also to return to its initial value, 3. This need not mean that a unit change in X_1 always has the same influence on Y—such would not be the case if the relationship was nonlinear. But it does mean that the influence of a particular value of X_1 on Y will not be altered by the direction of the change in X_1. In other words, the movement of X_1 from 15 to 20 may have a different influence on Y than an increase of

CHART 4.1

ILLUSTRATIONS OF REVERSIBLE AND IRREVERSIBLE
CAUSAL RELATIONS BETWEEN Y AND X

		Causal Relationship between Y and X_1			
		Reversible	Irreversible	Partially irreversible	
		Y	Y	Y	Y
Time	X_1	(1)	(2)	(3)	(4)
1	4	3	3	3	3
2	5	6	6	6	6
3	4	3	6	5	2

X_1 from 5 to 10, but in either case, the movement of X_1 back from 20 to 15 or from 10 to 5 will return Y to its starting point as well.

There are two types of asymmetrical causal relationships. The most extreme, illustrated in column 2, involves a purely irreversible $X_1 - Y$ linkage. As before, an increase between time 1 and 2 in X_1 leads to change in Y from 3 to 6. In this instance, however, the decline of X_1 to 4 by time 3 does not lead to a reversal in Y. As a matter of fact, Y remains unchanged. A purely irreversible relationship means that a change in one direction for the causal variable has a consequence for the dependent variable, but a shift in the opposite direction has no consequence for the dependent variable. Columns 3 and 4 illustrate asymmetrical causal relationships that are partially irreversible. In the first of these, we see that the downward shift in X_1 leads Y to decline but not to the point where it has started. Thus, with X_1 at 4 again in time 3, Y is at 5 rather than 3. In column 4, however, we see that the return of X_1 to its initial position has caused Y to decline to a level (2) even lower than it had initially been (3). For the purposes at hand, it is best to concentrate primarily on the most extreme of the asymmetrical relationships, to wit, one that is totally irreversible. However, the reader should keep in mind the possibility of partially asymmetrical causal linkages such that the changes in each direction are of different magnitudes.[2]

Distinction Between Reversible and Irreversible Causes

Suppose, five minutes after driving away from home in the morning, I remember wanting to take a certain book with me. If time permits, I can easily drive back and correct the lapse. If I have no time to spare, I will not turn back. In reaching this decision, I am implicitly distinguishing between *reversible* and *irreversible* events. On the one hand, my omission can be reversed by simply driving back to the house and retrieving the book. On the other hand, I am under no illusion about the reversibility of time, which will continue to move forward even as I move backward over space. If it was 7:30 when I left the house and 7:35 when I start back, I know it will be 7:40, not 7:30, when I reach the house again.

Even if an *event* is intrinsically reversible, the causal *process* may not be. The same process that leads my gasoline tank to become increasingly empty will not, if reversed, lead it to be filled again. If I turn my car around and drive home, my gasoline tank will not return to the level it had been when I first started out. This distinction, readily seen and understood in the everyday events we encounter, is totally muddled in our efforts to understand society— with disastrous consequences. The distinction can be expressed in very simple terms for sociological phenomena. If a change in some variable (X_1) causes a change in some other variable (Y), what happens to Y if X_1 returns to its earlier level? Assuming everything else is constant, a process is *reversible* if the level of Y also returns to its initial condition; a process is *irreversible* if Y does not return to its earlier level. Observe that it is the *process*—not the *event*—that is being described as reversible or irreversible. Thus, if Y were to return to its initial level through some other causal system, say the operation of changes in X_2 and X_3, this would simply mean that Y can be reversed. It would not mean that a reversible process is operating. As a matter of fact, Y could be fluctuating through the operation of two irreversible processes; a change in X_1 in one direction generates a change in Y even though a return in X_1 to its initial value does not lead to the return of Y to its earlier level. However, Y might go back to its earlier level with changes in X_2 and X_3. One must also remember that processes can be *partially* or *largely* irreversible rather than *totally* irreversible—in other words, there can be some degree of reversal in Y when X_1 goes back to its initial value (although even that may not happen). Needless to say, it is easier here to deal with those extremes where a process is either fully reversible or totally irreversible (as we shall see, there are certain processes that have an intrinsic total irreversibility). However, one must bear in mind the gradations that are often encountered.

In the natural sciences, there are theories and propositions that are clearly built on notions of reversibility, whereas others imply irreversible processes. Boyle's law, mentioned in chapter one as an example of the natural science model emulated in social science research, involves a reversible process. This law indicates that the volume of gas will decline and then increase over and over again in regular fashion as the pressure oscillates between higher and lower levels. This is an example—one of many that could be found in the physical sciences—of a reversible model. It is an *ahistorical* model; the history of the gas molecules is superfluous for determining what the molecules will do in the future under certain specified conditions (say, of temperature, pressure, etc.). The law states, pure and simple, that the gas molecules will behave in a certain way if subject to given pressure and temperature conditions—regardless of what the situation in the container had been yesterday or a year ago. Likewise, the concept of a "food chain" represents just such a reversible set of linkages in the bioecological context, in which the number of predators and their prey can move up and down indefinitely.

There are also many important irreversible processes in the natural sciences, ones where the causes of a given condition can be removed but the consequences remain (see Prigogine 1980). The chemical changes produced through electrolysis cannot be undone through a reversal of that process. It is almost certain that the giraffe would change or disappear if the causes leading to its evolution were to disappear, but it is dubious that the giraffe would return to the status from which it evolved even if those earlier conditions were again present. In similar fashion, if a heavy weight falls on someone and thereby breaks a bone, we know that removing the weight will not return the broken bone to its original condition. In the medical world generally, one is not too pleased to learn that some disease or damage is irreversible. All of these situations are characterized by the same causal process; namely, if X caused condition Y, then elimination of X will not mean the elimination of condition Y.

The social sciences are likewise characterized by both reversible and irreversible propositions. In Weber's classic essay on the role of the Protestant ethic in the development of capitalism, for example, he argued that the Protestant ethic was a prerequisite for legitimating and encouraging certain attitudes toward the acquisition of material goods and worldly signs of success. However, once such attitudes are established as acceptable, then these crucial dispositions will prevail even if the religious beliefs were to disappear (Weber 1958: 181–182). Likewise, we do not assume that the United States would become a colony of Britain again if the conditions that caused the American Revolution were to revert to an earlier state. In terms of the distinction between process and event, one must bear in mind that the issue is not whether the eastern part of the nation could again become colonies (the event itself) but rather whether such an event would occur if the earlier conditions were to return (a reversible process).

There is no shortage of reversible propositions in the social sciences. A classic proposition in social psychology, provided by Homans (1950: 112), is: "If the frequency of interaction between two or more persons increases, the degree of their liking for one another will increase, and vice versa." The implication of such a proposition is that the frequency of interaction between two persons could go up and down indefinitely without any alteration after each cycle in the level of affection. It is not likely that the rates would return to their initial levels if everything else is held constant, in the same way that Boyle's law generates a reversible proposition about gases, but the proposition is stated in this fashion. Likewise, when the economists use the random walk model to describe the price movements of stocks, a significant consequence is that the history or pattern of a stock's price movement in the past is of no value in predicting its future movement (see, e.g., the collection of pioneering articles in Cootner 1964). Indeed, the mathematics used to work with this proposition is derived from Brownian motion. Another example is provided by Blau's T-1.5 theorem: "The probability is that the rate of intergroup associations increases with declining group size for the groups distinguished by a given nominal parameter" (Blau 1977: 23). This could or could not be reversible, as stated earlier, since it is not immediately clear whether Blau is also suggesting that an increase in group size would generate a *decrease* in intergroup associations. However, that is precisely what he does have in mind: "A simpler equivalent formulation of T-1.5 is that size of the groups distinguished by a given parameter is inversely related to the extent of their intergroup relations" (Blau 1977: 24). (Incidentally, a cursory examination of the theorems presented in Blau's 1977 book will indicate that even such a major theorist as he is by no means clear with respect to whether his theorems are meant to be taken as reversible or unidirectional.)

CONSEQUENCES OF OVERLOOKING
THE DISTINCTION

Social research for the most part tends to assume that processes are reversible. *If a change in X makes Y change in a certain direction, then surely the opposite change in X would generate an opposite change in Y.* Reasoning of this sort pervades the sociological literature, either implicitly or explicitly, and of course fits in rather nicely with certain early natural science models, such as Boyle's law. Most social research descends from this model, although the various statistical procedures involved in multivariate analysis make it appear more complex. This assumption of reversibility is so much a part of our standard research procedure that it requires very little discussion here. Rarely are propositions stated in an asymmetrical fashion such that changes of X in one direction generate changes in Y that are not merely the mirror image of what is expected if X changes in the opposite direction.

While writing this section, I heard a speaker discuss the causes of the civil rights movement in the late fifties and early sixties. It was a particularly convoluted exercise, probably because it sought to do the intrinsically undoable, to wit, account for the specific timing of the movement within a narrow range of years. (Recall the discussion in chapter 1 of efforts that are so complicated that they become intrinsically undoable.) An objection was made from the audience not in terms of the undoable issue, but rather that the theory failed to account for the precipitous decline in the civil rights movement during the seventies. Specifically, the causal variables purporting to account for the rise had continued to increase during a period when the movement declined. The speaker was able to offer no more than a rather feeble response. Of interest, for the purposes of this chapter, however, is that the objection is a perfect example of the reversible processes implicitly assumed in much of our research. In point of fact, two irreversible processes could be operating such that: an earlier shift in X_1 in one direction leads to an increase in Y (the civil rights movement), whereas a later shift in one specific direction for X_2 leads to a reversal in Y. The key point should have been simply that the forces causing the decrease in the civil rights movement could be unidirectional in their causal impact; therefore, a separate force would have necessarily caused the earlier increase. Hence the speaker could have been correct about the causes of the rise even if they fail to account for the later decline. If the victim of a shooting dies even after the bullet is removed, we do not say, "Aha, if the bullet caused harm, then its removal should have eliminated the harm." We are still inclined to believe that the damage was caused by the bullet. All that is required is some sense of when a causal relationship is reversible or irreversible.

Speaking of injuries, one should bear in mind the tremendous damage that will occur when an irreversible process is erroneously assumed to be reversible—either because the theory is implicitly stated in such a manner and/or the empirical researcher makes such an assumption out of habit. Theories that are completely correct, if stated in a unidirectional form, may be negated by empirical evidence or found to be only weakly associated with the dependent variable when treated as reversible processes. Correct reversible theories, however, will tend to receive much stronger empirical confirmation. The interaction between research and theory—insofar as there is a meaningful one—will tend to favor reversible theories because they will be more likely to receive substantial empirical support. Of course, all of this is based on an assumption that I believe is quite true: even when an irreversible theory is generated, researchers will look for empirical ramifications that assume reversibility—except on those rare occasions when the theory *explicitly* makes this distinction and/or the researcher is especially alert to the distinction. All too often, with tragic results, our reasoning is as follows: If changes in X_1 really caused the increase in Y, then surely a reversal in X_1 would have caused Y to decline.

Multivariate data analyses are especially hurt when researchers or theorists are unaware of this distinction. If a model employs a variety of independent variables to account for a dependent variable, some of the linkages might quite easily be reversible and others irreversible. Attempts, under those circumstances, to talk about the relative importance of one as opposed to another independent variable are even more foolhardy than they would otherwise be.[3] Moreover, the belief that one has controlled or taken into account a variable's influence—whether this be through log-linear, regression, path analysis, standardization, or any other multivariate statistical method—is totally inappropriate when a procedure assuming reversibility is applied to a condition in which irreversible processes are operating. (These statistics are not necessarily inapplicable to reversible processes, as we shall see, but they do require a different approach to the matter which takes into account change in the *direction* of the independent variable.)

Theoretical selectivity will occur in other ways if the distinction between reversible and irreversible processes is blurred. When irreversible processes are erroneously treated empirically as if they are reversible, at times the empirical data will appear to validate the incorrectly stated (and/or tested) hypothesis and at other times the data will not be supportive. If in a given data set the independent variable tends to move largely in one direction (and that is the direction in which the irreversible process operates), then the process will appear to hold very nicely; if it were moving in the opposite direction, then the process would not at all behave the same way. A data set containing a mixture of shifts in both directions will, of course, generate some sort of weak result. If certain types of social processes tend to be reversible whereas other types tend to be irreversible, this means that social research will actually help confirm and encourage one set of theories while at the same time discouraging another set of equally valid ones—unless researchers are aware of these distinctions and adjust the demands of their empirical tests to appropriate models. Under these circumstances, it is entirely possible for empirical research actually to be counterproductive—tending to discourage some kinds of theories even though they are completely true.

Applied Consequences

The distinction between reversible and irreversible causal processes is as crucial for applied work as it is for basic research. Yet rarely does one encounter concern with whether a social problem was caused by one or the other type of process. This can have disastrous results since proposed solutions to social problems must first determine whether the initial causal force is reversible or not. In fact, the failures of applied social policies derived from contemporary social research and theory are in no small way due to the absence of such a distinction and the consequent inability to determine whether the observed process is one or the other type.

Suppose, for example, I wish to determine the causes of some severe racial difference in American society at present, a difference that will be called Y. If there are strong grounds for thinking that X_5 and X_6 are especially responsible for this difference (after all, why should X_1 always take the rap?), does this mean that social programs should attempt to alter the levels of those two causal variables? I would guess that this would be the normal next step in sociological logic. To be sure, one might be concerned about whether X_5 or X_6 was more easily altered by exogenous forces and/or whether the prescribed changes in one or the other X were more palatable to the larger population. But these questions and the policy itself would be absolutely and incredibly meaningless, if not downright harmful, if the processes linking X_5 and X_6 to Y are irreversible. For it would mean that the cause of the racial gap will not go away if the initial causes are removed.[4] If the causal process responsible for a social problem is totally or largely irreversible, failure to recognize this will mean policies that attempt to solve the problem by removing the initial cause (a plausible step only if there is a reversible causal relationship). Such policies are totally inappropriate, amounting to trying perpetually to close the barn door after the horse has escaped. In the case of the horse, an irreversible cause means that you get it back through a process different from the one that got you into the pickle initially. That is simple common sense, but many social policies are based on the assumption that a problem gets resolved by reversing the conditions that initially caused it. This makes sense, at best, only if it is first determined that the causal process is largely a reversible one.

Such projects are bound to fail; moreover, researchers and theorists are then likely to ask inappropriately if perhaps X_5 and X_6 were really not the main causes of Y (after all, policies based on such conclusions did not seem to work!). This disenchantment over a body of knowledge would not occur if a distinction had been drawn between reversible and irreversible causes. If both X_5 and X_6 are found to have irreversible causal linkages with Y, then we can see why corrective social policies based on such an assumption will not work. I believe this was a major difficulty in the "war on poverty" programs started under the presidency of Lyndon Johnson.[5]

In short, then, the reversible-irreversible distinction is of vital importance in three domains: the formulation of appropriate theories; the use of appropriate empirical tests; and the utilization of basic knowledge for applied policy decisions. In my estimation, sociological research will be inescapably marred if it remains insensitive to the distinction between reversible and irreversible processes. But perhaps this is putting the cart before the horse. One should first be certain that asymmetrical processes are widely found in society and that they cannot be dealt with in the ways presently employed. Before I suggest fundamental changes in current research procedures, therefore, let us consider why and how the most extreme type of asymmetry occurs, namely irreversible causal processes.

IRREVERSIBLE CAUSES

There are three different types of irreversible causes in sociological phenomena.

1. The social sciences have a variety of constant or invariant forces, just as gravity and the principle of selectivity are constant forces in the natural sciences. These invariances or constant social forces are basically irreversible social processes. Examples are: Simmel's classic proposition about the Tertius Gaudens, or the power inherent in a third party when the first two parties are in competition or conflict (Simmel 1950: 154–162); the Malthusian principle of the differences in the potential growth of human populations and the food available to them (Petersen 1975: 153–154); the invariant features of social organization proposed by Treiman (1977), which in turn generate certain constancies in the occupational prestige system; or the Marxist explanation of social structure in terms of the characteristics of the economic system and the relations between social classes

(Bottomore 1968: 46). In listing these propositions, it is not my intention to endorse them as necessarily true, but rather to illustrate the nature of such "constants" in social theory and their widespread existence.

It should be observed, however, that the outcome of these forces is often not formulated as inevitable or unavoidable. An *irreversible* causal force is not necessarily an *irresistible* force; rather, it is one that operates in only one direction. One might say that some features of Marxism are formulated as inevitable—at least, as it is proclaimed by some of its advocates at present—but certainly it is not inevitable that certain relationships occur in a three-person group, and Malthus himself allowed for humans to avoid the problem he postulated through their very own actions. Just as planes and birds can overcome the thrust of gravity, and human action may alter or delay the selective forces for survival, so too it is the case that societal constants are not necessarily irresistible.[6] But constants that operate in all situations specified do represent one type of irreversible force.

2. Irreversible processes also occur when a given causal sequence leads to a fundamental alteration of the dependent variable such that it will not respond in the same way to a reversal in the independent variable. This is easy to see in social psychological terms. People have memories that record events, and these records do not simply dissolve once the stimulus has disappeared. Hence any experience stored in the memory cannot be removed simply by withdrawing the cause of its initial transmission. This is rather obvious with people—consider how one is altered through marriage even if one is later divorced, or how an insult is remembered even if the offender later apologizes. Likewise, we know that it is much harder to unlearn habits than it is to learn them as anyone seeking to give up cigarettes has found out.

Groups and societies can also be altered in ways such that a later reversal in the independent variable will not generate a similar change in the dependent variable. For example, the history or tradition of a society becomes an entity itself. Regardless of what may have caused the tradition or history or sacred features of the society, it becomes the case that added value is placed on its existence which will not be altered by a shift in its initial cause.

3. Finally, processes can become irreversible even if the linkage

between the cause and effect is not intrinsically irreversible. This merits particular attention here since it is both especially common in social processes and not too obvious. The simplest way of describing a causal relationship between an independent variable and some dependent variable is as if it occurs universally, regardless of any other conditions. Thus we might say that changes in X_1 cause Y to change in a certain direction. The causal linkage can be described more precisely if we know of other variables that modify or affect the actual outcome of this relationship. For example, we might say that the process is restricted to advanced industrial societies or perhaps to a specific segment of the population such as those of a given age or educational level. Usually, because there is such a wide variety of other factors that influence Y, it is necessary to assume that the particular relationship between X_1 and Y operates without specifying all of the other relevant variables to be held constant, that is, all other factors that may themselves affect the Y variable. But what happens if there are other relevant variables that always are at certain levels when Y or X_1 hold particular values? Specifically, what happens when these other relevant variables are themselves the product of earlier developments in the very causal process under consideration? Under circumstances where X_2 is inextricably tied to the level of X_1 and Y, it is not clear that it makes much sense to assume a certain relationship between X_1 and Y net of X_2. It makes no sense to assume that other variables are held constant when they are inevitably at certain levels while the relationship under consideration is supposed to be operating.

If the outcome of a social process is a set of additional changes in other conditions—and if these later conditions make it impossible for the initial process to reverse itself— then assumptions to the contrary involve what can be called the "Ceteris Paribus Error." Whether it involves a theoretical statement, an empirical conclusion, or a policy decision, a Ceteris Paribus Error occurs if any of these is made with assumptions about combinations of other variables that in reality cannot exist. This is not the same as the commonly encountered issue of spurious relationships in which the investigator is asked to take all other known causal factors into account before determining the influence of the independent variable of interest. This is radically different because in the present

circumstance the levels of the control variables are in reality insepa-
rable from the level observed for the independent variable of interest
and/or the dependent variable. For all purposes, various mechanisms operate to make it impossible for X_1 to exert its influence in
the opposite direction even though there is reason to believe that it
would have done so if conditions remained identical.[7]

Consider a social process of the simplest sort, say, when an
increase in X_1 generates an increase in Y. This can involve a chain of
events such that a reversal in the initial value of X_1 in no way leads
to a reversal in Y. This will occur, among other ways, if a change in
Y generates a wide variety of changes in other conditions (X_2, X_3,
etc.) that then affect the further influence of X_1 on Y. As a
consequence, even if the X_1-Y relationship were purely a reversible one, it is almost certain that the changes in these other
conditions would keep a reversal in X_1 from causing Y to return to
its earlier level. As a matter of fact, we shall see next situations
where the return of the initial causal variable to an earlier condition
is only possible *because* it no longer has the consequences for the
dependent variable it originally had. In these cases, it is almost
immaterial whether the reversible form of the proposition is
theoretically correct because it is unlikely to be observed empirically. Empirical tests that implicitly assume reversibility end up
knocking our perfectly valid theories that would help us understand
social events if correctly understood. Indeed, the goal should be to
understand the conditions that keep the process from being reversible. Since this situation is rather widespread in social processes
and takes a number of different forms, a more detailed examination
is in order.

THE SPREAD OF ENGLISH: AN EXAMPLE
OF IRREVERSIBILITY DUE TO INEVITABLE
CHANGES IN CONDITIONS

The expansion of English as a world language illustrates rather
nicely the third type of irreversibility. Namely, we shall see how a
condition, once it is established, can create circumstances that will
perpetuate itself even if the initial causal variable is reversed. (The

following account is drawn from Lieberson 1981). English did not reach its preeminent position as the great language of international communication until relatively recently. For some two hundred years, beginning in the seventeenth century, the language of diplomatic interchange was French. At the Congress of Vienna, in 1815:

the victors employed French not only in dealing with the defeated France, but also among themselves—indeed the treaty was written in French. It was only at the close of World War I that English received important recognition as an equal to French in diplomacy. . . . In 1920 English was spoken in the League of Nations Assembly by delegates from six nations in which English was not an official language, whereas French was used by delegates from twenty-four nations besides those from France, Haiti, Belgium, Canada, and Switzerland (Shenton 1933: 381). By 1927, the numbers were even less favorable to English, with only two countries using that language in addition to those from nations with English as an official language. (Lieberson 1981: 352)

There is a variety of forces contributing to the growth of English as an international language, not the least of which is the expansion of the United States as a world political, economic, cultural, and scientific power. In addition, there has been a general intensification of international interaction such that it has become increasingly important to develop second-language skills. Advances in various transportation and communication technologies have made international interaction more and more significant and increased the relevance of English speakers from the United States. According to the data reported in a remarkable study by Shenton (1933), for example, there was a persistent increase in the number of international conferences held during the period between 1840 and 1931. There were more international conferences during just the last two years of this period, 1930 and 1931, than were held during the first forty years—despite the fact that the period ends long before there was any significant international air travel and before the relative affluence of the present time. An analysis of the representation at these conferences in the 1920s shows the relatively minor influence of the United States at that time. "Although the United States was represented at a large number of these international conferences, given the difficulties involved at that time, it was tied with Austria for eleventh place in the rankings. The nations were led by France, followed by Great Britain, Belgium, Switzerland, the Netherlands, Germany, Czechoslovakia, Italy,

Poland, and Sweden before the United States and Austria are reached" (Lieberson 1981: 370).

It is not my intention to weigh the relative importance of these different forces here. Rather, the point is to show how a condition, once established, may generate added conditions that will perpetuate it even if the initial cause disappears.

Shifts in the power of language groups, or in their numbers or in other forces that might be expected to affect language spread, will not necessarily have such effects. This is because the role of a language, once established, will tend to be perpetuated long after the disappearance of conditions that were initially necessary. Hence, it is quite possible for the English-speaking nations to decline in economic, political, or other types of power without a concomitant drop in the role of the English language. It also follows, then, that speakers of other languages can make significant gains in these domains without an immediate linguistic gain. (Lieberson 1981: 371)

A variety of forces contributes to the maintenance of a language's role as a medium for international communication, *after it is established as such.* For example, once people become bilingual in a specific language for the purposes of international communications, they will have little reason to shift to a new second language since they develop a vested interest in the language. Unless their own language is now a competitor for the international role held by some other tongue, such "third parties" will play a conservative role, definitely helping to maintain the existing international language (Lieberson 1981: 352–354). As a matter of fact, the existing pattern of language usage will tend to provide incentives for each new cohort to acquire the existing international language. Moreover, schools and bilingual educational programs will be in operation and there will be a set of teachers with the necessary skills. International practices, customs, and expectations, will be in operation (see Fishman, Cooper, and Conrad 1977). All of these are features that would not initially establish a language as an international force, but they come into effect afterward and tend to reinforce the language's role even if the initial cause disappears or returns to a level found at an earlier period. It is not that change is impossible—witness the shift from French to English or the earlier movement away from Latin and Greek as lingua francas. Rather, there is an asymmetric set of forces affecting these events, such that the forces necessary to establish a language are substantially greater than the forces necessary to maintain a language once it is established.

IRREVERSIBLE PROCESSES DUE TO THE ABSENCE OF A CETERIS PARIBUS SITUATION: A FORMAL ANALYSIS

If the preceding process is visualized formally—say, through diagrams showing causal arrows—the results are far more complicated than the causal models with which one normally works. It is more complicated not because there are more variables, however. As a matter of fact, figure 4. 1 contains fewer variables than do many path models. But figure 4. 1 is far more complicated because the linkages cannot be described in the simple single-picture way that one normally employs. And that is one of the problems that must be overcome. It is well known that social processes are complicated: the empirical researcher thinks that these processes are complicated because many variables are operating and a wide set of interrelations has to be taken into account; the theorist thinks that these processes are complicated because it is difficult for the researcher to measure fully and adequately the few forces that she or he is sure are the really "crucial" ones. Alas, the really complicated matter is the *form* that causal relations take—and neither group seems to recognize this. Recognition of the inadequacy of current forms, however, should prove to be highly rewarding. For it permits the researcher to pursue massively simpler and different empirical approaches; and it demands different goals from theorists. So, in the long run, attention to the complicated forms that causal relations can take, such as suggested in the series of panels described in figure 4. 1, is actually a beneficial simplification.

In Panel 1, we see a commonly described recursive relationship between X_1 and Y such that an increase in X_1 generates an increase in Y under the conditions observed at that time. (In terms of the example used earlier, Y is the position of English as a world language and X_1 represents a number of different variables that can

Panel 1. If X_1 is initially low:

$$X_1 \longrightarrow Y$$
(low)   (low)

$$X_2 \quad X_3 \quad X_4$$
(all are low or nonexistent)

Panel 2. If X_1 increases:

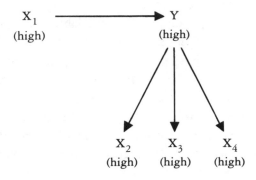

Panel 3. If X_1 returns to low:

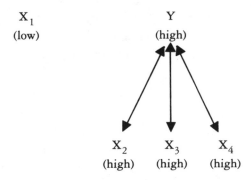

Figure 4.1. Formalization of an Irreversible Cause

affect this position—represented here for heuristic purposes as one variable.) At this point, where X_1, and Y are both low, conditions X_2, X_3, and X_4 simply do not exist or are at very low levels. (These variables represent events that will occur with varying degrees of lag after Y begins to go up.) Examples of X_2, X_3, and X_4 variables are: the availability of English second-language instruction in non-English-speaking countries; expectations that others will know English and hence that it will serve as a lingua franca; the presence of a large number of "third party" speakers of English who would be resistant to learning yet another nonnative language. Thus variables X_2, X_3, and X_4 are shown in panel 1, but no relationship is indicated between these variables and Y under these conditions

Panel 2 describes the change that will occur in X_2, X_3, and X_4 should an increase in Y occur owing to a change in X_1. At this point, X_2, X_3, and X_4 will develop as a response to the change in Y (i.e., to the increasing importance of English as a world language). In effect, then, if X_1 remains low, then Y will remain low and so too will X_2, X_3, and X_4. If X_1 does increase, then so too will Y and, in turn, X_2, X_3, and X_4. None of this sounds very different from the usual path approach. However, panel 3 indicates the divergence. Namely, once the latter variables are established, then and only then will a nonrecursive relationship develop with Y such that they support Y. (Panel 3 of fig. 4.1 describes the relationship between an established international language and the various supports that operate in the nations once it is established.) In the final panel, we face the situation in which X_1 shifts back to its initial low level; in other words, the original cause of Y's being high disappears. But at this point, such a change has either no effect or a modest effect on Y because of the support established through X_2, X_3, and X_4 (Panel 3).

Figure 4.1 illustrates three important points. First, it provides a clear example of processes that make it possible for social events to have lives of their own—a situation that is not mystical, but rather reflects changes in the causal linkages and directions over time. Second, we see how some conventional approaches can distort and inadequately describe complex social processes. Social researchers, whether they employ path diagrams or not, have a tendency to act as if there is a fully symmetrical model, in which the nature, magnitude, and causal direction of the linkages between variables are more or less unchanging over time. Finally, this example suggests that it is not simply a question of whether a process is reversible or not in the abstract with all other factors held constant. Rather, it is entirely possible—indeed, often probable—that a given process will generate changes that virtually guarantee that the earlier conditions will never again be duplicated. Thus a return of the initial causal variable to its earlier level will not have the same effect on Y as it once did simply because the ceteris paribus assumption will not occur. Changes in the Y variable create new changes in other X variables that do not change back in the same way. On this score, we should observe that the shift in X_1 back to an earlier position may or may not generate *some* change in Y in the opposite direction from what occurred earlier when X_1 was increasing. But even if the movement is in the opposite direction, it will not be of the same magnitude as what occurred earlier.

Consequences

The point of it all is that the consequences of a given event can have a life of their own, so that the causal conditions can be removed or return to an earlier stage without the consequences doing likewise. Whatever generated the Women's Liberation movement, for example, could now disappear and it is unlikely that the thrust and accomplishments of the movement would simply go away. A set of practices, expectations, organizations, laws, and the like are in existence which will not disappear if their original causes vanish.[8] If we think about it, there is nothing really mysterious about social events having a life of their own; it means that once an event is set into motion, the event may have consequences that in turn provide a reinforcement and support for its existence—even if these conditions did not exist at the outset and even if these added conditions were themselves generated by the event itself.

The presence of a reversible process is still of interest—in theoretical terms—but it is essentially untestable in this situation because there is no way in which all other conditions will be the same. There is also a good chance that such a proposition will be incorrectly studied with an empirical test that assumes reversibility (in which case, the variables are treated as if they are ahistorical, similar to the changes in the volume of gas generated by Boyle's law). Reversible processes that cannot be found in a ceteris paribus situation are likely to generate misleading empirical results. If the movement of X_1 is largely in one direction, then everything will appear to be fitting rather nicely, but woe unto those who either make policy judgments based on the assumption of reversibility or who do empirical research in which X_1 is moving in the opposite direction. Also pity the poor soul whose theory is examined with data in which there is also a shift in the opposite direction for X_1; the results will be weakened since Y will tend not to move back toward the opposite direction if the new conditions facilitating Y have by then been introduced. The strength of the relationship found between X_1 and Y will depend on the degree to which the first variable has persistently moved in one direction or not. If X_1 has changed in one direction, then a reversible process will be measured suitably if the changes are in the direction that supports the dependent variable. If X_1 has moved in the opposite direction, but only after Y has generated new nonrecursive linkages (represented by X_2, X_3, X_4, etc.), then the influence of X_1 on Y will be underestimated if the reversibility is assumed in the empirical work.

Further Examples and Discussion

Reversible processes can be blocked through other ways as well again simply because all the remaining conditions relevant to the outcome cannot be the same as they had been earlier. A couple of additional examples should suffice to show how the ceteris paribus assumption may never occur in reality. Suppose we start off, as we do in Panel 1 of figure 4.2, with a simple causal linkage between X_1 and Y. The low level of X_1 leads to a low level of Y; the increase in X_1 is followed by an increase in Y (Panel 2). What makes X_1 go up? Suppose it is another force, X_2; thus the increase in X_2 causes X_1 to increase and the latter change, in turn, causes an increase in Y (see panel 3). Everything is fine so far. If there is a simple reversible

Panel 1. If X_1 is initially low:

Panel 2. If X_1 increases:

Panel 3. Cause of increase in X_1:

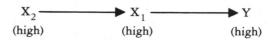

Panel 4. The cause of a decline in X_1 directly affects Y:

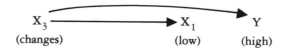

Panel 5. The cause of a decline in X_1 indirectly affects Y:

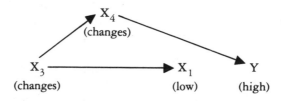

Figure 4.2. Further Examples of Irreversible Causes

relationship between X_1 and Y, then what might keep Y from returning to its initial value at this point in response to the return of X_1 to its initial level?

If the process initially causing an increase in X_1 is an *irreversible* one, then it means that the cause of the decline in X_1 back to its initial level is a reflection of a different causal process. If X_2, for example, had caused the initial increase in X_1 through an irreversible process, then it would mean that changes in something else would have occurred in order to deliver X_1 back to its earlier low level (say, changes in variable X_3). Under that circumstance, there is a strong chance—although it is not certain—that the conditions affecting Y are also different, because X_3 itself has a direct bearing on Y and/or because X_3 affects other attributes that influence Y. (These are shown in Panels 4 and 5 of figure 4.2.)

Although there are equilibrating systems, as a general rule the reversal of an important causal variable probably does not take place without a change in some exogenous variable. In turn, this means that there is a significant change in the entire system which almost guarantees that the ceteris paribus situation will not be met. In a certain sense, it is irrelevant whether the initial increase in Y was caused by a reversible or irreversible relationship between Y and X_1. For, in either case, it is unlikely that a reversal in X_1 will generate a comparable shift in Y. This is because the forces directly or remotely responsible for generating a shift in X_1 will likely also generate other changes that prevent all earlier conditions from holding. Hence, even if there is a return to an earlier value of X_1, the shift in Y will almost certainly not be the mirror image of its earlier change—it could be greater or possibly far less than the earlier change. (As a matter of fact, the ceteris paribus situation could be so remote from the earlier state of affairs that a shift backwards in X_1 could actually be accompanied by an increase in Y rather than anything else.)

CONCLUSION

Policies based on social research may fail for a variety of reasons. But it should be clear from this analysis that one of the prime candidates for failure is a policy that assumes that reversal of the forces that caused a problem will simply lead to a reversal in the problem of interest to the policymakers. In some cases, the causal linkage is an irreversible one; in other cases, the causal linkage is reversible but new support conditions have been established that make the initial cause irrelevant, either totally or partially, such that we say that the events have a life of their own. Further, there is also the ceteris paribus myth—the assumption that conditions are all the same when the initial causal variable is reversed. The myth occurs because, in many circumstances, some substantial changes in other features of the society are required before the initial causal variable will be reversed. This means that a new variable affecting X_1—whether reversible or irreversible—will not have a simple symmetrical influence on Y. One can ask, quite properly, if one is supposed to deal with these issues by controlling, cross-tabulating, or otherwise taking into account variables? The answer is yes and no. Controls of one sort or another cannot solve the issue of irreversibility. Normally, at least, control variables are treated as if they are ahistorical. To be sure, it would be possible to have more complicated temporal sequences than we customarily do. Since Chapter Six will deal with the control issue, for the moment it will be necessary to accept on faith that the whole control and cross-tabulation procedure is not what it is cracked up to be.

Asymmetrical causal forces tend to be neglected in social research. There are probably many reasons for this, not the least being the fact that they are difficult to work with. As a matter of fact, if a given causal process is viewed as totally or partially irreversible, then such an approach will vastly complicate the customary research procedures. With the present empirical systems and criteria for solid evidence, there is a bias against thinking in those terms—they are not tidy. Insofar as asymmetrical forces are operating in situations where researchers employ empirical devices appropriate for simple reversible forces, to that degree social research is missing the boat. For it is particularly likely to employ criteria that make it very hard to find the consequences of these irreversible forces.

A number of issues are raised by this distinction between types of causal processes—issues that must be confronted and resolved before theory, social research, and applied work can make further progress. The following questions will be considered in Part II of this volume:

1. How does the researcher know whether the process under study is symmetrical or asymmetrical? Moreover, if the latter, is there a way of telling if it is totally or partially irreversible?

2 What makes some causal linkages irreversible and others reversible? Are there certain kinds of linkages that are especially likely to be irreversible?

3. What further ramifications exist for theory construction, for empirical research, and for applied social research?

4. What modifications are necessary in the current statistical approaches that we apply to causal analysis?

CHAPTER FIVE

Variation, Level of Analysis, and the Research Question

Virtually all social researchers want data with variation in the characteristics of interest to them.[1] The notion is that existing theories will then be validated, and new ones developed, by determining what variables help account for the variation found in the data set. These two steps in the research process—the search for data sets that incorporate variation and, in turn, the effort to account for the variation that is found—are so ingrained and widespread that we probably take them for granted. It turns out that the logic underlying these steps is more complicated and shakier than practitioners seem to recognize. Moreover, the implementation of the variation goal often leads to levels of analysis and the framing of empirical questions in ways that are actually damaging to the advancement of knowledge. At issue in this chapter is the reasoning behind the steps, the impact they have on the formulation of empirical problems, and the consequences these procedures have for sociological knowledge. The pros and cons of the specific statistical procedures are not at issue here. A variety of statistical forms can be used; the choice depends on the nature of the data and the assumptions involved. For example, a log-linear model might be used to fit a complex data pattern obtained in a multidimensional cross-tabulation, or it might be a regression approach in which a "large" proportion of the variance in the dependent variable is accounted for. But, whatever the statistical approach, the goal is still pretty much to account for the observed variation. At issue here is the goal itself and the steps taken to achieve it.

VARIATION IS A STATISTICAL REQUIREMENT

Why is it important that we have variance? Why is it important that we explain the variance that we have? The first edition of *Statistics for Sociologists* (Hagood 1941), an important early text devoted to social statistics, observed that there were three preconditions for the use of descriptive statistics in sociology: plurality of units (as opposed to data for only a single unit); characteristics that are enumerable or measurable; and *variation* in the characteristics (104). What Hagood said about variation then is important to keep in mind now:

> If perfect uniformity with respect to a characteristic prevails throughout the units of a group, the description of the distribution of the characteristic in that group does not require statistical methods. But if some units possess the characteristic and others do not, or if some possess it in greater degrees than others, that is, if the units of a group vary with respect to the characteristic, a . . . criterion for the use of statistical methods is fulfilled. . . .
>
> The *variation* of individuals in a measurable characteristic is a basic condition for statistical analysis, and the concept of *variation* is fundamental to all statistical theory. If uniformity prevailed throughout the universe, there would be no need for statistical description, since any individual could be taken as a representative of all. (Hagood 1941: 104, 174)

The point is clear: if you want to do a statistical analysis, variation in the data is mandatory. As Mueller, Schuessler, and Costner (1977: 150) put it: "*Variation* is the foundation for all statistics. If all the values in a given set were identical, it would be superfluous to calculate an average—or for that matter, any other statistical measure—because any single measure already would represent all." Fair enough. But statistical analysis is ultimately a means for satisfying one or another sociological problem. Therefore, one must ask whether problems are sometimes posed in a certain way more because they meet statistical criteria and needs than because they are the most appropriate research question in terms of either substantive or theoretical issues. To be sure, a long-standing criticism in sociology is that quantitative social research is either nonproductive or fails to deal with the important issues.[2] But that is not the question here at all; the issue here is how to do it right!

MISINTERPRETATION OF VARIANCE EXPLAINED

The next step, after obtaining a data set with variation, is to explain it. It is not clear to me how we got to this state of affairs in social research, but it is clear that everything seems to ride on that criterion. In the OLS regression model, for example, researchers often act as if one variable is "better" than another if it can account for more of the variance; indeed, we even talk sometimes about the "explanatory power" of variables in exactly these terms; a procedure such as stepwise regression is based on finding the variables that account for the maximum amount of variance. We even belittle theories and/or variables that fail to account for much of the variance and we certainly worry about situations in which we cannot appropriately allocate the variance explained to separate independent variables because they are so closely intertwined (the problem of multicollinearity). "The more two variables covary or move together in a sample, the harder it is to ascertain the independent effect of one of them, holding the other constant" (Hanushek and Jackson 1977: 87). These are legitimate problems and issues, but they do reflect this central concern with variance explained or the equivalent thereof in other statistical procedures. In the case of log-linear models, for example, the estimated expected values are compared with the observed ones through goodness-of-fit statistics.

This concern with goodness-of-fit, or variance explained, or what have you, is not inherently bad or undesirable. If there is a model or theory about what is going on, then it is reasonable to see how well the data fit that model. (To be sure, this is a different matter from inferring a model from the data.) Given the desirability of finding a data set that fits some theory (to say nothing of the intellectual esthetics when a good fit is made), what objection is there to such a goal other than that the researcher may have generated a spurious association? After all, *not* worrying about goodness-of-fit or variance explained is certainly no assurance that a faulty explanation will not occur.

This process presents three major difficulties. First, there is a tendency to make explained variance or the well-behaved data set a good in itself. As a consequence, the researcher is prone to judge the optimal outcome in terms of the closest fit or the most variance explained. Although researchers sometimes know better, they have a propensity to weigh the substantive or theoretical *importance* of variables in terms of their contribution to variance explained or the equivalent thereof. Second, the pursuit of variance leads researchers to pick certain problems and ignore others, depending on whether they can obtain data sets that are "appropriate" (i.e., that incorporate variation in the crucial variables). This means more than merely a lopsided development in the social sciences; some of the most fundamental theoretical issues do not involve data sets with variation—at least as the problem is customarily approached. Finally, we shall see that the level of empirical analysis is often determined not simply by the substantive nature of the problem but by a *statistical* requirement, to wit, the need for variation in the data set so as to allow for variance-based statistical analyses. This propensity to pose problems at a certain level of analysis, simply because variation can be found at that level, is a remarkably deceptive and widespread practice that gums up our ability to evaluate various theories or generate conclusions about what is causing what.

The last two issues are key ones, and will be considered in detail later. But the first issue, the obsession with "explaining" variation, merits a brief discussion even if it is basically an offshoot of the second and third issues.

HAPPINESS IS VARIANCE EXPLAINED

We are all aware that association does not necessarily mean causality. Two durable examples of this follow:

In Table 13.2 we show the number of wireless receiving licenses taken out from 1924 to 1937 in the United Kingdom and the number of notified mental defectives per 10,000 in England and Wales for the same period. A glance at these figures shows that they are very highly correlated. The correlation coefficient is, in fact, 0.998. (Yule and Kendall 1950: 315–316)

A southern meteorologist discovered that the fall price of corn is inversely related to the severity of hay fever cases. . . . The price of corn is generally low when the corn crop has been large. When the weather conditions have been favorable for a bumper corn crop, they have also been favorable for a bumper crop of ragweed. Thus the fall price of corn and the suffering of hay fever patients may each be traced (at least partly) to the weather, but are not directly dependent upon each other. (Croxton and Cowden 1939: 10)

Despite a long-standing and keen awareness of the dangers, social scientists still tend to be uncritically happy when associations are found, and the stronger the better. The following quotation was written by three enthusiastic scholars arguing the case for mathematical sociology—at least as they visualized it. As a consequence, it is perhaps a less guarded and less inhibited description of what most empirical researchers seek or idealize, despite their awareness of the dangers listed earlier. Again, the issue applies to more than various regression models.

Many sociologists have tacitly assumed or explicitly suggested that axiomatic theory might be developed from weaker building blocks (i.e., theoretical propositions that explain about 10 or 20 percent of the variance). However, we agree with Otis Dudley Duncan, who suggested in his original critique (1963) that these efforts would be relatively fruitless unless the correlations were very high. Our experience with equation fitting has demonstrated that correlations must be approximately .98 in order for consistent continuities to appear across a broad range of data. . . .

The rule of determinancy prescribes the assumptions that natural phenomena are completely determined or very nearly so, and that it is always possible to find a correct answer—an equation that accurately describes or explains almost all the variance in the data relationships under investigation. It implies that scientists should push their investigations until they find an equation or set of equations serving to explain nearly 100 percent of the variance for the phenomena in question. (Hamblin, Jacobsen, and Miller 1973: 6—7, 212)

Is it reasonable, or even desirable, for a theory to account for the maximum possible level of variation in the dependent variable? Such a question is rarely asked; most researchers behave as if the ideal goal is to explain 100 percent of the variance in regression terms (witness the quote) or the equivalent with other statistics (such as obtained a low chi-square or L^2 in log-linear models).[3] Beyond the well-known issues of measurement error, instrumentation difficulties, sampling, and the like, there are *substantive* issues that might keep the researcher and/or theorist from seeking such a goal. There are grounds for cautiously reconsidering that which is presently a standard goal in social research.

First of all, it is always possible to generate an equation—a complicated one, to be sure—that can completely and totally fit any function whatsoever. In other words, if pairs of X and Y values are obtained through a series of random numbers, Taylor's theorem in differential calculus states that it will be possible to generate a function that will fit this set except under certain specified conditions.[4] Taylor's series, by the way, could be extended to cases where more than two variables appear (Allen 1956: 458−459). All of this means that in some circumstances a model could fit all of the data—and very precisely at that—but be of no "scientific" utility. Using Taylor's series, it would be possible to "account for" exactly every X-Y pair observed in a set of random numbers. A correlation of 1.0 would be obtained between the values of Y predicted by the equation generated through the use of Taylor's series and the observed values of Y. (By the criteria of "explanation" or "prediction," it would appear to be perfect.) Alas, before one searches for Taylor's series in that old calculus textbook, there is one catch. The values of Y predicted by the equation were fitted after the fact to the observed values of Y. As a consequence, if one randomly drew additional pairs of X-Y values, the existing equation would almost certainly do rather poorly. What is the point of all this? It is entirely possible, with Taylor's series, to fit such data without there being one lot of substantive meaning to the exercise. To be sure, the usual research project would require some minimal degrees of freedom, a statistical criterion that could not be met by this solution. But the Taylor theorem does serve to remind us that a model that closely fits the data is not inherently and inevitably wonderful.

The question is raised as to whether the analysis of some dependent variable in the typical multivariate approach is really any more appropriate than a curve-fitting exercise based on Taylor's series. How important is it anyway to account for as close to 100 percent of the variation as possible? In particular—above and beyond issues of measurement error, sampling, and other procedural problems—to what degree is it reasonable to expect a perfectly complete theory to account for less than all of the observed variation between units in the dependent variable of interest?

LESS COULD BE BETTER: HOW MUCH
VARIATION SHOULD BE EXPLAINED?

Seymour Spilerman and Wesley C. Salmon, sociologist and philosopher of science respectively, approach this question from rather different perspectives. Studying the chances of a community experiencing a race riot during the period between 1961 and 1968, Spilerman (1970) found that only two factors seemed to be operating: the number of blacks in the community and the location of the community (South or non-South). For the most part, after these two factors are taken into account, there is little intercity variation in the number of disorders that can be accounted for by such factors as: social disorganization, absolute deprivation of blacks, their relative deprivation, or political structure of the cities.[5] This result runs counter to those obtained in a variety of other studies for that period and earlier. Spilerman had been able to show that these other factors made virtually no contribution after number of nonwhites and region were taken into account (their zero-order influences were not, however, nil).

All of this is very nice, but since the R^2 between the two factors and the dependent variable is .468, one would normally ask if there are other unmeasured variables that might also help account for intercity differences in riot frequency and/or if there are measurement errors that keep R^2 from reaching 1.0. These questions are approached by Spilerman in his 1971 follow-up paper in which he asks whether it was reasonable to assume that there was nothing more to be explained:

Is it the case that by considering additional community characteristics the proportion of explained variation can be increased? Or, alternatively, is it possible that the total proportion of variation which can be *theoretically* explained is actually less than one?

The commonly employed measure of the inadequacy of an explanation, $1 - R^2$, is predicated upon an underlying explanatory model which is fundamentally deterministic. The concept of randomness is employed in that formulation to compensate for errors resulting from inadequate measurement and neglected effects. Presumably, by improving data quality and incorporating additional variables into an explanation, the proportion of explained variation could be increased and, theoretically, made to approach the value "one."

In contrast to that view of randomness as disturbance, a process may be conceptualized as inherently stochastic, and this type of explanatory model is consistent with there being a complete explanation (in the sense that all relevant knowledge has been incorporated) in which the R^2 value is less than 1.0. (Spilerman 1971: 433)

Spilerman then goes on to cite an example from subatomic physics: the decomposition of atoms is a well-known and understood process, he says, but it is impossible to predict the exact number of disintegrations or which particles will decay. He then approaches the racial disturbance question in an analogous manner. Using the basic distinction developed by Lieberson and Silverman (1965) between the immediate precipitants of riots and the underlying conditions that cause them, he develops a model in which both deterministic and chance factors operate. On the one hand, the structural conditions (underlying conditions) are viewed as responsive to deterministic forces such as various community characteristics; on the other hand, the occurrence of precipitating incidents is viewed as a random event. Accordingly, the actual number of outbursts is viewed as the product of this deterministic force and the random force. If this were the case and if this provided a complete account of the presence of riots, R^2 between the two structural forces (number of blacks and region) and the dependent variable would be less than 1.0.

Is this a complete explanation? How would one know if a lower R^2 reflected an incomplete or inadequate explanation? Ignoring measurement errors and other technical matters, social researchers would normally view an R^2 of less than 1.0 as an incomplete explanation; they would want to throw in more independent variables. (Notice the radical difference in outlook from the customary procedure, which would entail an unending pursuit of an R^2 of 1.0 and/or the conclusion that more is yet to be known about the process. Such research is perpetually vulnerable to the charge that the investigators did not take into account some other variables.) Obviously, one cannot simply allow researchers to decide arbitrarily that their results represent all there is to the problem.

Spilerman uses a simulation methodology to determine the R^2 that would be expected if the number of blacks was the sole underlying condition (South and non-South are analyzed separately). He finds that the observed R^2 in the non-South between number of disorders in each city and number of blacks is virtually identical to the R^2 expected under simulation of a model in which random precipitating events are combined with this one deterministic causal factor. The results for the South are not as strong—allowing for the possibility that other forces operated there as well (see Spilerman 1971: 434—435). How satisfactory is Spilerman's analysis? As he himself observed, it is not designed to deal with the massive fluctuations through the decades in the number of racial disturbances; however, Spilerman more or less wiped out other explanations for that period. He showed that an R^2 considerably below 1.0 in the explanation of intercity variation *within the period* need not lead to the conclusion normally made under such circumstances, to wit, that other variables must be affecting the dependent variable and/or that there are measurement errors or other problems of a technical nature which prevent the empirical demonstration of the factors under consideration. Instead, Spilerman attempted to show that, if his model provided a correct and full understanding, this was precisely the result to be expected. To my knowledge, the style of thinking represented in Spilerman's 1971 paper has not been taken up or pursued by sociologists generally. If one thinks about the issue in terms of the perspective developed in this chapter, one could apply the same type of question to virtually all empirical research activities. The procedure has radical implications for the normal way one seeks to maximize the explanation of variation.

For the purposes at hand, the approach to the statistical explanation of improbable events taken by the philosopher Wesley C. Salmon is quite similar.

> No one ever contracts paresis unless he has had latent syphilis which has gone untreated, but only a small percentage of victims of untreated latent syphilis develop paresis. . . . The probability that a person with untreated latent syphilis will contract paresis is still low, but it is considerably higher than the prior probability of paresis among people in general. To cite untreated latent syphilis as an explanation of paresis is correct, for it does provide a partition of the general reference class which yields a more homogeneous reference class and a higher posterior weight for the explanandum event.
>
> When the posterior weight of an event is low, it is tempting to think that we have not fully explained it. We are apt to feel that we have not yet found a completely homogeneous reference class. If only we had fuller understanding, we often believe, we could sort out causal antecedents in order to be able to say which cases of untreated latent syphilis will become paretic and which ones will not. . . .

A parallel example could be constructed in physics where we have much greater confidence in the actual homogeneity of the reference class. Suppose we had a metallic substance in which one of the atoms experienced radioactive decay within a particular, small time period, say one minute. For purposes of the example, let us suppose that only one such decay occurred within that time period. When asked why that particular atom decayed, we might reply that the substance is actually an alloy of two metals, one radioactive (for example, uranium 238) and one stable (for example, lead 206). Since the half-life of U^{238} is 4.5×10^9 years, the probability of a given uranium atom's decaying in an interval of one minute is not large, yet there is explanatory relevance in pointing out that the atom that did decay was a U^{238} atom. According to the best theoretical knowledge now available, the class of U^{238} atoms is homogeneous with respect to radioactive decay, and there is in principle no further relevant partition that can be made. Thus, it is not necessary to suppose that examples such as the paresis case derive their explanatory value solely from the conviction that they are partial explanations which can someday be made into full explanations by means of further knowledge (Salmon 1971: 56–57)

All of this suggests a simple conclusion: there are times when the goodness-of-fit criterion (or variance explained, or whatever the statistic's analogue) is grossly inappropriate, as it is customarily used. It would be nice to explain everything, but it may well be inappropriate and/or impossible. Suppose, for example, I wish to find out the factors that lead a small number of people to reach stardom in motion pictures, or at least leading roles. It might well be possible to find certain characteristics of the individuals which affect their chances, for example, personal attractiveness, persistence, race, connections, even acting talent! But among these characteristics, it may be largely accidental or intrinsically unknowable. Efforts to go beyond the establishment of probability functions for each type of characteristic or combination thereof, for example, talented-ugly-white-no connections, and so on, are doomed to failure. Curiously, if we looked at the small number of people who do make it to the top, we could no doubt provide ad hoc explanations of the unique combination of features that permitted them to make it. We could then even prescribe strategies for success that would be a curious mixture of incorporating the classes of events that do have probabilistic relevance for achieving a leading role with characteristics that have no bearing on success.

An analogy with coins is in order. Suppose a large number of unbiased pennies are each tossed ten times. The number of heads obtained with each coin will vary, although the mean will be roughly five. However, some coins will produce only two or three heads and others will yield seven or eight. (There is, of course, a chance that a series of tosses will give an even more extreme number of heads or tails.) At any rate, some well-known statistical propositions can be used to account for the overall distribution. But suppose we decide that we want to know why one particular coin gave us eight heads and another gave us only three. If, indeed, the coins are unbiased, then we are bound to failure. If we work at it long enough, I have no doubt that some individual characteristics of the coins will be found to help account for the differences among them in the number of heads in that particular round of tosses (perhaps: the year or the decade that the coin was minted; or the place of minting; or when the coin was tossed in the sequence of coin tossing; or the characteristics of the previous coin or two previous coins; or the number of heads obtained with the previous coin, etc.; or some higher order interaction such as between year or place of minting). As R. H. Coase put it, "If you torture the data long enough nature will confess" (cited in Wallace 1977: 431). But the results will not be meaningful in the sense that the subset of unbiased coins that generated a large number of heads in the first round will be no more likely to generate an unusually large number of heads on a second sequence of ten tossings than will the set of unbiased coins that came up with only two or three heads in the first sequence. Thus there is an excellent fit of the coins being tossed, but a very poor result with the characteristics of the individual coins.

What is the relevance of these various examples for the social research issue of concern here? First, a theory need not account for all of the observed variation—even if research conditions are ideal with respect to procedural matters such as measurement error, sampling, respondent availability, and so on. It is necessary, however, that the theory show why the existing level is all that can be accounted for. Second, the level of variation appropriate for analysis must be carefully considered; an explanation of the distribution of heads among all the coins makes sense, but an accounting of the variance between coins would not. Third, it is also necessary to consider what it would mean if we attempt to account for more variance than is appropriate. As the illustration with the coins should make clear, attempts to account for more than the appropriate level of variation are not innocuous. An overestimation of the appropriate level of variation to be fit has undesirable consequences. It can lead to the false conclusion that there is less than a full explanation or under-standing of the process under study when, in fact, there is a full explanation. It tends to encourage ad hoc accounts in order to maximize the explained variation—a procedure that will have no utility in the long run.[6] Overestimating the appropriate level of variation to be fit or explained makes it likely that a bad theory or idea will drive out a good theory simply because, at a given time and place, the former appears to account for more of the variation than does the latter. Finally, the attempt to account for all of the variation, when inappropriate, is but another form of attempting to accomplish that which is intrinsically undoable (as described in chapter 1).

GRAVITY: A LESSON FOR SOCIAL RESEARCH

By now it should be clear that a thoughtless and mechanical imitation of the natural sciences is certain to be fruitless. However, there is no harm in considering what they have done, as long as we are not bound to follow the model blindly. It is safe to say that the notion of gravity is an intellectual landmark and represents an accomplishment that we would be happy to match in the social sciences. It runs counter to our senses and accounts for incredibly diverse phenomena: the downward fall of bodies big and small to the earth at a uniform rate (assuming a vacuum); the movement of celestial bodies; the existence of black holes; and the feeling of weightlessness that occurs in outer space. The level of precision is awesome, at least by the standards of the social sciences. Consider that the existence of the planet Neptune was predicted on the basis of small discrepancies in the motion of Uranus—discrepancies that could not be explained by the gravitational fields of the other known planets. Indeed, Neptune's position had been correctly calculated within a degree of where it was found in 1846 (Nordtvedt, Faller, and Beams 1974: 288).

How might social researchers typically go about studying a

phenomenon such as gravity? A simple gravitational exhibit at the Ontario Science Centre in Toronto inspires a heuristic example. In the exhibit, a coin and a feather are both released from the top of a vacuum tube and reach the bottom at virtually the same time. Since the vacuum is not a total one, presumably the coin reaches the bottom slightly ahead of the feather. At any rate, suppose we visualize a study in which a variety of objects is dropped without the benefit of such a strong control as a vacuum—just as would occur in nonexperimental social research. If social researchers find that the objects differ in the time that they take to reach the ground, typically they will want to know what characteristics determine these differences. Probably such characteristics of the objects as their density and shape will affect speed of the fall in a nonvacuum situation. If the social researcher is fortunate, such factors together will fully account for all of the differences among the objects in the velocity of their fall. If so, the social researcher will be very happy because all of the variation between objects will be accounted for. The investigator, applying standard social research thinking, will conclude that there is a complete understanding of the phenomenon *because all differences among the objects under study have been accounted for*.

Surely there must be something faulty with our procedures if we can approach such a problem without ever considering gravity itself. First consider how similar the design is to that used in, say, the study of intergenerational occupational mobility (chart 5.1). Whereas in the gravity problem the dependent variable is the time it takes for each object to reach the ground, here the dependent variable is the level of SES achieved by each subject. In the former case, other characteristics of the objects are examined to see if they can account for variation among items in the velocity of their fall; in the latter, other characteristics of the individuals are considered, such as parental SES, subject's educational level, and so on. The parallel is quite striking. Again, the researchers would be happy if they have fully accounted for interindividual differences in the dependent variable.[7]

What is going on here? Something must be wrong if social researchers think that they have a full grasp of falling objects without ever invoking gravity. Yet, surely there must be *some*

CHART 5.1

COMPARISON BETWEEN STANDARD APPROACH TO OCCUPATIONAL MOBILITY
AND HOW SOCIAL RESEARCHERS MIGHT APPROACH GRAVITY

Body	Time to reach the ground (Y)	Density of object (X_1)	Shape of object (X_2)
Feather			
Small Coin			
Large Coin			
Lead Ball			
Paper			
Pencil			
Brick			
etc.			

Son	SES (Y)	Parental family's income (X_1)	Father's education (X_2)
A			
B			
C			
D			
E			
F			
G			
H			
etc.			

contribution to *some* form of knowledge if one fully accounts for the differences between objects in their rate of fall or between individuals in their socioeconomic status levels. Before I propose an answer to this issue, let us consider one more puzzle. Some years ago, I heard another sociologist object to Central Place Theory not on the grounds that the theory was false, but simply because he claimed that the model did not account for very much of the urban pattern observed in an advanced nation such as the United States. (In a nutshell, the theory provides a model of the location and size structure of cities under certain conditions where land usage is homogeneous and with no special city-forming geographic conditions such as rivers, oceans, mountains, etc. The model works quite nicely in parts of Texas, Iowa, and some of the prairie states [see the classic volume by Lösch 1954: chapter 22]). Clearly my friend was right; the theory cannot account for much of the overall urban pattern in the United States—nor should it, given the divergence between actual conditions and those assumed by the model. Nevertheless, if for the sake of argument we can assume that the theory is indeed valid, would we want to relegate it to a minor role because it helps us understand so little of what we observe in the nation's urban pattern?

Resolving the Question

Let us start with an elementary principle about the linkage between theory and research—one that is neither terribly hard to grasp nor particularly surprising, to wit: the nature of the question determines the nature of the data that are needed. In practice, this principle is not so easy to follow, particularly in nonexperimental work where one is obliged to work with existing and naturally occurring events. Data on the *phenomenon* of interest are not necessarily data relevant for the *question* of interest. In the gravity case, an analysis of various objects may tell us why they differ in the velocity of their fall, but not why they fall. Likewise, a study of interindividual differences in SES attainment may tell us why people differ in such characteristics, but it does not tell us why SES characteristics exist nor why the particular system of SES linkages occurs. (See the criticism raised by Coser 1975, and the defense of such practices by Featherman 1976.) There is nothing wrong, per se, with asking these questions. However, the falling bodies example illustrates the relative shallowness of the contribution compared to fundamental knowledge about gravity. Now does the same situation exist for much of our research on social processes using the same type of methodology? Do we gain a fundamental knowledge of the causes of intergenerational occupational mobility by considering the characteristics that have an impact on the variation in offsprings' attainment? Does that provide us with a fundamental clue as to the forces determining the dependent variable? The answer is, regretfully, probably not. We are so habituated to this type of logic that it is difficult for us to see this.

The variation issue is very subtle; it is not quickly resolved with a simple formula or a rule. There is absolutely nothing wrong with trying to account for the variation observed in some phenomenon. It is what is done with variation that is in error, not what is intrinsically problematic about variation. Looking at the velocity variable in chart 5.1, the dependent variable that we see is not *velocity* at all—rather, the dependent variable is *difference in velocity*. The "answer" that we can come up with is what causes differences in velocity, not what causes movement itself. In the case of occupations, the dependent variable is not occupational status, but rather differences in occupational status, and it is the latter that one explains. This issue applies to a lot of problems. I use occupational status solely because it is a widely known research topic with considerable interest at the present time.

The difficulty lies in the fact that the fundamental cause will often be a constant force and hence will not be amenable to variation-type analysis—at least, in the way that we normally proceed. A desire for variation should not mean the elimination of fundamental causal principles in empirical social research simply because variation is not conveniently found. Certainly it should not occur if it means substituting a concern with variation among falling bodies for a concern with the fall itself. When we look at different bodies falling to the ground in the earth's atmosphere, what we get is variation in the impact of the force. But we do not get at what the force is. So the first lesson to be learned here is that the *goal* of an empirical research project is the primary consideration, and the execution is secondary. In some cases, the aim is largely descriptive—for example, to find out the state of affairs with respect to poverty rates or trends in residential segregation or the frequency of violence in nineteenth-century France. It is one thing to have a problem that cannot be resolved—at least, at the present time or with the conditions faced by the researcher. But if the goal is analytical or theoretical, it is necessary to establish the goal first and make variation fit this goal, rather than the all too common practice of doing it in the opposite way.

The next point is that variation will be found even when powerful forces are operating. But a different way of thinking about the matter is required. In the gravity case, for example, there were a number of instances in which something was learned because of variation. In addition to the example cited earlier in which Neptune was discovered because Uranus deviated slightly from the motions otherwise expected, other examples can be cited from the same source (Nordtvedt, Faller, and Beams 1974): the total gravitational force produced on a body by many masses is a function of the characteristics of these masses vectored together (287); there are gravitational variations at different points on the earth due to local mass differences such as mountain ranges, mineral deposits, and ocean basins (289); g also varies systematically between the Equator and the Earth's poles (291).

So the issue is not to avoid statistical variability, but to use it properly by distinguishing its shallow applications from those where there are profoundly important regularities. Are there criteria that can and should be used to help guide us at least part of the way in reaching such decisions? Although there is no full solution—unless rules exist that will give us intuition, imagination, and verve—it is certainly an issue to be dealt with (as will be done in Part II of this volume). But as a rough rule of thumb and a clue to what lies ahead, we should be reasonably satisfied that we understand why an entity or process exists to begin with *before* turning to questions about its variation. This does not mean searching back to Adam and Eve in a historical sense, but it does mean that we seek out answers to fundamental questions before looking at minor variations. Again, as we shall see in Part II, there is more to be said on how to decide whether a question is fundamental or not.

Incidentally, if a case study involving a relatively modest amount of variation is to yield significant results, then data quality is an especially important consideration. As a rule, social researchers want large samples with considerable variation in the dependent variable; yet there is absolutely nothing wrong with small case studies if the data are good enough and the theory "clean" enough. After all, if Einstein's theory was tested through observations during a solar eclipse, we do not ask whether there was a large random sample of such solar eclipses. Now the social researcher may well chuckle about this because the beauty of physical events is that there is a high degree of confidence that the observations made in 1919 will be repeated over and over again. Certainly, progress in the development of measuring instruments is a very desirable business. Still, all of this suggests that the simple case study could be of considerably greater value than presently appreciated if it is possible to mount such studies with a very clear appreciation of some crucial issue *and* if the data are of very high quality such that the results can be taken seriously. The latter is no trivial consideration, and the current situation in social research is dreary. One does not really improve a situation with poor data by increasing the "N" and then hoping to deal with more variation.

As for the question posed earlier about Central Place Theory, the answer is very simple and again hinges on the statistical variation issue. If a "desirable" outcome is defined as accounting for the statistical variation within some data set, then any judgment about the "explanatory power" of a theory (in this case, Central Place Theory) will be affected by the nature of the data set. If we study the distribution of urban places in Iowa or in Bavaria (another area where it shows up very strongly), then we are likely to conclude that Central Place Theory is a wonderful idea. If we try it on New York State or the urban distribution within the entire country, we will not conclude that the theory is wrong, but we will conclude that it fails to help us account for much of the observed variation. There are two equally valid and at least partially separate questions involved here. The first refers to whether a theory is correct. The second refers to whether it helps us understand a given phenomenon. If the answer to the first question is negative, then of course it will not help us understand the phenomenon. But if the theory is correct, it need not help us understand the phenomena in a particular context. Thus, one cannot use a theory's ability to explain a given phenomenon as grounds for deciding if the theory is valid.

Given this fact, is it reasonable to use the amount of variation accounted for as a criterion for determining whether a theory is any good or not? A study of Iowa would show that Central Place Theory is great; a study of New York State would show that it is of minimal value. There is no "natural" unit of analysis to resolve this contradiction. A study of the urban distribution within the United States might lead to one conclusion; a study of the urban distribution within the world might lead to another. Moreover, even a study of the entire world would not necessarily be a "natural" context for evaluating the power of the theory since it would still be dealing with a sample of one time. Even if data are obtained for all urban places over time, it would still be a limited sample since we would not know about the future (and our knowledge of past urban developments would provide no reason for expecting urban events to remain constant in the future).

This leads to a rather radical conclusion: *It is impossible to use empirical data in nonexperimental social research to evaluate the relative importance of one theory vs. another (or, if you will, one independent variable vs. another).* Empirical data can be used to determine, under certain conditions to be specified in Part II, whether a theory is of use or not—but not whether it is more important than another theory. One can always say whether, in a given empirical context, a given variable or theory accounts for more variation than another. But it is almost certain that the variation observed is not universal over time and place. Hence the use of such a criterion first requires a conclusion about the variation over time and place in the dependent variable. If such an analysis is not forthcoming, the theoretical conclusion is undermined by the absence of information. The evaluation of one variable vs. another is possibly justified, but only if it is clear that the comparison is meant to hold only within the context of the observed variation (even then, it is of questionable value—see chapter 9).

Such conclusions are of limited value even if they are carefully restricted to the observed variation range in the variables. If there are any fundamental changes in the system, it is almost certain to mean different levels of variation and a different range in the variables' levels. Moreover, it is questionable whether one can draw much of a conclusion about causal forces from the simple analysis of the observed variation. This gets us back to the initial point in the discussion of gravity. To wit, it is vital that one have an understanding, or at least a working hypothesis, about what is causing the event per se; variation in the magnitude of the event will not provide the answer to that question. Thus, an explanation of the variation in the velocity of objects falling to the ground in a nonvacuum—an uncontrolled situation very much like those encountered in social research—would lead to the shallowest of conclusions about the cause of the fall per se.

LEVELS OF ANALYSIS

The "ecological fallacy" is well known in the sociological literature; there have been countless commentaries on it since the ecological correlation was first described by Robinson (1950). The fallacy occurs when the correlation of characteristics on one level (between spatial aggregates) is used to draw conclusions about the association of the same characteristics on another level (between individuals). Robinson, for example, showed that the correlation between race of individuals and their illiteracy in 1930 was far lower than the correlation obtained between these two characteristics when spatial areas were the units of analysis. The ecological correlation between spatial aggregates is not itself inherently erroneous; what is potentially fallacious is the assumption that the linkages at one level need occur at another level. In my estimation, the ecological fallacy is nothing more or less than a specific example of a widespread tendency in social research to mix up and confuse the appropriate levels of analysis. Galtung (1967: 45) has come very close to capturing this process in what he calls "the fallacy of the wrong level," which, "consists not in making *inferences* from one level of analysis to another, but in making direct *translation of properties or relations* from one level to another, i.e., making too simple inferences. The fallacy can be committed working downwards, by projecting from groups or categories to individuals, or upwards, by projecting from individuals to higher units."

Suppose we consider the relationship between a higher and lower

level (to be labeled "H" and "L" respectively). The group level could
be represented by H, and L could represent individuals; or the
letters might represent, respectively, societies and subsocietal forms
of organization. At any rate, what happens when data on one level
are used to draw inferences about either theoretical or empirical
events on another? Just to make life simple, I will assume that the
linkage on one level either occurs or does not occur on the other
level; we will not worry here about all the nuances raised in the
ecological correlation literature about the magnitude of the association or the standardized or unstandardized regressions, but just
about the presence or absence of the same association on another
level. Hence, if anything, the potential complications are understated in this analysis.

Starting with Robinson's landmark paper and Galtung's fallacy,
one can develop the following proposition:

If the conceptual or theoretical issue is on a given level of analysis, then the
empirical evidence obtained at a *lower* level will not be relevant for determining
the merit or validity of the theory.

The association observed at one level need not necessarily hold at
another level—this is the point of the ecological fallacy. But beyond
this danger, associations on the lower level are irrelevant for determining the validity of a proposition about processes operating on
the higher level. As a matter of fact, no useful understanding of the
higher-level structure can be obtained from lower-level analyses. If
the same process operates at both levels, then the higher-level one is
uninteresting since it has no unique transformational or structural
features; if the process is different at both levels, then obviously the
lower-level information will be providing a misleading picture. In
terms of advancing knowledge, then, the use of lower-level data to
test propositions on a higher level and/or to infer the empirical
patterns on a higher level cannot win.

The opposite process, in which higher-level data are used to draw
conclusions about theoretical or empirical conditions on a lower
level, is a somewhat different matter. If the process observed on a
higher level is found on the lower level, then the use of data from the
H-level will indeed lead to a correct conclusion about the L-level if
certain statistical conditions hold.[8] If these conditions do not hold,

then the process observed on a higher level is different from the process found on the lower level and an erroneous inference will be made. But the key difference is that L-level processes found on a higher level are essentially uninteresting in terms of advancing our knowledge about the higher level. This is because we are especially interested in processes and events that are distinctive to the level, that is, not merely the sum of lower-level forces. By contrast, if an H-level process is also found on a lower level, it is interesting information about the lower level.

Consider further the situation where data on a lower level, L, are used to draw conclusions about what is going on at the higher level. Suppose the procedure "works," such that the same relationship operates on both levels. However, the use of L-level data to draw conclusions about an H-level proposition involves more than the question of whether the inference is correct or incorrect. Also of concern is the consequence of making an erroneous vs. a correct conclusion. *When the relationship is different on the two levels, that is exactly when we should be most interested; for societal processes are not simply a function of the summation of the subunits but have an organic entity themselves.* (This is the whole point of Durkheim's Social Fact [1950].) Accordingly, we cannot win when using lower-level data to draw inferences about the empirical events on a higher level or to test theories of what is operating on a higher level. The most interesting features of the higher level—features that are not simply a sum of the lower-level units—will never be correctly found under such a procedure. If the higher-level events are merely a summation of the characteristics of the lower-level units, then a relatively uninteresting finding occurs, that is, relatively uninteresting from the perspective of understanding the distinctive structural qualities of society. If the L-level and H-level relationships are different, then the most interesting and important process will never be known since the researcher will draw the wrong conclusion when using L-level data to infer H-level processes.

Variation Again

Why do researchers employ empirical data on one level to deal with a problem operating on another? There are several major reasons for this discrepancy between the empirical level and the theoretical level (a widespread discrepancy, as we shall see), but any answer must begin with the fact that the data are often unavailable for the level of interest, particularly in a form that the researcher desires. In my estimation, substitution is particularly common when the data for the most appropriate level do not have sufficient variation. As a consequence, the actual data used are at a different level from that for which the theory or problem is posed. The reasoning is deceptively simple: here is an empirical consequence that we might expect if the theoretical proposition is valid. Hence, although the data are less than ideal (i.e., on a different level), if the data follow from that proposition, we have more grounds than we would otherwise have had for supporting the theory (or, conversely, rejecting it).

This type of thinking is revealed in the initial debate about ecological correlations. One of the big issues was that correlations between large spatial units tend to overestimate the magnitude of the associations that might be found on the individual level or with smaller spatial units. Again, it was a question of variation accounted for. This was not the only objection to ecological correlations, but it was certainly a major factor.[9] (Perhaps the other major objection represents an even worse failing—if such is possible—namely, the failure to understand that the societal or group or aggregate level is not merely the sum of the individual units. More about this shortly.) As we shall see, this unrelenting desire to find variation is rather pervasive and has led to certain blunders, to wit, the failure to recognize that the application of lower-level data to higher-level issues can make *no* contribution to knowledge.

CRIME IN THE UNITED STATES:
AN EXAMPLE OF AN INAPPROPRIATE LEVEL

Two superb sociologists, Judith and Peter Blau, provide us with a concrete opportunity to consider the level of analysis issue. They start off with a paradox:

> Crimes against persons as well as property crimes are correlated with poverty, yet the United States, a very affluent country, has one of the highest crime rates in

the world. At comparable levels of urbanization and industrialization, the homicide rate in the United States is more than ten times that in Western Europe. (Blau and Blau 1982: 114)

Using a general macrosociological theory put forth by Blau (1977), the authors hypothesize that racial differences in socioeconomic position cause criminal violence.[10] The study is not concerned with individual differences in crime rates, they are careful to indicate, but rather with the social conditions that cause violence to vary from place to place and over time (1982: 114−115). The empirical test is accomplished by examining differences in crime rates among 125 large metropolitan areas in the United States. They report that, "findings essentially support the hypothesis advanced here, though with some modifications. Socioeconomic inequalities, between races and within them, are positively related to high rates of violent crime in SMSAs, and when they are controlled, poverty is not related to these rates" (1982: 126). As an added bonus, they are able to provide an alternative noncultural explanation for the higher rates of violence in the South based on racial differences in that region.

What is wrong with this? Blau and Blau are careful workers, and I have no complaints about their procedures except for a single crucial matter. They use data on one level to cope with issues and theories posed on a higher level. Why does the United States have such a high rate of criminal violence? They deal with this question by looking at intranational variation, to wit, differences within the United States. To my knowledge, at no point do the authors even discuss why data on nations are not considered. One can understand the logic behind these steps. If, as their theory suggests, pronounced racial differences cause violence, and if in turn the United States has very high rates of violence because of the exceptional magnitude of the racial gaps, then would we not also expect variation in the racial gaps within the United States to cause different rates of criminal violence? Maybe and maybe not.

In effect, the issue is why do nations differ on some attribute. The crux of it all is found in the logic underlying an analysis of covariance (ACV). We must forget all of the usual multivariate issues involving control variables, and so on, and just visualize a simple bivariate relationship between Y (crime) and X (racial differences) obtainable for entire nations and for various cities in each of the K nations. We can visualize four regressions: in the first, *a*, Y for nations is regressed on the X values for each nation; in *b*, Y for each city in a nation (the United States) is regressed on the appropriate X; in *c*, Y for each city in all of the nations is regressed on the appropriate X; and in *d*, Y is regressed on X for each city in Iran.

The initial theoretical issue is represented by the relationship *a*, one that would be found in the direct comparisons between nations. If the high level of violence in the United States is to be suitably accounted for by the variable suggested by the Blaus (assuming here and elsewhere it is net of all other factors that affect crime), then presumably the United States will show up rather high on the regression line in figure *a*. Such data are apparently not available— or, at least, not used in this study. Instead, we see that intraurban variation in one nation, the United States, is used (regression *b*). Is this adequate? There is nothing about the nature of social processes that requires the relationship within subunits to be the same as that across units. In other words, regression *b* could be quite different from that in *a*—yet the researcher is assuming that one represents the other. The regression within the United States, *b*, could be negative and the one between nations, *a*, could be positive, for all we know. The whole point of societal processes is that they are more than the sum of subunits.

The notion that an entity is more than the sum of its parts may seem almost mystical, even if it is crucial for understanding the essential nature of the social order. Moreover, since just about any result we come up with could have a possible alternative explanation, this does not help convince the unconvinced very much. Let us go further, then. For the regression among cities in the United States to represent adequately what is going on among nations, it is necessary that there be no nation effect per se, that is, no between-group effect.[11] This means that if a series of regressions were computed separately for the cities of each nation, we would find identical regressions of Y on X in each. (To be sure, the distribution along the slope might be different because not each nation would have the sample range of interracial differences, but a given level of interracial difference would lead to identical crime rates in any and all nations.) Except for sampling errors, the effect of the K nations would be nil, and c would show an identical result for the regression of Y on X within each of the K nations. I do not say that this is true, but rather that this is what is assumed to be operating if the regression within the United States is an appropriate surrogate for a. Someone might argue that b does represent what is going on generally in a regardless of whether the assumption about c holds. In other words, yes, there might be a K effect (a nation effect, or a between-group effect), but still the relationship within the United States approximates the overall relationship. That is conceivable, but it would require either luck or an extraordinary case of optimism to believe that data for the United States represent the average nation of the world.

To clinch the matter, consider whether one would use data on intercity differences in present-day Iran to test the hypothesis. I rather doubt it, but in terms of the logic implicit in the use of lower-level data to test propositions and hypotheses on a higher level, it would be perfectly appropriate. If variation only within the United States can be used to test a proposition explaining why the United States is where it is relative to other nations, then we have seen that it is legitimate to do so *only* if there is no unique United States effect that sets it off from other nations (the procedure is not appropriate if there is a unique United States effect). But if there is no unique United States effect, then it follows logically that the analysis of variation within another nation would be just as good. In other words, if the assumption about c holds—and that is crucial to justify the use of b data to infer a results—then it would follow that the relation obtained in d for Iran would be equally good since it would be identical to that obtained for the United States and/or for all nations (b and a respectively). Try submitting an article using Iranian data to account for high crime rates in the United States!

Fallacy of Nonequivalence

This is not just a simple nicety that fancy methodologists might indulge in when talking about "ideal" conditions, as opposed to what some hard-working researcher has to contend with out there in the real world. It is far more fundamental than that. For if we are

interested in the higher levels of processes and events, it is because
we operate with the understanding that they have distinctive qualities that are not simply derived by summing the subunits. In other
words, societal processes have societal causes, causes that cannot be
flushed out by analyses on a lower level. Efforts to use lower-level
data to determine the nature of processes on a higher level, or to deal
with theories of higher-order processes, commit what can be called
the fallacy of nonequivalence.

Is it common to find lower-level observations being used to deal
with theories that are posed on a higher level? If this is frequently
the case, then we have one of the major reasons why theory and
research have so little to do with each other. If the empirical data are
compiled on a lower level than the problem, then in effect they are
totally irrelevant for drawing any conclusions about the problem. I
believe that this practice is extremely common in social research,
particularly if one bears in mind that the incorrect level of analysis
error is not simply confined to psychological reductionism, but
rather to any step in which lower-level aggregate data are used to
deal with higher-order aggregate propositions (as in the Blau and
Blau example). Moreover, if investigators are unaware of the
dangers stemming from the nonequivalence fallacy, the interpretation of apparent contradictions and inconsistencies can be more
difficult and needlessly confusing. If one investigator finds a relationship between X and Y on the H-level and another finds a
different relationship on the L-level (but which purports to deal
with the higher-level theory), there is apt to be confusion about an
apparent inconsistency, which really is no problem if levels are kept
straight.

A linguistic example illustrates how easy it is to fall into such a
trap. If one asks whether urbanization is correlated with language
change within a nation, the answer is often in the affirmative; the
more urbanized subareas of the nation seem to experience more
language shift. However, if one asks whether urbanization causes
language shift in nations, the answer is to the contrary; Lieberson
and Hansen (1974) examined this question longitudinally and
found essentially no relationship over time. The reasons for this
discrepancy are not entirely clear, but it does appear reasonable at
this point to speculate that, "urbanization in at least some nations

has nationalistic, political, and economic consequences which intensify resistance to change and then spread back into the hinterlands. . . . Under these circumstances, a language group's migration into large urban centers may retard long-term change even when there is a differential rate between the urban and rural areas" (Lieberson, Dalto, and Marsden 1975: 59; for the evidence, see 57–59). This is a very nice example of how easy it is to work at the wrong level; the relationship found within nations need not hold for the nations as the unit. There is nothing wrong here as long as the levels of analysis are kept straight and not crossed over.

IMPLICATIONS FOR CURRENT
AND ALTERNATIVE APPROACHES

1. The variability approach—regardless of the particular statistic used—tends to be applied prematurely and inappropriately to sociological problems. It is premature to think about variability in an event before knowledge is developed about the fundamental cause of the event itself. Explanation of a variable's variation should not be confused with an explanation of the event or process itself. Contrary to the assumption commonly made in social research, we cannot learn the fundamental cause of an event by studying the factors affecting its variation; at best, we can only learn how secondary characteristics might modify the consequences of a fundamental cause. The earlier discussion of the way social researchers might approach gravity should make it painfully clear that we are geared toward the lesser problem; learning why bodies drop at slightly different speeds in a nonvacuum is relatively insignificant compared to learning why they drop to begin with.

It is fruitful to distinguish between the properties of a system and the properties of the units within the system. Social researchers at present tend to look at the properties of the individual units (differences among bodies falling to the ground or individuals' socioeconomic attainment) rather than of the system (say, gravity or rules of social mobility). Researchers act as if knowledge of the former will lead to fruitful inductions about the latter. There is nothing to be gained from entering a debate about research "strate-

gies" or the best procedures for advancing knowledge, but there is
no intrinsic reason for expecting the properties of the system to be
logically deduced from observing variation in the behavior of the
individual units. The latter may provide the significant facts from
which some bold leap can be made, but keep in mind that the larger
system or process is constant for all of the individual units or bodies.

2. There are absolutes or virtual absolutes in the social sciences;
and there is nothing more misleading than "explanations" derived
from variation models. For example, except for relatively short
spans of time, it is safe to say that essentially all nation-states seek to
control the nature and number of immigrants allowed to enter. If we
want to explain that phenomenon, we should do so directly in terms
of whatever theory we want to generate. But it is almost certain to
be rather different from what we conclude by accounting for the
variability between nations and over time in the numbers allowed to
enter. Likewise, suppose we want to determine the consequence of
race riots on the position of blacks in cities during the ensuing years.
A typical approach at present would involve an analysis of intercity
variance in riots (number experienced and/or severity) and the
relevant dependent variables, such as changes in black-white gaps,
election of blacks to public office, hiring programs, public and
private expenditures on certain programs, and so on. Such an
approach would be standard social research, but it would have a fatal
flaw. It would take into account the consequences of a given city's
riot experience on later events, but it would not take into account
the consequences of riots for *all* cities regardless of their specific riot
experiences. If the Congress, for example, adopted an urban rodent
control program because of the riots, then this would be a constant
for all cities regardless of their unique experience. We would lose
sight of that in examining variance among cities.

3. New ways are needed for linking theory with nonexperimental social research. This involves criteria that are, at one and the
same time, more demanding and more permissive than those currently used. A data set with variation in the dependent variable is
not necessarily a prerequisite for determining the validity of some
theory. Moreover, when it is appropriate to deal with variation, the
researcher must be careful to work at the proper level of analysis.
Lower-level data can make no significant contribution by them-

selves to knowledge of the relationship on a higher level. If the relationship is different on the two levels, then the inference is obviously in error. If the relationship is the same, then we have not learned anything about the structure of the higher level since, by definition, this would mean something more than the sum of the subparts. The fallacy of nonequivalence occurs all the time because researchers turn to lower levels of analysis in order to obtain sufficient variability in their data sets.

4. A complete theory may well account for less than 100 percent of the variability; something substantially less than this level is not necessarily due to the operation of other forces or problems with the data. It is certainly possible that the theory is wrong or incomplete or the data inadequate, but it is also necessary to consider whether the criterion for the maximum proportion is in error. Obviously, the amount of variation that a theory expects to explain cannot be a figure that is arrived at by a subjective or post hoc statement conveniently made equal to the actual proportion accounted for. Appropriately rigorous criteria must be used. One must keep in mind, however, that in many cases an analysis of the variance explained, goodness-of-fit, or other statistical procedure used to account for variability, is not at all an appropriate step for evaluating the theory.

5. A theory must indicate the appropriate level of analysis. This must be made explicit because, as we have seen, there is otherwise a danger of leaping to the wrong level. The fallacy of nonequivalence means that conclusions at a lower level are not inevitably true at a higher level—indeed, if they are true, they are less interesting from the point of view of the higher level of analysis.

6. It is erroneous to assume that the importance of causal forces—in either an absolute or relative sense—can be determined by the amount of variation "explained" by them in some empirical study. The variance and range of both the dependent variable and the independent variables will almost certainly vary from setting to setting, and in turn this will affect the relative importance attributed to each independent variable (see Duncan 1975: 55–66). In this regard, there are grounds for asking in Part II of this volume if the theory should indicate the expected level of initial variation.

7. To indicate how far off the mark one can get with a variation-

based approach to determining causal importance, let us consider the following multivariate example. Suppose high values of X_1 always cause high values of Y, but there are also other causes of high Y (X_2, X_3, etc.). In the available data, high values of X_1 are rarely found, but these other causal conditions do exist and the researcher concludes that very little of the variance in Y is accounted for by X_1. This is a perfect prelude for totally misleading and surprising results. All we need is a new situation in which the other causes are absent and/or high values of X_1 are quite common. An apparently unimportant variable—"unimportant" by the variation criteria in the first study—now seems to be generating lots of high Y values. We have neither a surprise nor a social change; rather, there was a misleading conclusion earlier which failed to distinguish the in-frequency of high X_1 from the influence of high X_1 when it was found. The only change is in composition—not in causal process.

Jeffrey G. Reitz, in describing his superb study of ethnic assimilation and maintenance in Toronto (1980), came up with an excellent example of how misleading the variance-explained criteria can be. He considered the relationship between language learning among immigrant groups and the groups' occupations and income. Obviously, the acquisition of English is a very important condition for good jobs and incomes. Accordingly, after a few years' residence, virtually everyone learns English in Toronto. Therefore, language learning does not help us understand very much of the income or occupational differences among individual immigrants in Toronto or their groups. If I want to know why some immigrants earn lots and others very little, I cannot turn to language learning because virtually all of the immigrants—rich and poor—have learned English. However, if I want to use this result to conclude that there is no economic incentive or consequence in learning English, I would be wrong. I would be wrong because the importance of the independent variable (learning English) on the dependent variable (income and occupational position) is so great that virtually everyone learns English. As a consequence, my ability to explain much of the variation in the dependent variable is limited by the importance of the independent variable's influence. If my question is, "Why do people differ in their incomes?" then it would be appropriate to leave out language or relegate it to a minor role. But if I desire to know what affects income in Toronto—not income differences among people—then I would be sadly mistaken to think that the acquisition of English is unimportant and may be omitted. The analysis of differences or variability is an analysis of just that—it is not to be confused with the analysis of causes, especially those that are so widespread that they help explain very little of the variation.

CHAPTER SIX

Control Variables

It is widely believed that the application of control variables is both desirable and possible. In one form or another, the control approach is viewed as a way of determining the influence some specific characteristic has on a dependent variable net of the influence due to other characteristics. A variety of statistical procedures is available to control or otherwise take into account the influence of variables.[1] This routine everyday procedure must be one of the most widespread practices found in contemporary social research. It is very much an accepted part of the logic of social science, even for those who are primarily not researchers, and is practiced with probably very little reflection.

Given the ideal implicit in most nonexperimental social research, we can understand the prominence of this perspective. Most social researchers have in mind an experimental model in which there is some form or another of *control* over the conditions under study. In trying to account for a given dependent variable, typically we can think of a large variety of possible causes; accordingly, it usually appears both reasonable and desirable that the influence of each cause be isolated from that of other possible causes. If high values of X_1 appear to cause high values of Y, and if X_2 also appears to affect Y, then what could be more reasonable than determining the influence of X_1 by controlling for the observed linkage between X_2 and Y? A standard "error"—one dreaded by all social researchers—is someone else discovering the omission of an important control variable. In one form or another, we constantly encounter the following argument: "The investigator did not control for X_{14}; had such a control been made, then the influence of X_8 on Y would be quite different from the result obtained by the investigator." In addition, if control variable X_{14} cannot be measured adequately or is not used for some other reason, someone disinclined to accept the empirically determined influence of X_8 can claim that the observed effect would be radically different if only X_{14} were tossed into the statistical hopper.[2]

This is not a happy state of affairs. It makes it even more difficult for the results of empirical research to alter people's initial beliefs about the nature of the causal process operating. In all fairness, this is apparently the state of affairs in the natural sciences as well (see Kuhn 1962), but we will let them worry about their own problems. The social researcher's problem is compounded not only by the resistance to changing established paradigms but also by the fact that there appear to be so many different possible causes—albeit of varying magnitude—for just about any given dependent variable. Because it is almost certain that not all will be included in the study—or if included, adequately measured—a nasty uncertainty plagues us all. Application of this control model involves such widely recognized problems as: model specification; multicollinearity; problems in determining the causal order; complications when the variables also differ in the quality of their measurement; possibilities of extremely complicated nonrecursive systems; and other difficulties. The issues to be considered here, however, are more fundamental than these. To begin with, should we attempt control procedures? If so, under what circumstances should such steps be taken? Under what circumstances are control procedures *not* justified and, in such cases, what happens if they are applied? If controls are not applied, what can we learn in complicated multivariate problems?

A NONTRADITIONAL VIEW

In my estimation, the assumptions implicit in the control procedure are actually invalid in many instances and certainly are of far more limited utility than most of us seem to assume in our research. Accordingly, I wish to propose a radically different view of what the control process can accomplish and how its results are to be interpreted. The next two paragraphs present the initial thesis; the remainder of the chapter is dedicated to the reasoning that supports it.

In quasi-experimental research, the use of a control is likely to be appropriate only if the control proves to be unnecessary, that is, when the control (say, X_2) does not alter the initial relationship (say, the influence of X_1 on Y). If the initial relationship is significantly altered after the influence of a control is taken into account, then usually one cannot immediately conclude—as researchers currently do—that the control puts us closer to the true net influence of X_1 on Y. Rather, such a result could also mean that an approximation of a true experimental situation is inappropriate and hence controls cannot be applied. Therefore, if the control variable does appear to have an influence, it may or may not be the case that the results obtained with controls provide a closer approximation of the true substantive relationship. Before such a conclusion can be drawn, it is necessary to determine first whether the social processes involved permit a quasi-experimental approximation of the experimental model. If the answer is negative, then the application of controls is inappropriate and must not be done since it fails to accomplish what most researchers assume such a step accomplishes. It is ironic, then, that the application of controls is likely to be appropriate only when the control has no effect on the dependent variable or is unrelated to the independent variable of interest.[3]

If controls do not alter the initial relationship, then there is evidence that the quasi-experimental assumption is appropriate and the initial uncontrolled relationship is sound; if the initial relationship is altered, then for the moment one cannot make any substantive conclusions whatsoever. Rather, further analysis is required in order to decide whether or not the implicit experimental model is appropriate without further analysis. Only then, if the answer is in the affirmative, can one freely apply the controls.

A little patience is needed since this view of control variables probably runs counter to one's initial disposition. The task here is to justify these propositions and evaluate current practices in terms of them.

SELECTIVITY AGAIN

The selectivity problem raised in chapter 2 is serious enough and difficult enough to justify a new way of interpreting the use of control variables. Recall that if the $X_1 - Y$ relationship is unaffected by X_2, then there is no fundamental disagreement with the conventional conclusion, although the reasoning process is somewhat different. From the perspective taken here, such a result helps to confirm the appropriateness of the quasi-experimental simulation and in that sense helps to justify the use of controls. By contrast, the conventional researcher assumes that controls are justified be-fore examining the results. In either case, however, we end up with the same conclusions: substantively, X_2 does not affect the $X_1 - Y$ relationship; methodologically, the control procedure is appropriate.

It is another matter if the relationship between X_1 and Y changes significantly after the influence of some control variable, X_2, is examined. Under that condition, the perspective advocated here departs radically from the conventional approach to control variables. If we find that X_2 affects the $X_1 - Y$ relationship, it means that there must be some association occurring between X_1 and X_2.[4] As a consequence, when one takes X_2 into account, through whatever statistical procedure is appropriate, the issue remains as to whether a selective process underlies the relationship between X_1 and X_2 and, in turn, whether it has an influence on Y which badly warps what is believed to be the influences of X_1 and X_2. The experimental model, implicit in the simulation, involves the notion of random assignment of subjects to the different controls.

Let us consider again the private-public school issue raised in chapter 2. What is the influence of school type (X_1) on educational performance (Y) before and after the influence of, say, some family background characteristic (X_2) is taken into account? When the two types of schools differ with respect to some other characteristic of the students, such that there is an association between school type and family background characteristic (X_1 and X_2), then random assignment of X_2 has obviously not been operating for the different subpopulations of X_1. If the initial $X_1 - Y$ relationship is altered by the control variable, then the quasi-experimental simulation has not yet been achieved since obviously significant influences on Y are not randomly distributed. How well is this solved by taking into account differences between public and private schools in their X_2 distributions? For those parents with a given level of income (control variable X_2), is it chance that some of their children attend private schools (one level of X_1) whereas others have children attending public schools (another level of X_1)? If chance (or because of selective forces that have no bearing on Y), the researcher has indeed moved closer to simulating an experimental model by controlling for X_2. By contrast, if selective forces operate which themselves affect Y, the researcher has not necessarily moved closer to simulating the experimental model by controlling for X_2. In the school case, if parents with a given level of income are differentiated by chance (or some characteristic unrelated to Y) in terms of whether their children go to private or public schools, then controlling for parental background in wealth does indeed accomplish its goal. But if the answer is in the negative, such a step does not simulate the experiment, as shown in chapter 2. If private and public schools differ in the background characteristics of the parents of the children attending each type of school, "controlling" for such differences does not at all deal with the question of why they exist to begin with. This is not a simple philosophic question of going back to first causes, because the researcher cannot satisfactorily control for the influence of parental background unless confident that there are no differences within background categories between those attending one or the other type of school. Evidence exists that there are differences in the background of those attending each type of school (that is why the control was necessary to begin with). So if controls make a difference, then the best conclusion in most circumstances is that one is not ready to go ahead with the experimental simulation; one would first have to find out why there is an association (either negative or positive) between the two causal variables. If subjects with a given control characteristic are nonrandomly assigned to the X_1 situation, is it random *within* each level of X_2?

At present, we misinterpret the results obtained when a control variable (say, X_2) is found to alter the influence of the test variable (X_1) on the dependent variable. Researchers now act as if the controlling procedure provides a closer approximation to the test variable's influence because it removes the impact of at least this one entangling causal factor, X_2. This may or may not be the case, but it is a presumptuous and inappropriate conclusion if it is made simply because the X_2 control is found to alter the initial X_1-Y relationship. One may well argue, and quite correctly, "This is precisely why we want to use controls for a given variable." The problem lies, however, not in the motivation but in what such a result tells us about our ability to execute such a solution. There are certain preliminary considerations that must be dealt with before controls are applied. So the next step is not to reach a substantive conclusion about the net influence of the test variable on some dependent variable. Rather, it is to determine whether other influences are also nonrandomly distributed in a self-selective way and then to deal with these forms of self-selectivity. (Remember that such a finding can only occur if the control variable is correlated with X_1.) Only after these issues are satisfactorily dealt with can the researcher simulate the experiment (which hinges on random assignment) and thereby apply controls. One has to know *why* there is an association between X_2 and X_1. Until the association is understood, it is improper to control for X_2 in order to ferret out the net influence of X_1. This is because a selective process is probably operating which is not taken into account by the control. Indeed, as was shown in chapter 2, the application of the control can create a more misleading conclusion about the influence of X_1 on Y than would occur without any controls.

This is a central difference from current practices. Researchers do not like to think about the unmeasured selectivity that remains even after controls are applied—although I believe that most would acknowledge this if confronted with the issue. In my estimation, most researchers would respond by claiming that their results are still closer to the net true influence than is observed before the available controls are applied. But it would be a claim or an act of faith, certainly not based on any sound empirical evidence. In an earlier chapter, it was shown that some controls need not be better than none. An incomplete set of controls need not get us closer to the true relationship than is accomplished if no controls at all are applied. Witness, for example, the care and caution shown by Greeley (1982: 13 – 14, 111) in discussing the selectivity issue with regard to those attending Catholic schools.

In the example discussed in chapter 2, the researcher wants to know the influence of X_1 (public vs. private school) on Y (test performance) net of the influence due to X_2 (students' family income). Suppose a researcher finds that wealthy children are more likely to attend private schools than are the children of poor people and, in turn, that parental income affects test performance. Before taking into account or otherwise controlling for parental wealth, one must first understand more fully the nature of the association between school type and parental income. Specifically, are there underlying nonrandom factors that differentiate those wealthy children going to public schools from those who attend private schools? Likewise, are there underlying nonrandom factors differentiating poorer children in terms of the type of school that they attend? If there are, do these selective factors also affect the dependent variable? Even if wealth per se has an independent causal influence on test performance, we cannot gauge even that influence (and hence the impact of X_2 on the measured relationship between X_1 and Y) until we understand these underlying selective processes. Control procedures are often applied to situations in which there are self-selective processes that must first be considered and adequately understood. (This may sound as if an argument is being made to push the study back to the days of Adam and Eve, but such is not the case, as will be seen in Part II.) In many cases, if these processes are considered carefully, it is likely that the researcher will conclude that a control variable approach is totally inappropriate. In that sense, if we find that X_2 alters the $X_1 - Y$ relationship, the most appropriate conclusion is a methodological one—not a substantive one. To wit, it is a clear warning that the random assignment model, which is the fulcrum for any control procedures, cannot yet be applied.

SELECTIVITY AND CONTROLS:
AN EXAMPLE AND ELABORATION

A paper by Card (1981), "Long-Term Consequences for Children of
Teenage Parents," is representative of a more or less standard and
widespread kind of thinking about control variable procedures. A
close examination will be rewarding. The investigator uses an
attractive longitudinal data set to compare offspring born to teenage
parents with the offspring of parents who were at least twenty years
of age at the time of the birth. (For convenience, I will refer to the
former as "adolescent" or "teenage" parents and the latter as "older"
parents.)[5] The children of adolescent parents "were different from
their classmates in terms of their cognitive, personality, and interest
profiles while in high school, and in terms of their educational
attainment and marital histories eleven years after high school"
(Card 1981: 147). As one might expect, the two subsets of parents
differed in their background characteristics; teenage parents were
more often black and poor, and their children were later more likely
to be living in households without a mother-father combination.
The next step is a "natural" one; it has been taken by social
researchers over and over again through the years (note that CAP
and COMP refer respectively to children of adolescent parents and
children of older parents):

> To what extent were the differences between the two groups when they were
> teenagers and young adults attributable to differences in the age of their parents at
> their birth, as opposed to other demographic and family background differences?
> Could any insight be obtained regarding the process leading from adolescent
> parentage to its outcomes? These were the research questions tackled next. First,
> the direct effect due to adolescent parentage was studied by investigating the
> extent to which differences between CAPs and their classmates persisted after the
> demographic and family background differences were controlled. Then the role of
> family structure as a variable intervening between adolescent parentage and its
> outcomes was assessed via two sets of multivariate analyses conducted on data
> from the 15-year-old cohort: (a) a series of analyses of covariance and multiple
> classification analysis using matched samples of first-born CAPs and COMPs, and
> (b) an integrative path analysis using the entire analysis sample. (Card 1981: 147,
> 150)

As one might expect, the application of these various controls
alters the initial crude linkage found between age of parent at child's
birth and later characteristics of the child. For example, differences

in personality, interests, and educational expectations all disappeared (Card 1981: 150). Other associations remain even after these controls were applied, although their magnitude is changed. What could be a more typical piece of social research? But it all makes sense if we can assume that there is a true possibility of matching these parents up when we control for the socioeconomic characteristics of parents, birth order of child, and any and all other characteristics that might influence the offsprings' behavior independently of the test variable under consideration. Let us work out the logic of this. (Although restricting ourselves to the controls for socioeconomic status, we recognize that controls would normally be applied to more than this cluster.)

The procedure makes sense *if* we can assume that "teenage" parents who are at present of a given socioeconomic position are identical to "older" parents occupying the same socioeconomic position. Problems exist for the social researcher even if conditions deviate only slightly from the experimental ideal. Suppose we start by assuming that the following four conditions operate:

1. At the time of puberty, it is possible to predict the socioeconomic level that will be attained by the subject when reaching adulthood.

2. For whatever reason, persons destined to be of low socioeconomic status have a greater chance of having a child when they are teenagers than are parents destined to be of higher socioeconomic status.

3. From the pool of adolescents destined to be of low socioeconomic status when they become adults, some are randomly assigned to have children at an early age and others must wait.

4. From the pool of those destined to reach higher socioeconomic status, some are also randomly assigned to have children during their teenage years and others to wait until later. The only difference from condition 3 is that a smaller proportion of this group are assigned to have children when they are teenagers.

If these four conditions hold, we can be truly confident that controlling for socioeconomic status is a reasonable procedure. Among those of a given socioeconomic level, we can be sure that there are no aggregate differences between teenage parents and those who waited (except for random errors). We would then be very happy to control for SES and know that everything was all right in terms of determining the influence that age of parents has on later events for their offspring. But our exuberance would only be justified if future SES was so inalterably fixed at the age of puberty that it did not matter whether one had a child or not as a teenager.

Deviations from the Experimental Ideal

Despite these random assignment assumptions, it would be another matter if early parenthood itself has some bearing on the SES eventually attained in adulthood. In point of fact, the evidence supports such a conclusion (see, e.g., Waite and Moore, 1978, for the influence of early parenthood on women's educational attainment). This means that adults will differ later on a variety of dimensions that reflect whether or not they became parents at an early age. Suppose we therefore reconsider SES, but this time in a more realistic way. Again we will use a random assignment model to determine whether someone will or will not become an adolescent parent. But this time, instead of assuming that adult SES is determined by the time someone reaches puberty, we will recognize that it is not possible in the adolescent years to make a completely accurate forecast of SES outcome because various experiences during adolescence and adulthood also play a role. Accordingly, working with what we know about these future parents at the time they reach puberty, we will devise some prediction of their likely SES as adults—recognizing that these predictions will be imperfect regardless of the early pregnancy issue. Let us visualize two classes of future parents: in one class, there is a high probability that they will be low SES as adults, and in the other class, there is a high probability that they will be high SES as adults (for convenience, they will be referred to as Probable Low and Probable High destination parents, respectively P_l and P_h). For the parents in the two classes, the same procedure as described before will again be followed: a random sample of low-destination parents will have children before they reach their twenties; a random sample of high-destination parents will also have children while they are adolescents, but the proportion in the latter case will be smaller.

Since the SES ultimately achieved is affected by age of parenthood, the analysis is complicated by the consequences that having a child at an early age has on the path for SES attainment. The net effect is that what appears to be a simple controlled comparison is not really a simple controlled comparison. Moreover, the controlled comparison need not provide the researcher with a better picture of what is going on than would the uncontrolled zero-order observations. An example may make all of this clearer. I believe that the results are so counter to the assumptions normally made in the control procedure that the patience required in going through this example will be rewarded.

Let us assume that half of the population at the time they reach puberty can be said to have a strong probability of achieving high SES at a certain adult age. Likewise, let us assume that the other half of the population has a strong probability of reaching low SES as adults. Among the P_h set, if they do not become teenage parents, 90 percent can be expected to reach high SES and 10 percent will be incorrectly predicted, that is, they will end up in low SES positions despite their promising background characteristics at the time they reach puberty. (All of the relevant hypothetical figures are shown in chart 6.1.) The predictions are equally accurate for the P_l population if they do not become parents in their teens, but the prediction is in the opposite direction: 90 percent of those predicted to reach P_l status will indeed do so, but 10 percent will fool us and end up in high SES positions despite the pessimistic prediction. It is reasonable to assume that the probability of high SES is reduced for those

CHART 6.1

HYPOTHETICAL DISTRIBUTION OF RELATIONSHIP BETWEEN ADULT SES,
AGE AT PREGNANCY, AND SES OUTLOOK AT PUBERTY

Age at pregnancy	SES probability at puberty	SES distribution at adulthood	
		low	high
Adolescent	Low	.95	.05
Adult	Low	.90	.10
Adolescent	High	.15	.85
Adult	High	.10	.90

members of both the P_h and P_l population who are randomly assigned to teenage fertility. The probability of high SES goes down from .90 to .85 for the P_h group, and from .10 to .05 for the P_l group.

Suppose, through a random process, we now assume, on the one hand, that 45 percent of the low-destination teenagers (P_l) have children during their adolescence and 55 percent do not have children until they reach at least age twenty. On the other hand, suppose that 20 percent of the P_h population are randomly assigned to a teenage pregnancy and the remaining 80 percent do not have children until later. How would this work out? Looking at chart 6.2 we see, for example, that .21375 of all parents would have

CHART 6.2

SES OUTCOME, ASSUMING DIFFERENCES BETWEEN P_i CLASSES
IN THEIR AGE AT PREGNANCY, BUT RANDOM
ASSIGNMENT WITHIN EACH CLASS

SES probability at puberty and age at pregnancy	Outcome		Proportion of population with indicated characteristics
P_l Adolescent	$(.5)(.45)$	$(.95) \rightarrow$ Low SES	.21375
		$(.05 \rightarrow$ High SES	.01125
P_l Adult	$(.5)(.55)$	$(.90) \rightarrow$ Low SES	.2475
		$(.10) \rightarrow$ High SES	.0275
P_h Adolescent	$(.5)(.20)$	$(.15) \rightarrow$ Low SES	.015
		$(.85) \rightarrow$ High SES	.085
P_h Adult	$(.5)(.80)$	$(.10) \rightarrow$ Low SES	.04
		$(.90) \rightarrow$ High SES	.36

the following combination of characteristics: parents when they are teenagers, who belong to the Probable Low SES category, and who indeed end up as low SES adults. This is owing to the combinations of probabilities such that: .5 of all parents are P_l; .45 of such people are randomly assigned to teenage parenthood; and the chances of reaching low SES for teenage parents of the P_l population is .95. Hence $(.5) \cdot (.45) \cdot (.95) = .21375$. Each of the values is obtained in analogous fashion, with all eight of them summing to unity, 1.0. Thus in the last example, .5 of all parents are in the P_h probability class, with .8 of them assigned to post-adolescent pregnancies, and .9 of these will attain the high SES predicted for them. Hence $(.5) \cdot (.8) \cdot (.9) = .36$.

Chart 6.3 is a simple cross-tabulation between parents' SES and their age at parenthood. Visualize how the figures in each cell would be interpreted if they characterized the offspring with respect to some dependent variable (a personality trait, or perhaps educational attainment, or offspring's age at first marriage, etc.). Such a cross-tabulation would normally be viewed as a reasonable step toward determining the influence that age of the parents has on their offsprings' characteristics, controlling for another feature (SES) that both affects the dependent variable and is correlated with the independent variable. So why not control for SES in order to get closer to the true relationship? The answer is found in the cells of chart 6.3; the figures refer not to some dependent variable but rather sum up the results of tabulations provided in chart 6.2. The figure in each cell is the percentage of parents whose characteristics at the time of puberty would lead one to expect low adult SES. Thus the 93 percent shown in the upper left-hand cell is obtained by the two relevant random processes operating in chart 6.2. We saw that .21375 of all parents would end up in this cell who were low-expectation parents and that .015 of all parents would end up in this cell even though they initially had high SES expectations. Hence, of all those in this cell, 93 percent are parents who had initially low SES outlooks, $.21375 \div (.21375 + .015) = .93$. The important point is that the percentage with initially low SES expectations (P_l) varies between the cells and therefore undermines the comparisons made after the control is applied. Within each SES category, the percentage with unpromising background characteristics is greater for adolescent parents. Among those with low SES, P_l is 93 percent for teenage parents vs. 86 percent among the older parents. Likewise, for high SES parents, a bigger segment of adolescent parents were P_l, 12 percent, compared with 7 percent of older parents. In other words, the parental background characteristics within each socioeconomic category are different, depending on whether or not they had a child during their teenage years. This occurs despite the fact that there was no self-selectivity within classes with respect to becoming a teenage parent, that is, parents were randomly assigned to one or the other pregnancy ages.

CHART 6.3

PERCENTAGE IN P_l CLASS AT AGE OF PUBERTY, CLASSIFIED BY THEIR ACTUAL
ADULT SES AND AGE OF PARENTHOOD

Actual SES of parents	AGE OF PARENT AT TIME OF BIRTH	
	Adolescent	Adult
Low	93	86
High	12	7

What does this exercise with hypothetical but realistic conditions mean? It means that there would still be problems even under relatively optimal conditions such that all of these random processes are operating. We must remember that this is assuming a closer approximation to the true experiment than is usually justified in the analysis of naturally occurring social data. Holding SES constant, we would still not know if the differences between children in the two pregnancy classes reflected the direct or indirect consequence of age of pregnancy *or* whether the observed gaps were due to differences between their parents that existed prior to pregnancy.[6] We would not know this because the two sets of parents would still differ in background characteristics, that is, in this case, in whatever characteristics are involved in being assigned to the P_l or P_h class. In this particular case, it is true that the parental difference in the P_l percentage is smaller when compared across a given SES class than when compared among all parents. For all adolescent and all parents it is, respectively, 69 vs. 41 percent P_l, whereas it is 93 vs. 86 percent for low SES parents and 12 vs. 7 percent for high SES parents. "So what," one might be tempted to say, "the controlling procedure is not perfect, but it does get us closer to the truth than would occur otherwise." Alas, this will not do; the hypothetical figures assumed only a very modest effect of pregnancy on detouring parents from where they were likely to go anyway.

The example used assumes that early pregnancy generates very modest downward deflections in SES; the assumption in chart 6.2 is that an adolescent pregnancy increases the probability of low SES in adulthood from .90 to .95 for the P_l population and from .10 to .15 for the P_h class. Suppose we recompute matters under the assumption that early pregnancy more severely undermines high SES opportunities for the P_h class. Here we will assume that the probability of low SES for the P_h population experiencing adolescent fertility is now .55, as opposed to .10 for those P_h who become parents at a later age. As a consequence, 80 percent of adolescent parents with low SES as adults had characteristics at puberty that placed them in the P_l group, and 20 percent of high SES teenage parents were in this probability group (chart 6.4). The P_l percentages in the adult pregnancy column are identical to those shown in chart 6.3 because the assumptions about the mobility consequences for older parents remain unchanged.

The conclusions that would now be made are radically different. Comparing chart 6.4 with 6.3, we again observe that adolescent parents who later attain high SES levels have a much greater P_l component than high SES people who did not become parents until a later age. Indeed, the gap in P_l (20 vs. 7 percent) is now greater than existed earlier for fertility comparisons within the high SES population. However, the direction of the uncontrolled distortion has shifted for low SES parents. An even larger proportion of nonteen parents are P_l than are teen parents, 86 and 80 percent respectively for low SES adults.[7] In this case, the uncontrolled $P_l - P_h$ distribution within each cell which operates when comparisons are made within class lines will upset the results and probably lead to erroneous conclusions. Insofar as the early dispositional characteristics of the parents affect their own children's outcome, controlling for SES does not isolate the age-of-parent influence even under these unusually generous assumptions of nonselectivity. Chart 6.4 shows that the unmeasured push in these hypothetical conditions would be in one direction for high SES parents, and the unmeasured force is in the opposite direction for low SES parents.

CHART 6.4

PERCENTAGE OF PARENTS IN P_l CLASS (USING AN ALTERED ASSUMPTION ABOUT SES CONSEQUENCES OF TEENAGE PREGNANCY FOR P_h POPULATION)

Actual SES of parents	AGE OF PARENT AT TIME OF BIRTH	
	Adolescent	Adult
Low	80	86
High	20	7

Assumption Altered from Chart 6.2

		$(.55) \rightarrow$ Low SES	.015
P_h Adolescent pregnancy	$(.5)(.20)$		
		$(.45) \rightarrow$ High SES	.085

This result deeply undercuts the belief in the advantages of replication—namely, the simple argument that the replication of a study over and over again will confirm whether a given relationship really holds. Unmeasured forces, in the manner described earlier, may differ from situation to situation, depending on the nature of the combinational rates, such as those shown in charts 6.2 and 6.4. As likely as not, the repetition of a study will really be telling us whether or not the uncontrolled forces and the nonrandom associations are operating in the same way in the various contexts and periods being studied. This is hardly what the investigator thinks he or she is obtaining when the study is repeated in several contexts.

It is certainly possible to cope directly with the issue raised. Shown in chart 6.5 is a hypothetical three-way cross-tabulation between: Age at Pregnancy (teen vs. older); SES of Parent (say, high vs. low); Parental Characteristics at Their Age of Puberty (probable high vs. probable low SES as adults). With such a tabulation, the relevant dependent variable for the offspring could be compared so as to take into account directly the influence Age at Pregnancy has. (For example, the offspring of older and adolescent parents with identical P; and current SES.) But it is crucial to have sufficient information and cross-tabulations so as to be confident that the relevant differences are fully taken into account when comparing outcomes for the dependent variable with respect to the causal variable of interest. It is not impossible to do, at least theoretically, but it entails a movement backward over time so as to develop a high level of confidence about the branching conditions generating the populations found in each control category. Keep in mind that this would work only if adolescent pregnancy was a random outcome within a given subgroup.

CHART 6.5
HYPOTHETICAL THREE-WAY CROSS-TABULATION

Parental SES	SES probability at puberty	Age at pregnancy adolescent	adult
Low	Low		
	High		
High	Low		
	High		

It Is Usually Worse

These results are really much better than the researcher would normally have the right to expect. In reality, not only is there a problem because of the causal order issue but also it is almost certain that teenage pregnancy is not randomly assigned within different subgroups of the society. If blacks, for example, are more likely to experience teenage pregnancies than are whites, it is almost certain that blacks are not randomly assigned to one or the other pregnancy category. Rather, teenage blacks experiencing parenthood differ on the aggregate from teenage blacks who did not become parents.

And, in turn, these differences may well include characteristics that affect their offsprings' life chances. Hence the offspring of the two subsets of black parents may differ in the aggregate from each other in ways that do not reflect the fact that their parents were teenagers or not teenagers at the time of their birth. That is, within a given control class—race, in this case—whether or not someone became an early parent is probably related to characteristics that affect the offspring's behavior. Until these types of factors are fully taken into account, when we look at differences between the offspring of adolescent and older parents, we do not know how much and in what ways to attribute these gaps to the independent variable of interest (age at parenthood) as opposed to selective nonrandom forces operating within the control category.

CONTEXTUAL ANALYSIS AND CONTROLS

In a brilliant paper, Robert M. Hauser (1970) developed some rather telling criticisms of what is widely known as the "contextual effect." Briefly, a contextual effect refers to situations where the group context itself influences the dependent variable; it is found after all the compositional differences between the groups are taken into account through one or another of the usual controlling procedures. One can easily see how such a way of thinking might be attractive for school studies. For dependent variables such as test scores or aspirations, for example, does it make any difference if students are in school with lots of middle-class children? Since we know that class origin affects aspirations, obviously the researcher would normally not be content with examining the simple correlation between class composition in each school and the percentage of students planning to become president of the American Sociological Association or even president of the United States. The standard step would be to see if the linkage is simply due to the differences between schools in class composition and any other relevant controls. If a contextual effect operates, then presumably schools would differ above and beyond these background effects. In other words, middle-class children in a predominantly middle-class school would have higher aspirations than middle-class children in a predominantly working-class school. Likewise, for working-class children, those in a middle-class school would have higher aspirations than working-class children in predominantly working-class schools.

In Hauser's paper, he observes that high schools differ in their sex composition and that the students in schools with high sex ratios (relatively more males than females) tend to have higher aspirations. Coining a clever term, "the consexual effect," he then asks if sex composition influences aspiration net of other differences between the schools. He finds that the contextual effect is relatively modest at best after the influences of student's intelligence score, father's education, and sex of the student are simultaneously taken into account (see Hauser 1970, table 8, p. 654).

> The sex-ratio context explains little of the variation in aspirations. The four-fold point correlation between sex-ratio context and educational aspirations is 0.140, which accounts for less than 2 percent of the variance in aspirations. When sex, intelligence, and father's education are entered as predictors in a multiple regression equation, they account for 15.4 percent of the variance in aspirations. The addition of the sex-ratio context to the regression equation increases the explained variance only to 15.9 percent. The increment in explained variance is statistically significant at the .05 level, but it is hardly of much substantive importance. (Hauser 1970: 660–661)

Hauser goes on to show that the sex-ratio effect would be even less important (in variance explained terms) if each of the schools had been treated as an independent entity rather than grouped (661).

What do we learn from this exercise? I will not dwell on the use of variance explained as a criterion for determining the importance of variables since that issue was discussed in detail in chapter 5. Moreover, the contextual study illustrates once again the inappropriate application of controls to situations where the randomization assumption cannot hold. We are in fact back to another variant of the private-public school issue. It is only under certain conditions that the controls for father's education, and the sex and intelligence of the student, would help to eliminate or greatly reduce confounding causal features—namely, only if the controls are not substantially associated with unmeasured attributes that themselves significantly influence the phenomenon under study. If a school has an unusually large number of students whose parents are well educated and another school has relatively few, can it be assumed that the children of well-educated parents going to the first school do not differ from those going to the second school after parental education, sex, and intelligence are taken into account? And the same can be asked about those children whose parents have minimal levels of education: Do those attending schools where they are in the minority differ from those who attend schools where many of the children are in the same circumstance? It is highly unlikely in this circumstance; hence it is questionable what one learns by controlling to begin with. For all we know, the contextual effect studied by Hauser is actually stronger than meets the eye on the zero-order level. This would be the case if the unmeasured factor(s) responsible for this non-random sorting actually work against the contextual effect. At any rate, there is no need to belabor the point; the control variable style of analysis used to evaluate the contextual effect is a weak one for the reasons elaborated earlier.

Of interest here, however, is a set of questions raised about the use of control variables. Are there problems for which the control approach can be judged as inappropriate on a priori theoretical grounds, regardless of what the data look like? Further, when the use of controls is justifiable in theoretical terms, under what conditions is it practical or not to use them? When not practical, what is the alternative?

As for the first question, Hauser presents a brief but important argument that runs counter to the contemporary usage of control variables—an argument that is rarely followed. He suggests that "it is not necessary to control for individual attributes when you are really interested in the covariation of structural or aggregate variables. Such controls may be desirable when the object is to find out how structural or aggregate variation occurs, but this is not ordinarily the case in contextual analysis" (Hauser 1970: 661). As a matter of fact, one can show that this is part of a more general set of problems for which the application of the normal control procedures would be incorrect. Chapter 10 describes when it is inappropriate to consider the influence of some structural variable after using various controls. It sets out some principles to enable us to know both why and when such a radical deviation from our current practices is appropriate. At this point, however, there is a more immediate issue to consider about controls.

THE NATURE OF THE CONTROL VARIABLES

The misuse of control variables, illustrated in the contextual study and found in many others, including some by myself, raises the question of whether there is an alternative way of thinking about the control problem. There are three basic facts: secondary public schools in the Nashville area differ in their sex ratio; students differ in their educational aspirations; and those students in schools with relatively high sex ratios tend to have greater educational aspirations than students in schools with lower sex ratios. The issue for Hauser—and for most social researchers in that situation—is to explain this association between sex ratio of school and aspiration level of students. Since such factors as father's education and student's intelligence are not randomly distributed among the schools (along with sex composition), it is necessary to take their influence into account before attributing any causal influence to school composition per se. And off we go into the wild blue yonder of control variables, making assumptions about the control variables that would only make sense in a true experimental situation involving random allocation of subjects. Never mind the fact that we do not have a true experiment such that there is nonrandom allocation of subjects.

Assuming that the use of a multivariate approach cannot be rejected on a priori theoretical grounds, what would be a reasonable alternative to such a procedure? The research must start by recognizing why it is impossible to assume a true experiment. This means dealing with the fact that characteristics are not randomly assigned to the units of analysis (in this case, schools); the independent variable of interest (the sex ratio) varies between schools; the control variables (such as father's education and student's intelligence) also vary between schools. Rather than sweeping these matters under the rug, one must decide whether a control procedure is justified.

Instead of starting with the association between the independent variable of interest and the dependent variable, the researcher must initially determine whether there are unobserved sorting processes operating and, if so, whether they affect the specific dependent variable under study. First, is there unmeasured selectivity underlying the correlations between the control variables and the independent variable of special interest?[8] Second, why do these independent variables differ between the units of analysis (cities, nations, groups, societies, schools, individuals, or whatever)?

Appropriate answers to these two questions are necessary if the researcher wants to use a control variable approach to the empirical problem. But until they are satisfactorily answered, the use of controls is an outrageously inappropriate step. And I make that statement fully congnizant of the fact that it applies to a substantial part of contemporary nonexperimental research. Fortunately, in some circumstances, satisfactory answers can be obtained with relatively little effort. However, for researchers pursuing the truth rather than a result that others are willing to accept as part of a mutual self-deception, in many instances the answers to these questions will no longer permit the use of control variables.

LINKAGES BETWEEN THE INDEPENDENT VARIABLES[9]

In the study discussed earlier, an association was found between father's educational level (one of the control variables) and the independent variable of interest (sex composition of the school). Comparing seniors whose fathers are highly educated with those whose fathers have minimal education, one finds that a relatively smaller proportion of the latter attend schools with high sex ratios. The opposite holds for the children attending schools with low sex ratios (Hauser 1970: 651). Let X_1 and X_2 represent two measured independent variables and Y represent the dependent variable (in this case, educational aspirations of the student). For convenience we will assume that X_1 is the independent variable of interest (sex ratio) and X_2 is a control (father's education). If a variable is present in the study which is both unmeasured *and* is not caused by either

X_1 or X_2, it will be designated by X_3. Variables of that nature may or may not exist in a given study. For ease in presentation: X_1 is a dichotomy, X_2 is a trichotomy; and X_3, if it exists, will be a continuous variable. Low, medium, and high values of the trichotomy will be represented respectively by the subscripts l, m, and h. Chart 6.6 should make it easier to follow the different possible relationships between X_3 and both sex ratio and level of father's education. The first subscript designates the sex ratio and the second subscript indicates father's level of education. Thus $\overline{X}_{hm}$ indicates the mean value of X_3 for those children attending schools with high sex ratios and whose fathers have medium levels of education.

If an association exists between the control variable and the independent variable of interest, there are three different ways X_3 could be involved.[10] These are:

1. Pure random assignment with different probability weights.

2. Nonrandom assignment but where the conditional factors do not influence the dependent variable of interest in the study.

3. Nonrandom assignment in which the conditional factors influence the dependent variable of interest.

These types are extremes and all three forces could be operating in varying degrees in any given case.

A Purely Random Assignment of X_3

Although an association exists between the control variable and the independent variable of interest (such that the distribution of X_2 varies by level of X_1), the level of X_3 may not have any relationship to the sorting process that operates. In the case at hand, if a purely random assignment model is operating, then the offspring of highly educated fathers who go to high schools with one type of sex ratio are identical on the aggregate to the offspring of those similarly educated fathers who go to the other subset of high schools. In terms of chart 6.6, it means:

$$\overline{X}_{ll} = \overline{X}_{lm} = \overline{X}_{lh} = \overline{X}_{hl} = \overline{X}_{hm} = \overline{X}_{hh}.$$

As far as the first question goes, under these conditions there is every reason to proceed with control variables because the experimental situation is indeed approximated. I say *approximated* because if it was an ideal experimental situation, the X_1 populations would not differ on X_2, which they do. However, once these differences are taken into account, that is, controlling for X_2, there is nothing more to worry about in terms of the first question.[11]

Nonrandom Assignment of X_3

Should the random model not hold, the control approach may or may not be justified. It is appropriate if the conditional factors have no bearing on the dependent variable and, under certain specific conditions, may also work even though X_3 does affect Y. However, an adequate measurement of X_3 would be absolutely mandatory in many settings before one could proceed with a control variable approach. There are thus three different subsets of conditions to be considered when a nonrandom assignment of X_3 occurs.

Nonrandum assignment of X_3, but where X_3 does not influence the dependent variable. Suppose, for the sake of illustration, that highly educated fathers send their children to high sex-ratio schools because they want their children to be in a relatively masculine environment. This would mean that the children of well-educated fathers are not randomly assigned to one or the other type of school; namely, the children of educated fathers who have a certain attitude are more likely to attend high sex-ratio schools than are the children of comparably educated parents with a different attitude. But if that parental characteristic has no bearing on the dependent variable of interest in the study, then a control for father's education would be fully justified as sufficient.[12]

Acceptable control procedures when there is a nonrandom assignment of X_3 and where X_3 does influence the dependent variable. The control variable approach is not necessarily endangered even if $\overline{X}_3$ does vary between combinations of X_1 and X_2. No problem will occur when the control is applied as long as $\overline{X}_3$ differences are associated only with the controls; a problem will occur if $\overline{X}_3$ is also (or instead) associated with the independent variable of interest (sex ratio cate-

gories). Using Chart 6.6 as a reference, in this case no problem
exists if:

$$\overline{X}_{ll} = \overline{X}_{hl},$$
$$\overline{X}_{lm} = \overline{X}_{hm},$$
$$\overline{X}_{lh} = \overline{X}_{hh}.$$

When sex ratio comparisons are made after X_2 is taken into account,
the influence of X_3 on Y is of no consequence insofar as the level of
X_3 is the same among the sex ratio categories being compared. To
be sure, this ignores all sorts of interaction effects with which the
researcher would actually want to deal. (The contemporary re-
searcher would very much want to know, for example, if the $\overline{X}_{ll}/\overline{X}_{hl}$
ratio differed from the $\overline{X}_{lm}/\overline{X}_{hm}$ ratio or if either was different from
$\overline{X}_{lh}/\overline{X}_{hh}$.) But in terms of deciding whether the explanandum is
affected by the independent variable of interest, at least some
conclusion can be reached even if X_3 is unmeasured and does affect
aspirations. The key proviso is shown in the preceding equations, to
wit, that $\overline{X}_3$ be identical within a given control variable so that sex
ratio influences cross-tabulated by the control are not contaminated
by X_3.

CHART 6.6
LINKAGE BETWEEN INDEPENDENT VARIABLES

Sex ratio (X_1)	Education of father (X_2)	Mean of unmeasured variables (X_3)
	Low	$\overline{X}_{ll}$
Low	Medium	$\overline{X}_{lm}$
	High	$\overline{X}_{lh}$
	Low	$\overline{X}_{hl}$
High	Medium	$\overline{X}_{hm}$
	High	$\overline{X}_{hh}$

Unacceptable control procedures. A problem occurs if an unmeasured
variable, X_3, affects Y *and* differs among high sex-ratio schools

and/or low sex-ratio schools as a function of the control variable X_2 such that:

$$\overline{X}_{ll} \neq \overline{X}_{hl},$$
$$\overline{X}_{lm} \neq \overline{X}_{hm},$$
$$\overline{X}_{lh} \neq \overline{X}_{hh}.$$

In this situation, the researcher cannot blithely use control procedures. As noted earlier, application of the control procedures can actually generate results that are further removed from the truth than would occur if no controls were applied. As a consequence, the influence of sex ratio on the dependent variable cannot yet be determined until the influence of an unmeasured variable, X_3, is taken into account. One is tempted to say that this is because X_3 is *correlated* with the independent variable of interest, X_1, but that would be misleading. Although my concern in this volume is primarily procedural rather than statistical, I want to point out that this represents one of the most widespread and fatal errors in social research. It does not matter whether there is a correlation between X_3 and X_1; what *does* matter is that the mean and/or distribution of X_3 varies by level of X_1. This condition is obviously met if there is a correlation between the two variables. However, in the absence of such a correlation, it does not necessarily follow that X_3 is uniformly distributed at all levels of X_1. In turn, if X_3 affects Y, then it will affect in one way or another the observed impact of X_1.

What can one do under these circumstances? If the control approach is to be followed, one has to somehow measure X_3 in order to control or take into account its influence such that one of the conditions described earlier is attained. Observe, incidentally, that controlling for X_3 is not yet sufficient. For one must in turn then be confident that some other attribute, X_4, does not differ between levels of X_3, and so on. All of this leads to an unwelcome conclusion—unwelcome because it undercuts current procedures. An incomplete application of all relevant controls does not necessarily mean a partial approximation of the truth. Rather, the results of such a procedure are as likely to be further from as closer to determining the true influence of the independent variable of interest. Mastery over the relevant variables is at present viewed as on a continuum in terms of the benefits that ensue: the more you are able to deal with relevant controls, the more good (i.e., closer approximation to the truth) will occur. Alas, in many research contexts, measurement and mastery of the control variables is not a matter of degree in terms of the knowledge that ensues. Rather, it is either doable and hence beneficial insofar as a true experiment is thereby simulated *or* it is not doable at all. A partially adequate set of controls is an inadequate set of controls and an inadequate simulation of the experimental model. For each time that it provides a closer approximation of the truth, there is another time when it provides a more distorted approximation. This leads to some interesting and important questions that should be central issues for contemporary social statisticians:

Is there any way of determining whether a fully adequate set of controls has been administered such that the conditions acceptable for controls are in operation? The problem is especially severe for variables that are either inadequately measured or not measured at all.

Are there variables that can be used appropriately for controls even when the conditions are not totally suitable for a control variable approach? If the answer is in the affirmative, then in turn does this mean that there are conditions and variables especially likely to be disasters when not fully taken into account? Moreover, if in the affirmative, is there a way of determining the conditions when a partial set of controls is less or more likely to be an approximation of the true relationship?

If one cannot cope with the nonrandom conditional factors that are operating, is there any alternative way of empirically approaching the problem or does one throw up one's hands in defeat?

WHY DO THE INDEPENDENT VARIABLES VARY BETWEEN THE UNITS OF ANALYSIS?

Why do the independent variables vary between the units of analysis? This question must be thoroughly considered before control variables are applied. In the school context problem, why is it that schools differ in their sex ratios? Why does the level of father's education vary between schools? At first glance, it may appear as if the researcher is being asked to go back endlessly in time before the application of some standard control such as age, sex, education, or income is to be accepted. This is hardly the case.

We can understand why public high schools would differ from one another in the SES characteristics of the seniors attending them. After all, SES residential segregation in cities by itself would lead to SES differences between local schools.[13] If only because SES affects standard IQ test performances, this would lead one to expect at least some differences between schools on this characteristic as well. So it is not implausible that two of our important control variables would differ from school to school.[14] What about the independent variable of interest? Why would the sex ratio vary between schools? The ratio of boys to girls in the eleven schools varied rather widely, from 1.33 to 0.34 boys per girl (Hauser, 1970, p. 647). Hauser has some plausible reasons for this.

> Although sex ratios varied markedly from school to school, this variation was not a result of any explicit policy with regard to admission of students. Recruitment to the eleven schools was based on neighborhood of residence. It is probable that the sex ratios of the schools varied less as a consequence of neighborhood variations in the sex ratio of persons of high school age than as a consequence of dropout, grade retardation, and enrollment in private schools. Reiss and Rhodes (1959, chap. 2:10) found that on the basis of a one-year follow-up of the students covered in the 1957 Nashville survey, white boys were more likely to drop out of school than white girls. . . . In order to ascertain the plausibility of dropout and grade-retardation differentials as an explanation of school sex-ratio differences, the sex ratios for students in lower-grade feeder schools were calculated down through the seventh grade for each of the sex-ratio contexts. Within each context, the sex ratio varied inversely with grade in school, and there was no difference in sex ratio between the two contexts below the tenth-grade level. (Hauser 1970: 648)

What does it mean if the causal variable of greatest interest in this project, sex ratio of the schools, is generated by areal differences in the dropout rate, grade retardation, and enrollment in private schools? With processes of this sort, it is virtually guaranteed that selective forces were operating to create the sex ratios found in each school and to alter the characteristics of the children attending each school. And these forces have a bearing on the dependent variable.

(This ignores the additional fact that residential location may itself have been affected by the nature of the neighborhood school.) The number of girls, for example, whose fathers have low levels of education is slightly in excess of the number of boys, respectively 159 and 144 (a ratio of 1.1). By contrast, among seniors attending the public high schools who have highly educated fathers, the ratio is 1.7—126 girls and 75 boys (Hauser 1970: table 3). This almost certainly suggests differential treatment of boys and girls such that families with highly educated fathers are especially likely to send their sons to private schools.

The moral of this example is rather simple. Knowing what we do about the forces generating variation between schools in the independent variable of interest, it is something of a deception to pretend that there is any way one can directly simulate the experimental model by applying controls. The controls cannot have the meaning that researchers want to give to them—and could give to them—if there was a random force generating different levels in the independent variable or if the researcher had systematically varied schools as part of a controlled experiment. There is an important dropout process operating by the time we get to high school seniors, in terms of both those quitting school altogether and those who shift to one or another type of private school. This means that any comparison, to begin with, is subject to a significant unmeasured process affecting who or what is available for comparison. If the reasons for the sex-ratio differences between schools are taken seriously, it seems inappropriate to use control variables in the way that they were. Clearly, the study's first question would be why are these attributes distributed the way they are and what consequences does that have for the simulation of the experimental model?

CONCLUSIONS AND COMMENTS

There is an ironic quality to certain of the conclusions in this chapter. The use of controls is generally most attractive to researchers in the very circumstances where they are likely to be least appropriate. Situations in which the initially observed relationship is altered, after controls are applied, are the very ones where there is a strong chance that the experimental analogue is inapplicable. However, there is no problem with the current procedure when the initial relationship remains unchanged after controls are applied. There is no problem because, in order for such a conclusion to hold, we have seen that it entails patterns that are compatible with a quasi-experimental simulation. Hence the use of controls is most likely to generate erroneous conclusions in the very circumstances when the need for controls seems most acute. Given this conclusion, it is important to develop an alternative procedure that is appropriate when controls are not justified. This will be attempted in Part II of this volume.

In this regard, then, situations when control procedures appear most important, that is, when their application alters the outcome for other causal variables, are the very situations when they cannot be applied without further consideration of other selective forces. Until further analysis justifies the use of controls, the observation of apparent control effects should be viewed as an important warning that controls are not the correct way to treat the data because a quasi-experimental approximation is totally inappropriate. In other words, we have to look at the problem not from the perspective of determining the net influence of some characteristic on another. Rather, we have to decide first whether there is justification for the assumption implicitly underlying the entire procedure, to wit, whether there are grounds for taking data generated by naturally occurring events and assuming that they can be manipulated to approximate a quasi-experimental situation.

Before controlling, perhaps the best thing to do is figure out why the set of variables go together to begin with. There are two questions here: Why does the nonrandom pattern exist, and what influence does the nonrandom pattern have on the comparisons that are being made when controls are applied? These linkages may themselves be reflecting something that would change the meaning of the partials, multiples, and so on, that are found. Researchers usually focus on the linkage between independent variables and the explanandum—to a much lesser extent do they attempt to understand the linkages between independent variables.

One might argue at this point that there is really nothing new here. This would, I feel, be an irrelevant response. Irrelevant because whatever may be the official rules of the National Research League (NRL), they do not represent what is actually practiced. Social scientists know that a table of organization does not necessarily reflect the actual functioning of an organization. Likewise, incredible chasms often exist between what a group says are its norms and what it practices. So too is the case for actual research procedures with respect to control variables, as can be seen in current research. So whether this is a novel revelation or simply a discovery about the emperor's clothes is immaterial. The fact is that control variable issues raised in this chapter are pertinent to what is actually practiced.

At the very least, variables should not be controlled until we first know why the controls operate the way they do. By that is meant not merely understanding the influence that the control has on the explanandum but also learning why the control is nonrandomly distributed with respect to other independent variables. In other words, if the control influenced the explanandum but the control was distributed equally in all conditions of interest, then we would normally not have to take the control into account.[15] This means that an early step is understanding why the control is not randomly associated with the independent variable of interest. What is the social process that leads to the association of the control variable in some form or another with another independent variable? Until that is known, there is no point in controlling, especially since there is a strong chance that there is selectivity within the control on what is being controlled. Until we know what these selective processes are, and can then suitably cope with them, there is no point in applying the control.

This is a reasonable position and an important consideration. However, suppose someone argues that it would lead us further and further back in a causal chain that would probably never end because of the probable selective nonrandom assignment association of variables at all points back and back ad nauseam. There are two responses. First, it may indeed be the case that there are circumstances where the control procedure is simply inappropriate, pure and simple. If there are, then it is too bad in the sense that a ritualistically applied set of procedures is invalid. But it does mean that we are better off knowing this than pretending that something is right when it is not. Second, it seems to me that we would be better off trying to work in situations where fewer controls are needed, either because we generate theories that do not have to contend with the issue or because the problem is worded in such a way as to eliminate the need for such a large number of controls. This must not mean picking trivial problems. That would be counterproductive in terms of actually advancing substantial knowledge. But I believe that we overdo the multivariate approach altogether and will attempt to show, in Part II, an appropriate way of thinking theoretically that undercuts the control simulation.

At the very least, we need to rethink the logic of controls and set up a statement about the conditions under which such procedures are appropriate and inappropriate. Any development that sets out rules and logic for this would be extremely valuable. Such an attempt at this point would be premature. First, as chapter 7 will show, there are theoretical dimensions to control procedure that need airing. Second, the functions of the project must also be considered before the control procedures can be appropriately evaluated. Is it to determine policies for actions (say, if we raise variable X_{14}, will this lead to an increase in Y which the society desires to see occur)? Is it to develop theoretical notions about how the social universe operates? Or is it simply to describe the set of events that occurs (in the way that a journalist might attempt if there was sufficient time and resources)? A judgment about the use of control procedures is not independent of the nature of the research goal. This is unrecognized at present; there is no conception in social research that the nature of the question influences the way a given data set is analyzed. In fact, judgment about the appropriateness of controls for a given data set can depend on the specific type of problem being pursued.

CHAPTER SEVEN

More about Current Practices

This is the last chapter in which the primary goal is a critical evaluation of current research; sooner or later, we must start to consider alternative procedures.[1] The heart of my concern is again with the present-day pursuit of the undoable. This entails certain *theoretical* facets to the control issue, but first we will examine the assumption that there is only one true or correct interpretation of empirical results. A study's goals and the theory driving the research (the two are *not* the same) affect the interpretation of results in ways that are not appreciated at the moment. As matters now stand, researchers seem to assume that there is ultimately only one correct conclusion. Without suggesting an intellectual anarchy in which any conclusion is as good or valid as any other, I wish to put forth certain relativistic propositions about the interpretation of research results. A review of these matters will expose additional weaknesses in current practices and, it is hoped, help clear the way for a different approach to social research.

THE INTERPRETATION DEPENDS ON THE RESEARCH GOAL

There is a variety of reasons for gathering and analyzing a set of data. One function of research is "simple" fact-finding—for example, what is the level of residential segregation between blacks and whites and/or has it changed in the past ten years? Such an activity sometimes means that social researchers are doing nothing more than a superior sort of journalism, that is, providing information about the society in as rigorous and careful a manner as is possible. There are those who look down on this activity, but their disdain is unwarranted. After all, who is better suited to serve this function than social researchers? It is self-destructive for social scientists to denigrate such work on the grounds that it is atheoretical. Fact-finding of this nature can require great elegance and craftsmanship, it is socially useful, and social scientists are uniquely skilled to accomplish it and interpret the results.

A second research function is more complicated than this; it involves an effort to account for a given pattern or set of events. Again using residential segregation as an example, the researcher wants to know whether segregation is affected by a city's size, its age, region, percentage of blacks, industrial composition, and so on. In this case, the investigator wants to determine the apparent causes of a given state of affairs.[2] This type of causal analysis is viewed as being theoretically driven because the analysis is geared toward accounting for as much of what is going on as possible— based on the ideas (or theories) that the researcher and others have about what might be causing the pattern. Such analyses usually relate more to application of a theory or set of theories than to development or evaluation of a theory. This is because the focus is on accounting for a given event, rather than on the power of the theory itself. Hence, in the typical multivariate analysis, the researcher might take note that a prediction generated by a given theory does not seem to operate as expected, but this is unlikely to lead to the conclusion that the theory is invalid. It is another matter if there is only one theory supposedly able to account for the events. Also, serendipitous knowledge may develop in this circumstance when the expected explanation does not seem to operate. As a general rule, however, such studies are concerned primarily with explaining the event and only secondarily with weighing the theories that are meant to explain them.

A third research function entails evaluating a given theory and/or comparing the relative merits of competing theories. This is very difficult to execute effectively simply because it is difficult to find situations in which a "crucial test" is more or less approximated. The problem is hardly unique to the social sciences, but the subject matter that social researchers deal with and the expectations they have about theories certainly do not make it any easier. About the only feature here that is relatively easy is the study in which an investigator seeks to find a place in the sun for a given theory, that is, show that certain forces predicted by a given theory do operate to influence events of interest. Using the segregation example, one might want to see if, say, percentage of blacks has a bearing on the level of segregation. This often leads to a study with a form similar to the second type—except here the focus is on the value of a given causal notion, whereas the other type is concerned with explaining something. Pursuing this goal, the researcher would be concerned with whether or not composition affects segregation after other causal forces have been taken into account.

A fourth function of research is to suggest policy or applied consequences. For example, one might ask: How shall we go about reducing residential segregation? To answer this question, it would seem reasonable to investigate what appears to be causing segregation now and see what would have to be changed in order to reduce it.

These different goals can be readily understood and appreciated, even if the boundaries between them are sometimes rather arbitrary. But what we do not recognize is that a given data set can be perfectly appropriate for meeting one of these goals but, at the same time, be of virtually no use for another of the goals. If that is the case, and I will try to show why it is, then there are three very important consequences for current practices:

1. A given data set can provide considerable information for one research goal without necessarily providing relevant information for another goal.

2. The same data set will require very different kinds of analysis, depending on the goal that is being pursued. There could well be four correct or ideal ways of analyzing a data set, depending on which goal is being pursued.

3. If the above points are valid, then it also follows—and this is rather counterintuitive—that knowledge about one question might be of little more than remote value in trying to answer some other question.

An Example

Expanding on a paper by Lord (1969), the quotation below from Cohen and Cohen raises some interesting questions about partialing procedures in the analysis of covariance (ACV). The biological example illustrates rather nicely the point that different goals can require radically different data sets and analyses.

> An agronomist, investigating the difference in yield (Y) between "black" and "white"varieties of corn (set B), grows 20 pots of each under the same conditions to maturity. Upon harvesting, he finds a considerably higher yield of marketable grain for the white variety. But he also observes that the white variety averages 7 feet high at flowering time (set A), compared to 6 for the black variety. The yield-on-height slopes being the same, he performs an ACV and finds that the adjusted mean yield difference is near zero and nonsignificant. What does this mean? (Cohen and Cohen 1975: 397–398)

The facts are very simple: two varieties of corn differ in both their yield and in their average height at flowering time; when height is taken into account, there are no differences between the varieties. How do we interpret these results? Most readers, I suspect, are inclined to believe that there is indeed a *single correct* interpretation of these events. This is true in the sense that there can be a correct interpretation for a given goal or research function. As a simple description of the events, it seems reasonable to conclude that, *under the planting conditions experienced in the study*, one variety yields more corn than another variety and that the former also has taller plants.

The same data, however, may generate different conclusions for other research goals. Suppose we now ask a second question from the data: What causes the varieties to differ in yield? Both varieties of corn, when matched by height, have the same yield. But this does not mean, to use the thinking that social researchers are apt to apply to such a situation, that height explains away yield. Despite the common regression lines for yield on height, it would make no causal sense to conclude that the yield differences between varieties are explained away or fully accounted for by differences in height. For it is the case that the corn variety is the identical cause for both the yield differences and the differences in flowering height. As Cohen and Cohen (1975: 398) observe, in the analysis of covariance, "the dependent variable is no longer yield (Y), but yield adjusted for flowering height (Y·A). The use of ACV does not change the fact of the yield difference of the two varieties." A few pages later, they cite another example of inappropriate partialing procedures:

Consider the fact that the differences in mean height between the mountains of the Himalayan and Catskill ranges, adjusting for differences in atmospheric pressure, is zero! (Cohen and Cohen 1975: 400)

In point of fact, the typical causal analysis in social research is really nothing more than the manipulation of the available data. This is not surprising, but the results are based on the assumption that the statistical manipulation of the available data will establish the causal linkages that would have been found had a controlled experiment been possible. The validity of the results will therefore depend on how closely the naturally occurring data approximate what would be found in a true experimental situation. There are, at times, incredible possibilities of incorrectly manipulating the data sets.[3]

This last point requires no elaboration here since it is simply a restatement of the points made in the previous chapter. As for the theoretical goals of empirical research, it is best to wait on that until we figure out a more positive approach to social research. However, almost anyone who has tried to make data address a crucial theoretical issue should be able to testify that they do not work very well for that purpose. As the data are rarely that "clean" and the possibility of alternative explanations is usually so great, it can be the highest form of pretension or self-deception for a researcher to conclude that some theory is wrong because the data seem to contradict the expectations generated by the theory.[4]

Applied Issues

Judging by present practices, a contention that does require elaboration here is that the empirical data needed for policy or action-oriented research are of a different sort than what is used to describe and analyze the forces causing the current situation. Put another way, no matter how well executed an empirical study of the causes of a given phenomenon may be, it is not usually possible to go from the results of such a study to policy conclusions. In my estimation, one source for the present disillusionment with social science is the fact that policies generated from the conclusions obtained in earlier "basic" research proved to be largely failures. And, in turn, they were failures precisely because there was no recognition of the fact that simulated causal explanations of existing patterns usually cannot answer the questions needed for policy decisions. An understanding of the mechanisms generating the current situation, even if very thorough, is not the same as understanding the consequences of changes in the current situation.

This is quite different from taking the relationship observed between volume and pressure to set out a procedure for raising or lowering the volume by appropriately changing the pressure.

Cohen and Cohen provide a lucid example of how applied conclusions (ways of increasing the yield of corn) need not at all follow from explanations of the existing events (differences in yield), no matter how satisfactory the latter may be.[5] Although accepting the possibility that differences in flowering height account for the yield differences between the two corn varieties, and recognizing the validity of the statement that black and white plants of the same height have the same yield, they object strenuously to what they call "subjunctive" formulations such as: "*If* black and white varieties *were* of equal height, *then* they would have equal yields."

We cannot know what the consequence of equal height would be on yield without specifying the means of producing equality in height. We might add fertilizer or water to the black variety, or stretch it when it is young, or use other means to actually equate the varieties. There is no reason to believe that such alternative methods of equating height would have the same consequences, or that any of them would result in equal yields. More technically, such intervention in the process might well change the groups' yield-on-height regression lines, so that those used for adjustment in the analysis are not necessarily descriptive of "what would happen if . . . ." Only if heights were equated by excluding short black plants or tall white ones could the regression lines be assumed to hold, and the interpretation be admissible. But this is not what we usually wish to know. Only by making the appropriate changes which accomplish height equality in a new experiment and determining the consequent yields can the question be answered.

Unfortunately, operations analogous to these in behavioral and social science applications are more often than not simply impossible, and such subjunctive questions cannot be answered by ACV, or indeed, by any method of analyzing data. (Cohen and Cohen 1975: 398)

This is quite analogous to drawing applied consequences from social research conclusions about the factors causing the current state of affairs.

The statistical explanation of a given set of observations must be distinguished from action-oriented conclusions drawn from such efforts. In this case, it is one thing to draw conclusions about what accompanies the yield differences in corn varieties. (And even here it is not as simple as we would like because of the danger of applying inappropriate controls.) But it is a totally different matter to draw conclusions about possible consequences of unobserved acts on the dependent variable of interest—here the consequences for yield if black corn were to reach the same average flowering height as the white variety. The projection of existing statistical linkages into unobserved patterns is usually one of the great goals of social research because it then permits policy conclusions that deal with a series of *what if* statements. Should social policymakers wish to reduce the gap between the two types of plants, as it were, then it is vital that they be able to know in advance what will happen if various policies are followed. In this case, what would be the consequence of increasing the flowering height of black corn? The problem is that there is some set of interactive forces, as Cohen and Cohen observe, such that it is unlikely that the steps taken to increase the yield will leave unaltered the regression of yield on height observed for black corn. In effect, the observations made earlier are sufficient to provide an understanding of the present set of processes that operate to generate the differences in yield. But these observations are insufficient for drawing policy conclusions because the observations tell us nothing about the consequences of altering the height distribution of black corn.

The relationships observed between the control variables and the explanandum are not necessarily readily manipulated to change the explanandum. This is because the model and statistics necessary to account for the observed set of affairs are normally different from those needed in describing or accounting for the desired set of relations. To understand what is going on at present requires, in many social research situations, a different kind of knowledge than that needed to anticipate the actual dynamic consequences of certain changes in the observed patterns. If we find that differences in X_3 fully explain differences in Y, we normally have no business making the assumption that whatever we do to change X_3 will itself have no bearing on Y independent of the shifts in X_3. Indeed, these changes (social side effects, as it were) may be more powerful than the influence of X_3. Moreover, there is no assurance that even the net influence of X_3 will remain unaltered under these new conditions. As we shall see, in many settings there are strong grounds for expecting a radical alteration in the current relationship between X_3 and Y.

There is, in short, an important difference between statistical exercises designed to explain the differences between various attributes (say, types of corn, or people, or groups) and statistical efforts geared toward determining the best way to achieve a reduction in these differences. All of this ignores the additional factor developed in chapter 4, to wit, that causal processes are often asymmetrical in social events. If the forces causing a given dependent variable are asymmetrical, it means that they could be removed without changing the dependent variable. If such is the case, then without doubt it means that empirical analyses of the causes of the event would not tell us how to alter the phenomenon being explained.

A LITTLE MORE ON CONTROLS

The examples from Cohen and Cohen show how easy it is to generate disastrous conclusions when controls are applied incorrectly; a formal procedure is needed for deciding when and how controls are to be applied. As matters now stand, researchers control for any and all variables whenever they believe that the variables precede the variable of interest or, in certain more restricted cases, when the variables occur simultaneously. At the very least, one needs a model of the causal linkages that operate between not only the control and the dependent variable but also between the control and other controls and the independent variable of special interest to the investigator. Otherwise, it is all too easy to fall into the social equivalent of the mountain example given by the Cohens. Do the lowly Catskills differ from the noble Himalayas in height? Of course they do. Do they differ after you take into account some control variable, such as differences in atmospheric pressure? There is no height difference at all! The flaw is easy to find in this case; the control variable applied here—atmospheric pressure—is dependent on the explanandum and hence the causal direction is misdirected when height is considered net of its own consequence. A simple moral lesson is that controls cannot be blithely applied without first considering the causal direction of the relationships involved.

One might well argue that path models at present accomplish these goals, and this would be partially correct since such modelling procedures obviously do help clear up our understanding. But it is not enough. First, many path models throw in disturbance terms which obviously include more than mere measurement errors. Second, the models usually include unanalyzed relationships between causal factors (represented by double-headed causal arrows). Third, there is no explicit logic or rule available as to how far back one should go in the causal set. Some researchers seem to feel that they can throw in anything that seems to have temporal priority regardless of whether it is thought through.

For a control variable to have any impact, it must be linked to both the dependent variable and some other causal variable of interest. Before controlling, however, the researcher must have some understanding of why these associations exist. In a certain sense, we are talking about determining the linkages between the control and the independent variable in a more careful way before controls can be simply applied to the influence of the independent variable on the explanandum. Is the linkage due to some special cause-and-effect pattern that reflects relatively independent causes? What are these conditions? This is rarely considered as one blithely controls for some variable. Yet it is the central issue in interpreting the results of the control—to say nothing of drawing policy conclusions based on the statistical analysis. We have to know, then, if there are special conditions operating under the situation being studied which have led the control and the causal variable of interest to have the relationship with each other that they have. This cannot be answered by controlling for everything that precedes the dependent variable in temporal order.

CAUSAL ORDER AND CONTROLS

Most social researchers implicitly assume that the causal order of events has some sort of temporal structure and, moreover, that the two can be linked in one way or another. A variable that precedes another variable in the temporal order of events may or may not be the cause of the latter variable—that is an empirical question—but it is certain that the variable occurring later in time will not be viewed as the cause of the variable that preceded it. This viewpoint affects decisions about what variables are to be controlled or otherwise taken into account when analyzing the causes of a given dependent variable. Events that temporally precede the dependent variable are included then as possible causes in quasi-experimental research.

The phrase "controlling for all relevant variables" does not mean that one should automatically control for all variables that might be available to the researcher, including possible dependent variables. It means that one should control only for variables that are either prior to one or both of the variables being related or that may be intervening between them. Even this rule can give misleading results depending upon the purposes of one's investigation. But at the very least, we can indicate that one should not control for dependent variables. (Blalock 1961: 67)

The cruel truth is that such thinking is inappropriate for many social processes. I fully agree with the position that you cannot use later events to explain earlier events. However, it does not follow that one should view the causal explanation of a given event as necessarily revealed by the analysis of variables preceding the explanandum. It would make sense if one could assume that the variables preceding the dependent variable are there by chance. In reality, their very existence often reflects a more fundamental underlying force. Much is to be gained in understanding social events by looking at the outcome—not at the causal linkage of a particular independent variable. The *first* question is simply whether Y occurs (or, in quantitative terms, its magnitude), not whether a specific X precedes it. In turn, if Y occurs, it is necessary to know what is driving the system which leads Y to occur, and that may be quite different from what particular X variables precede Y in one or more specific contexts and periods. To be sure, the force driving the outcome could itself be viewed as a product of an even larger and greater force—a matter we need not worry about right now. In any case, the presence or absence of certain independent variables has to be visualized as generated by the more basic cause such that their connection to the dependent variable is not to be taken for granted. From this perspective, the presence or absence of such X variables is of interest, but only secondary to understanding adequately the forces that generate their presence or absence.

One may well raise two serious objections at this point. First, do we not end up attributing all sorts of causal wonders to some rather vague and poorly measured "basic" cause while, at the same time, rejecting prosaic attributes that actually show empirical connections with the dependent variable? Such a criticism is indeed appropriate (see, e.g., the excellent statement by Hirschi and Selvin 1973: 130–133). Before the advocate of some fundamental or basic cause can casually sweep out all sorts of prosaic social research variables, it is absolutely mandatory that reasonably rigorous procedures be followed. We will have to guard against the quick and easy substitution of lofty and sweeping generalities for the rigorous demands of empirical social research. Second, one can also ask if the preceding paragraph is nothing more than an argument for considering whether there are intervening variables operating—a procedure that is very much in line with the logic behind the use of control variables. After all, if the presence of X_4 and its linkage to Y is due to some more fundamental force (X_{28}), should that not show up as we look at the chain of relationships? The answer is no. Ultimately, we get to exogenous variables that we simply take as givens, but we have no logic or procedures worked out as to when we are willing to stop at a certain point in the causal chain and declare the remaining variables as exogenous. Our normal controlling procedure deals with the question of what happens to Y and X_4 when X_{28} is at different levels, not with *why* the observed range of X_{28} is what it is (or simply why X_{28} is present, if it is a qualitative variable).[6] These are totally different questions, and much harm is done by the failure of modern social research to see the difference. Let us correct this immediately.

Association vs. Presence

In the typical research situation, we ask if the various levels of some independent variable, say X_1, affect the level of Y. We might control for the value of X_2 found in each unit and its effect on Y. If X_2 preceded X_1 and if there were theoretical grounds, a simple causal model could be developed in which X_1 was an intervening variable between X_2 and Y. Researchers are fully prepared to deal with such an occurrence; they are also fully prepared to deal with the possibility of interactions such that Y reflects more than the linear combinations of two or more causal variables. As a general rule, however, researchers do not consider whether the set of different causal variables is generated by an underlying structure. Some specific examples follow.

Starting with a physical example, rivers are dynamic entities with features that continuously change. The existing channels not only move but some may also actually close and others open; the delta can expand; the rate of discharge changes; the river's depth at any point varies, and so forth. Although various factors influence these changes, a researcher will approach all of these phenomena with the understanding that no matter what else the river may do, it is going to end up flowing in a generally downward direction. All other causal factors are bound by that principle. There can be modest or short-term reversals in the opposite direction, but that is still the underlying causal force. An incredible array of factors influences the actual form that the river takes—and these factors are rigorously developed—but one has to start by recognizing a certain inevitable outcome that binds and constrains all other causal forces. A similar case can be made about evolution. By starting with the notion of competition and the resultant consequences for the survival of the fittest, one can interpret and understand all sorts of specific principles and diverse causal patterns. How misleading it would be to look at some specific species and examine its changes over time without regard to the underlying notion of what directions are possible.

Using a social science example, let us consider what happens when such basic forces are ignored. In the area of race relations, a white-black difference with respect to some dependent variable (say, occupational composition) is usually analyzed by taking into account a wide variety of other factors that seem to have an influence (age, education, residence, etc.). The question usually posed, in one form or another, is: How much of the occupational gap can be explained by these factors? This has its utility insofar as it enables investigators to determine: (1) if the occupational differences are due to more than the influence of other group characteristics, such as black-white differences in educational attainment; and (2) the impact of the existing set of social processes operating in the society. But this type of analysis does not lead us to ask whether the outcome is partially determining the set of "causes" that appear. Rarely does one ask whether the immediate causal factors may exist at least in part because they have certain consequences. In other words, there is a strong possibility that the presence (magnitude) of these factors and/or their observed causal linkages is actually generated by the underlying forces driving toward the observed outcome. From this perspective, if the *apparent* causal factors were not present, then some other causal factor would occur with the same consequence. There are certain specific and limited functions that can be filled by analyses that fail to take into account the primary or underlying force driving a certain outcome. But they should never be confused, as they are now, with an understanding that takes into account *why* the surface causes exist. To put it in its simplest form: Societal rules may change to create a certain outcome.

Consider a nice neutral example—the test for a driver's license. Clearly one can determine the impact various tests and rules have on the chances of different subsets of people passing. But it would be a serious error to think that the observed linkages explain why a given percentage of the applicants pass the test. We would be missing the point if we failed to consider an underlying force that affects the testing process: namely, that one way or another, only a small percentage of the applicants will eventually be kept from passing the driver's test. If too many fail, chances are strong that the rules will be changed and/or the enforcement of the standards weakened in order to raise the percentage passing the driver's exam. The outcomes will be determined by certain rules, but the rules are changed to affect certain outcomes. This two-way interaction is likely to be missed in most control variable analyses (notwithstanding the development of both recursive and nonrecursive models and the warnings of Blalock which will be cited later). It is all right to ask: What are the characteristics of those most likely and least likely to pass? What is the linkage between certain specific characteristics and the chances of passing? But these questions have meaning only if it is first recognized that there is an underlying force driving the system toward a certain outcome. Insofar as virtually everyone can pass the existing test, then somewhat higher standards can be used; insofar as virtually nobody can pass the test, then the standards must be relaxed. Results will be altered either through shifts in the difficulty of the questions and tasks and/or the levels required for passing.

If such a basic principle operates, then it follows that the observed empirical relationship could in no way tell us why X percent of the population in a given state passes the driver's test. The observed relationship indicates who is especially likely to pass or not pass the present test and how that sums up to the overall percentage with passing grades. But the observed relationship is not a given—rather it is itself one that in part fluctuates in order to meet a certain outcome. Researchers all too often tend to confuse these issues and, to the detriment of social science, derive theoretical principles or generate applied programs on the basis of superficial causal relationships.

One more example before going back to the racial and ethnic matter. I have taught at a number of universities with varying levels of student quality. At institutions with high quality students on the average, my course standards tend to drift upward; at lower quality institutions, the opposite shift occurs. Perhaps this says something about me, but I think it illustrates a certain shift in which the apparent dependent variable (the percentage of students obtaining a given grade or passing) actually controls the phenomenon that, on a superficial level, appears to be the causal variable (the difficulty of the tests and the standards applied). In this case, the tests and grading standards are true independent variables insofar as they explain *who* gets what grades within the class. But they are not independent of the overall outcome, and hence shifts in the testing material occur in order to generate a certain outcome.[7] Again, the grades obtained by a class are only superficially explained by the test given and the standards used. Insofar as there is an underlying causal principle operating—namely, the notion that the grade distribution should fall within a certain broad range (not everyone fails or gets an A, etc.)—then the tests and/or the grading standards will shift in order to generate that outcome.

Now what about racial differences in occupational composition? One may speculate that if whites were disadvantaged because blacks had the more favorable educational distribution, then the chances are strong that either the linkage between education and occupation would be altered or the educational gap would disappear. This is less likely to be the case if the influence of education on occupation and black-white educational distributions both work to the detriment of blacks. To control for education in looking at the occupational differences between blacks and whites is to miss the driving force underlying the surface relationships. In this particular case, the dominant group attempts to use its dominance to advance its own position.[8] To be sure, there are differences in the educational distribution of the groups and, within each group, education affects occupation. But the existence of the two combined facts (both the observed causal linkage *and* differences in educational attainment must occur for occupational disadvantages to result for blacks) is not to be taken for granted as an inherently inevitable relationship. Therefore, we can be sure that the education-occupation linkage is affected by its own consequences for the dependent variable. That is the crucial point: the influence of the X_2 control variable (education) on Y (occupation) should be viewed not only as affecting what the influence of X_1 (race) on Y would otherwise be but also as holding a form and having a magnitude of consequence which is partially a consequence of what its consequences are. To put it all in a nutshell: *Those who write the rules, write rules that enable them to continue to write the rules.*

This is not the place for a discourse on the issues surrounding teleological interpretations (see Nagel 1961: 401−428 and 532−535 for an illuminating discussion of teleological explanations generally, as well as their role in different disciplines, including the social sciences). But it is readily apparent that such an approach to causality would seriously undermine the quasi-experimental research model as it is currently practiced. The joy of the true experiment is that the researcher is able to manipulate the causal forces under study and examine the consequences of such manipulations with the confidence that they were not initiated by some more basic underlying force. Quasi-experimental social researchers are denied this opportunity. One is not obliged to pretend that the associations between all of the different variables are random; there are tools for examining the complicated network of associations operating *within* the system of variables.

The problem lies in the starting point of the study, the exogenous variables that the researcher is obliged to assume occur or do not occur in some sort of random or at least unknowable way. The implicit logic of the statistical manipulation is: "Here is what the linkages would mean if the experimenter had been responsible for generating these values for the exogenous variables." But in truth the experimenter was *not* responsible. Now this does not rule out all possibilities of quasi-experimental research. But quasi-experimental research, as it is currently practiced, rules out all possibilities of a teleological model of causality—or simply of a model that is capable of taking into account the almost certain fact that the exogenous conditions observed are not a random sample of all possible exogenous conditions, but occur in ways that are relevant to the dependent variable under consideration. When that operates, the researcher can no longer casually assume that even the observed network of causal linkages within the endogenous set of variables occurs without reference to the powerful forces external to the system. Yet to account for the exogenous variables, that is, to make them endogenous, would lead one into an endless causal chain going farther and farther backward without any logical end in sight and yet without resolution of the problem. We must get out of this box, and an empirically oriented approach will be offered in Part II. As Blalock notes:

> Those variables that have been left outside of the causal system may not actually operate as assumed; they may produce effects that are nonrandom and that may become confounded with those of the variables directly under consideration. Through devices such as randomization we can get by with reasonably plausible simplifying assumptions about outside variables. But . . . randomization cannot be used to rule out the disturbing effects of all types of outside variables. (Blalock 1961: 21)

PART TWO

Toward a Solution

CHAPTER EIGHT

And Now What?

And now what? As has been said before, the first step toward reaching a solution is to recognize that there is indeed a problem, that something is wrong. I have argued that several of the most widely accepted procedures in contemporary social research are often based on models and assumptions that are patently inappropriate and that, in such circumstances, their application is counterproductive. There is no point in arguing the matter further; the first part of this volume has either convinced the reader or not. Assuming there is agreement, then at the very least we must recognize that "business as usual"—even if the alternative does not appear clear—is often nothing more than "ritualism as usual." Researchers, editors, scholars, students, the consumer of applied research, and everyone else involved in the research process must question and challenge assumptions that are now taken for granted as inherent parts of our thought processes. There is no point in continuing to do something that sooner or later must be rejected and replaced.

Obviously we would like to have an alternative. In proposing the initial steps toward reaching a solution, I will continue to assume that a rigorous science of society is an enterprise that is well worth pursuing. The goal is not to show that social science is intrinsically unobtainable. Rather, it is to eliminate the unthinking imitation of a crude physical science model that characterizes so much of social research. The remainder of this volume provides some suggestions or guidelines that might be of use to thoughtful researchers and theorists who are not bound to follow current procedures mechanically but who, nevertheless, are not quite ready or willing to abandon the enterprise. It is really arbitrary to assume that Part I of this volume was exclusively a critique of current procedures and that Part II is purely a set of alternatives. A careful discussion of current practices implies suggestions for alternative procedures; however, alternatives cannot be suggested without a critical understanding of existing work.

It is for good reason that Part II is called "Toward a Solution" rather than "The Solution." There is no solution, pure and simple, and this is not a cop-out but a matter of sensible and unpretentious thinking. Programmatic statements are easier to write than to take seriously. The approach used to gain new knowledge about a subject is very much affected by the existing body of knowledge. It is not possible to predict what will be learned in the course of work performed by a large community of scholars (in other words, at present we do not know what it is that we will later know!) and yet it will affect how we later think about the topic. The knowledge that we have about society is going to affect what problems we research and how we research them; in turn, our research procedures will affect our future knowledge. What would a programmatic statement for astronomy look like before Copernicus, and what would we think about it afterward? Likewise, our way of approaching social processes is going to be influenced by the existing body of knowledge, as witness the shift that has occurred in the approach toward gender differences in recent years. In the case at hand, as we learn how to deal better with the control variable issue or with alternatives to experimental simulation or with causality or with what the basic theoretical questions are, who is to say where this will lead us?[1] It is important to recognize that a long-run programmatic solution is not possible. What will be provided here, rather, is a set of proposals for dealing with the issues raised earlier. In the course of pursuing this goal, I have taken the liberty of stating my hunches in a relatively assertive manner, sometimes even in the form of principles or working hypotheses that may be of value in taking a step or two out of the dark. It is hoped that, at the very least, they will be stimulating to others who can then move us further along.

The goal is simple enough—to do a better job of understanding and explaining social events than we now do. The issues that must be addressed are reasonably clear. What should we be doing at the present time? How can we determine when the current approach is appropriate and when it is not? If there are questions that are inappropriate to ask and procedures that should not be used, what are the alternatives?

CHAPTER NINE

Rethinking Causality

SYMMETRIC AND ASYMMETRIC CAUSES

Neither researchers nor theorists can continue to neglect the distinction between symmetric and asymmetric forms of causality. To my knowledge, most standard statistical research tools are applied with symmetrical causal relationships in mind. The researcher seeks to determine whether a change in one variable is associated with a change in another variable, possibly net of the influences of various other attributes. In any case, this is implicitly done in the form of a symmetrical test or description. The question of whether an increase in X yields an increase (or a decline) in Y is not distinguished from the question of whether a decline in X yields a decline (or an increase) in Y. When we begin to pursue this question, I suspect we will find that many social processes are at least partially asymmetric, if not entirely or overwhelmingly so. If that is the case, then research operations are badly confounded if they fail to make the distinction. There is no problem with a fully symmetrical relationship since movements back and forth with respect to a given independent variable will keep producing the same shifts back and forth in the dependent variable. But when that is not the case, there will be rather serious errors.

Theorists must share responsibility for this sad state of affairs. As far as I know, rarely are theories posed with this distinction in mind.

174]

In my estimation, this is easily corrected on both the theoretical and measurement ends. In terms of statistical measurement, researchers would have to determine whether the directional shift in the independent variable affects the dependent variable. For a crude test, one might even consider it as a dummy variable to be considered along with the independent variable. If, of course, there was no evidence of asymmetry, the researcher could report this, pool the data accordingly, and go on. But I suggest, as a working hypothesis, that we will find asymmetrical relationships quite common. (This test assumes the use of longitudinal data—a matter to be considered shortly in this chapter.)

I might add that asymmetry has very important ramifications for applied social issues; its existence implies that some policies based on observed empirical relationships could easily backfire. Suppose a statistical analysis shows that there has been a general trend for X to be increasing and Y to be decreasing. A policy aimed at raising Y could easily assume that reversing X would do the trick. But, as we have seen this would only make sense if the Y-X relationship is symmetrical. In a completely asymmetrical linkage between the two, a reversal of X will have no effect on Y and it will appear as if something is radically wrong with the initial analysis. In point of fact, it will reflect the failure to keep this distinction in mind. Social applications are especially vulnerable because they are apt to be based on the analysis of data sets in which the independent variable has been changing largely in one direction. As a consequence, it becomes very difficult to sort out the question of whether the observed relationship is symmetrical or not.

Several distinctions are appropriate here that should be of value for researchers and theorists alike. As noted in Chapter Four, an asymmetric cause means an irreversible *process* in only a very restricted sense—it does not by any means imply an irreversible *outcome*. Causal asymmetry simply means that an outcome generated by a given cause cannot be reversed by simply eliminating the cause or turning back the cause to its earlier condition. There are other causes that could change the dependent variable. This distinction should affect the analysis of proposed solutions, as well as what is done on a theoretical plane and in the analysis of data. It is also useful to distinguish between the two sides of an asymmetrical relationship. If X changes in one direction, there will be changes in Y; if X changes in the other direction, there will be no changes in Y.[1] The two sides of an asymmetric relationship will be referred to as the *responsive* and *nonresponsive* sides respectively, depending on whether Y shifts or remains fixed when X changes.

This confusion between the two causal types means that all sorts of theories are inappropriately rejected. One often encounters the following logical form among those evaluating a given proposition: "I don't think it is true that an increase in X caused Y. Consider how, in situation Q, the decline in X did not lead to the disappearance of Y!" Some such thought process is repeated over and over again in the social sciences. This makes sense only if we view the particular X-Y relationship as symmetrical, that is, with a fully reversible causal linkage. Otherwise, it is perfectly possible that an asymmetrical pattern operates in which Y is responsive to increases in X but unresponsive to decreases in X.

As matters now stand, we need to work out a set of procedures for identifying whether a given empirical relationship appears to be symmetrical or asymmetrical. In many cases, the relationships will fall somewhere between the extremes, and we will need to be able to describe the magnitude of symmetry or, in some way, describe the separate directions. Unless this is done, we have a set of systematic errors. Our current procedures will work very well with fully reversible events, of course, and they will also work nicely (in the sense of fitting the data) with asymmetrical causal relationships if two conditions occur: (1) the independent variable is largely shifting in one direction, and (2) the direction of that shift is indeed in the responsive direction such that X affects Y. In that event, current statistics will abstract out what is at present going on with the asymmetric process, but conclusions or applications based on changes in the opposite direction will be in error. Current procedures are a disaster right now if there is an irreversible causal linkage and the independent variable is largely going in the unresponsive direction *or* if the independent variable has been moving in both directions. (In the first of these, the researcher will conclude that no relationship exists even though an asymmetrical one exists but could not be studied. In the second case, the strength of the relationship will be overestimated for the nonresponsive side and underestimated for the responsive side because of the failure to analyze shifts separately.)

This means that the interplay between social research and theory, when the distinction between reversible and irreversible causes is ignored, has a strong bias toward finding only a certain subset of causal relationships and, in certain circumstances, there is a bias toward underestimating the magnitude of the causal linkage. Insofar as certain types of causal linkages are reversible and others are irreversible, social research is presently warped toward missing certain relationships, underestimating others, and misapplying some relationships to situations where the causal linkage is irreversible.

One type of cause is no more desirable than the other; relationships are not intrinsically reversible or intrinsically irreversible. Rather, symmetry or asymmetry is changed by the context under which it is considered. But it is vital that this distinction be applied if we want to understand the phenomenon under question in the societal context in which it is studied. In situations where the causal variable has moved over a wide range in both directions, everything is possible; we can examine the influence of X on Y when X goes up and again when it is shifting downward. In those circumstances, it is possible to determine whether the relationship is roughly of the same magnitude in both directions. In other words, conclusions can be made about whether a relationship exists at all and, if so, whether it is symmetrical or asymmetrical. However, if X has moved largely in one direction and a causal linkage appears to operate in that direction, then it is impossible to decide if a symmetrical relationship exists. One can conclude that movements of X in the observed direction do cause changes of a certain nature in Y, but it is not possible to say whether this is a symmetrical relationship or if Y will be nonresponsive to the opposite changes in X. Likewise, if no causal linkage appears to exist between X and Y in circumstances where X is largely changing in one direction, it is possible only to make that direct conclusion and it is certain that a symmetrical relationship does not occur. But the researcher has no grounds for deciding when no causal relationship exists between X and Y or when an asymmetric relationship occurs in which only the nonresponsive side has been observed such that changes in X in the opposite direction would affect Y.[2]

BIAS IN DEVELOPING AND
EVALUATING CAUSAL PRINCIPLES

For reasons that are easily understood, researchers and theorists are influenced by their own experiences, particularly those that are relatively recent in either time or place. This affects one's own work and the way others are evaluated. Scholars are often negative about research or theories that appear to contradict their own. This is understandable not simply because of the ego invested in a body of work but also because one's work fits into one's experiences and at least appears to be harmonious with those experiences. For this reason, a temporal or experiential bias exists in developing and evaluating causal principles.

All of this is reasonable—after all, why shouldn't our experience influence the way we think about social processes? However, it creates a special bias for research and theory when formulated in a probabilistic manner—and most of contemporary social research and theory (of an empirically compatible nature) is done in that manner.[3] Because of this propensity to be influenced by the most familiar, we tend informally to weigh events differently even though they are all, in theory, of equal significance. If we find an association that does not make sense out of those instances of the dependent variable with which we are most familiar, we will tend to reject the results or its theoretical implications. This tendency to explain it away occurs even though a probabilistic approach would maintain that the relationship would not be expected to explain all of the events. However, if the same association seems to make sense out of the events with which we are most acquainted, we will be more tolerant of the failure to explain less familiar events in the same set. In that case, we are more likely to view the theory as a probabilistic one which is not expected to explain everything. In a nutshell, the problem is that the evaluation of a given interpretation will be greatly affected by the way in which certain specific instances of the dependent variable (perhaps the most recent, or familiar, or most important) fit into the framework. This is a special kind of bias or distortion since, from the point of view of the probabilistic approach, the usefulness of an explanation of a given percentage of occurrences of an event should not be affected by how well that explanation handles the most recent or most familiar example of that event.

All we can do in this case is watch for this bias in our tendencies. There is no simple way to avoid the problem, but we should be aware of it. It does mean—and this is not desirable for those pursuing probabilistic approaches—that the most recent and most familiar incidents are going to affect the way in which theories are generated and data interpreted, even though they are presumably no more or no less important than other events of the same set.

CAUSAL ANALYSIS AND CROSS-SECTIONAL DATA

Nonexperimental social research often uses cross-sectional data gathered at one point in time to infer the causal influence of different conditions. Both Brown and Gilmartin (1969) and Carlsson (1970) found that an enormous proportion of the research literature is based on cross-sectional rather than longitudinal data. Although the situation may have improved in recent years, even a quick examination of the journals suggests that the practice is still widespread. A common example comes to mind: Data are obtained for a large number of cities at one point in time in order to determine the influence of city differences in population composition on some behavioral variable. The cities differ with respect to some attribute of interest, say, simply in terms of their total population size. The researcher then seeks to determine if such an attribute affects the dependent variable of interest, say, some type of crime rate. The meaning of an association would seem to be fairly clear. A positive association makes one think that increases in city size cause increases in the crime rate, and decreases in size cause declines in crime. No doubt the reader can think of lots of objections to these conclusions: You should control for this, that, and the other thing; why city size rather than metropolitan area?; or perhaps there is something about size and the quality of crime records.

These are more or less the standard types of objections that might be raised. Of concern here are two different issues: the implied longitudinal causality that is unexamined, and the distinction between symmetric and asymmetric forms of causality. The conclusion reached earlier in this hypothetical study would imply that, over time, shifts in crime follow from shifts in the size of the community. The results are based on the following notion: If we started with a whole set of cities of a given size and then followed them over time, they would presumably differ in their rates of population change and this would be accompanied—possibly with certain unspecified lags—by shifts in the crime rate. Whether this would be the case is not very clear from a conventional cross-sectional analysis. In this regard, I would like to advance some thoughts that might not be too popular with researchers.

Let us start off with a simple principle that is both methodological and theoretical. *All causal propositions have consequences for longitudinal change.* These changes could be in the past, or the future, or the present, but in one way or another a given causal proposition has implications for change over time. If X is a cause of Y, then changes over time in X in one or both directions (depending on the symmetry of the causal linkage) should generate changes in Y. To put the matter in rhetorical form, how can there be a causal proposition that fails to have longitudinal consequences? Let us now consider a second principle: *Longitudinal data provide the only fully appropriate "test" of a causal proposition's validity. Cross-sectional data are certain to be relevant only under special circumstances. If it is possible to assume that the values of the dependent variable were all initially the same, only then are there grounds for believing that the situation observed cross-sectionally at a later point in time provides a reasonable opportunity to study the hypothesized influence of the causal principle under consideration.*[4] This would not eliminate other issues that longitudinal data would have to face, such as spuriousness, measurement errors, and the like, but unless this assumption is valid or can be approximated, cross-sectional data can easily fail to support a causal proposition without its necessarily meaning that the proposition is false. The opposite problem is even more likely to occur—namely, cross-sectional data will appear to be harmonious with a given causal proposition when the causal proposition is invalid, that is, is not found to operate when actual changes over time are considered (for an example of this, see Lieberson and Hansen 1974). At any rate, regardless of the frequency with which these different combinations occur, it follows from the two principles stated earlier that cross-sectional data cannot be casually substituted for longitudinal data in measuring the predicted consequences of a given causal proposition. These two principles suggest some research guidelines:

1. Many causal conclusions based on cross-sectional data will be radically altered if they are examined longitudinally.

2. Conclusions based on cross-sectional data are not of equal merit to those based on longitudinal data, all other conditions being the same, such as data quality, sufficient N, and so on.

3. If a cross-sectional analysis does not imply longitudinal change, then it cannot be a causal analysis.

4. It is not possible, with exclusively cross-sectional data, to determine if the relationship is symmetric or asymmetric since data for at least two points in time are necessary.

5. Exclusively cross-sectional data cannot take into account the presence of any lags in the influence of the causal variable on the dependent variable.

6. Policy applications based on cross-sectional analyses—even when the analysis is correct—could be inappropriate given the absence of any measurement of lags.

7. Cross-sectional analyses can actually underestimate the magnitude of some causal linkages because of their inability to deal with lags and to distinguish symmetric from asymmetric causal forms.

8. It is vital for researchers working with cross-sectional data to do more than simply state that they are aware of these problems; really do wish they had longitudinal data; and believe that cross-sectional data will provide some approximation of what the results would be like if longitudinal data were available. This is nonsense (and the author admits that he is not without guilt). Cross-sectional data are all right only under certain special circumstances, and it is incumbent on the researcher to justify such use not because better

data are unavailable, but because the assumptions indicated can be met in the specific case. Otherwise, it is best to forget the problem as a doable research problem at the present time. After all, there are so many potential research problems existing at any given time that there is no need to pursue ones that have such a low chance of having any fundamental scholarly utility.

9. A key feature in determining whether cross-sectional analysis is appropriate, aside from the issues of lags and symmetry, is whether the investigator has any grounds for assuming that the conditions for the units under study were initially identical. More imagination and effort could be put into testing whether the assumptions are valid for a given cross-sectional problem. Consider, for example, the results obtained when cross-sectional linkages between language diversity and the level of national development were carefully examined with at least some effort to test out the longitudinal implications of these cross-sectional results (Lieberson and Hansen 1974). Aside from the procedures used in this specific problem, the researchers were able to suggest some simple procedures that could be used in testing the validity of this assumption for other problems (538–539).

10. It is perfectly appropriate to use cross-sectional correlations if one wishes to examine the current association or pattern between characteristics, but such data cannot automatically be used to draw inferences about causal models of change (Lieberson and Hansen 1974: 538).

11. In conclusion, any serious causal proposition implies that a change will occur over time in some dependent variable if the causal force itself changes. The change could have virtually instant consequences or it could take a long time for its ramifications to occur. Cross-sectional data are not a good way to deal with a causal proposition because they are not a straightforward examination of longitudinal change. Sometimes they are all right, but using them requires reasoning that involves more than simply saying that these are the only data available. It requires explicit consideration of the lag problem and it also gets complicated by the symmetric-asymmetric distinction. Moreover, there is the question of whether one can assume that the observed cross-sectional variation in the dependent variable represents changes that have occurred from some

earlier position after there were changes in the independent variable under consideration. It is not too often that such assumptions can be made.

SPECTACULAR CAUSES AND EVENTS

An old issue in geology deals with the relative merit of two different types of causal approaches: "uniformation" and "catastrophism." The latter assumes that dramatic changes in the earth had sudden and rather dramatic causal antecedents, whereas the former assumes that constant and uniform action from forces such as wind and water eventually reshape the surface of the earth (Lasker and Tyzzer 1982: 20). The development of uniformation by Charles Lyell was a major step in modern geology and offered a significant alternative to the use of supernatural or religious forces in explaining important changes in the earth's surface. This emphasis on slow change produced by uniform forces was significant, for obvious reasons, to Charles Darwin's theory of evolution.

We will let the geologists worry about the relative utility of these approaches for understanding great mountain ranges, rivers, bodies of water, canyons, and the like. But there is something here for us to consider in social research and in the theories that we construct. I believe that there is an unrecognized propensity to assume that dramatic or massive social changes must have their cause(s) in other massive changes, or at least ones that are sudden or dramatic in character. Likewise, moderate or less dramatic changes in the society tend to be interpreted in terms of less spectacular causal variables. If we think about the matter, there is no reason for such a relationship to exist between cause and effect. It should be clear, upon reflection, that a spectacular change in a causal variable could have modest changes for some dependent variables. But it may not be so clear that the opposite may be true—that modest changes in causal variables can have massive consequences. To be sure, this is an open empirical question. But I think that there is a bias or propensity at the moment to assume that big changes must have big causes.

What do we mean by "spectacular" or "dramatic" changes

anyway? Such labels are often greatly flavored by the specific times so that only a few years later the same event seems like a modest or barely noticeable blip in the set of processes being observed. Other events, which appear to stand the test of time in terms of how significant they were, are often discernibly different only because of what later occurred—not in terms of what they looked like at the time.

Another impediment to our understanding of major social changes is that we can only see them after they occur. This might appear to be different from physical events such as the slow carving out of the Grand Canyon by the Colorado River and other natural forces, where such changes occur over long spans of time and are visible throughout.[5] Social changes seem to have an all-or-nothing quality, a certain cataclysmic nature to them. However, this is more a function of their suddenly becoming visible to us. The eruption of such changes to the point where they are visible and readily measurable should be distinguished from the underlying changes that have gone on through a long span of time and are due to broader forces of a less idiosyncratic nature. It may well be that there are social processes occurring that have enormous implications for other changes that do not surface immediately. When their consequences do appear, it seems so sudden and powerful that investigators are inclined to look for the cause in a force of comparable suddenness. In point of fact, one can also look for causes in longterm changes that are finally manifested. The race riots of the 1960s in the United States were shocking, and it appeared as if a massive change was suddenly occurring in the attitudes of blacks and in racial inter-action. Likewise, there were great changes surrounding the war in Vietnam with respect to the acceptance of war on the part of young adults in the country. A vigorous and aggressive feminist move-ment may also appear to be a sudden eruption. But in directly pursuing the explanation of such phenomena, the investigator is likely to find out only why the event erupted when it did. This is an interesting question but much less significant than one that ad-dresses the fundamental underlying changes in the basic dependent variable. There is probably not much to be gained in a causal approach that views these dramatic events as either *the* dependent variable or as a close surrogate for it.

This is not the place for a lengthy evaluation of Ogburn's Cultural Lag Hypotheses. But if we accept the notion that indeed some parts of a society change more rapidly than other parts, it would fit in very nicely with the notion of change just advanced. For the Lag Hypothesis helps us understand how some changes may appear to erupt suddenly without its necessarily meaning that there was a precipitous underlying cause. In this regard, the Cultural Lag Hypothesis could be seen as one of several possible ways in which a sudden observed change need not itself have been caused by equally abrupt massive change in some independent variable.

BASIC AND SUPERFICIAL CAUSES

A fundamental distinction needs to be drawn, one that will greatly affect both the way research is done and how theories will be developed. On the one hand, there are the *superficial* or *surface causes* that appear to be responsible for a given outcome; on the other hand, there are the *basic causes* that are actually generating the outcome. As we shall see, this distinction is not approximated through the many statistical exercises that seek to decide causal importance in one way or another by determining how much a given factor appears to account for the dependent variable after various controls are applied. The task proposed here is both different and more difficult because causal variables or forces are not intrinsically superficial or basic, rather, their role may vary from situation to situation. Moreover, it is rarely possible to distinguish between basic and superficial causes if the researcher is working exclusively with data for a single point in time—no matter how elegant the statistical tools, the size of the sample, and the potential for multivariate analysis. In addition, the basic causes in a given set of situations may well be unmeasurable; researchers at present have a difficult time employing causal forces that they have not measured, particularly as factors accounting for shifts in the observable. Finally, it is also possible to use causes that are *too* basic for the question at hand.

In the typical research situation, the investigator encounters a complicated network of linkages between a relatively large number of different causal variables and the explanandum. To be sure, the different variables are not found to be of equal "importance." The notion behind all of this is that indeed there are many different factors contributing to a given outcome.

> In most social science work, a primary factor is that models are not sufficiently precise to indicate every possible influence on the behavior in question. Social science explanations are, at best, partial theories that indicate only the few important potential influences. Even if one could establish the list of all influences, this list would be sufficiently long to prohibit most analysis. Generally, researchers are trying to estimate accurately the importance of the influences that are central to policy making or to theoretical developments. To do this, one hopes only to obtain a data set where the influences excluded from the formal statistical analysis are sufficiently small and random so as to warrant exclusion. (Hanushek and Jackson 1977: 12)

Hanushek and Jackson are, in my estimation, actually understating the degree to which researchers seek to throw in as many possible causal variables as they can. It is not uncommon for social scientists to distinguish their disciplines from the natural sciences in just these terms, to wit, that the natural sciences are blessed with a more limited set of causes operating in any given situation.

Let us make a radically different assumption—that the dependent variable in a typical setting is actually responding to a small number of causes (which may include an important stochastic element). A complicated network of causal relations will also appear, but these are largely superficial causes that do not have any true impact on the dependent variable, which is actually affected by a very small number of basic causes. The situation can be rather confusing. In a given research situation, it is not too easy to separate empirically these causal forces from the complicated network of linkages that are actually observed. But at least conceptually we can distinguish the surface or superficial cause from a basic cause in terms of their actual impact on the dependent variable. Some working definitions are in order. First, variables are intrinsically neither basic nor superficial causes, but will vary by the specific context. Within a given context, a *superficial cause* is one that appears, by statistical simulation of the controlled experiment, to affect causally the dependent variable in a symmetrical or asymmetrical way. But, in practice, shifts in either direction have no actual consequence for the dependent variable.[6] A *basic cause*, however, is one that in a given context actually does affect the dependent variable such that changes in its level will alter the dependent variable. A shift in the surface cause will not affect the magnitude of the dependent variable—no matter how close the association between a surface cause and the dependent variable. Thus the conventional statistical analyses do not usually allow us to distinguish basic from superficial causes.

In the example used earlier, if educational differences between the races are a superficial cause of the racial gap in income, then a drop in the racial educational gap will most likely simply alter the regression of income on education and/or possibly increase the apparent relevance of some other superficial variable. Under any circumstance, the net consequence will be no change in the racial income gap. A change in a basic causal force, however, will mean a change in the dependent variable regardless of the form through which it works its way. If educational differences were purely a superficial cause of the income gap, to deal in ideal types, then a change in the educational composition of blacks vs. whites would not lead to any shift in the income gap but only in the partial regression of income on education. Thus the change in education would have no direct consequence for the income gap. If educational differences were a symmetrical basic cause of the income gap, then regardless of the apparent shifts or stability in the superficial apparent causal models, a change in educational differences would be associated with a change in income. Instead of looking at all of the complicated network of controls, direct and indirect effects, recursive and nonrecursive linkages, the first and most fundamental step is to ask whether a change in the independent variable in a certain direction leads to a change in the dependent variable.

The strength of the association between the independent and dependent variable does not tell us whether a basic or superficial cause is operating. A superficial cause could easily be strongly associated with the dependent variable, whereas a basic cause could be unmeasurable or, if measurable, be less closely associated with the dependent variable than a superficial cause. Likewise, the magnitude of the change in the dependent variable associated cross-sectionally with each independent variable is no clue to whether the cause is superficial or basic. From this perspective, much of the contemporary research approach—and this holds regardless of the statistic used—is oriented toward evaluating causes improperly, namely, in terms of either the association or the magnitude of the shift in the dependent variable. One may theorize as to what is going on, but the empirical test is of the sort described above.

If this perspective is valid, then it means that a given dependent variable has certain basic causes which, if changed in a specific situation, will generate changes in the dependent variable. Other factors that appear to be associated with the dependent variable may also change, but if they are purely superficial causes, then the *outcome* for the dependent variable will be unchanged. If a cause is a superficial one, its shift over time will not lead to changes in the dependent variable. Instead, a new set of apparent linkages will develop between the superficial cause and the dependent variable such that there is no real shift in the dependent variable during the period under consideration. There is the same actual outcome as before, but it appears as if the linkage has changed.[7] In a given context, changes in surface causes will have no bearing on the outcome; changes in surface causes will merely shift the causal network around to generate the same outcome. In the educational example used earlier, the role of education—if it was a superficial cause—might decline and the role of specific contacts or discrimination might go up, but the outcome would remain un-affected by shifts in education. However, if education was a basic cause, then its changes would alter the dependent variable re-gardless of whether other attributes change. Again, a possible causal factor is not intrinsically basic or superficial, although some tend to be more commonly found in one or the other circumstance. The term *superficial* refers to causal linkages that appear to exist in a given setting only as the byproduct of the operation of certain other forces in that context. The same attribute in one context may be a surface cause, and in another context it may be the basic cause. We can use the term "pseudocausality" to refer to the mistaken identification of superficial or surface causes as if they were real causes.

Why would the strength of an independent variable's linkage with the dependent variable, or the magnitude of the change in the dependent variable, both fail to tell us whether the independent variable is a basic or superficial cause? Why should there be so many apparent causes anyway that we have to sift them out? We have to view any outcome not only as being driven by the principle under consideration—say, the propensity of groups in control to maximize their rewards—but also as being affected by other powerful forces in the society (in this case, perhaps the differential reward structure operating within the white-dominated society, limitations proscribed by the society's ideology, historical accidents, and the like). Insofar as we have a contradiction between various dimensions of the society—for example, the clash between status ascription and an ideology that emphasizes achieved status—then the exact form by which black-white income gaps will take place can be expected to fit, as much as possible, with the outcomes of these various causal principles. Being consonant with the ramification of such other causal principles is not the same as being caused by them. Moreover, since there are an enormous number of causal principles operating in the society, the outcomes generated by each may crisscross with other outcomes and requirements in the society in a very complex and involved way. As a consequence, there is this mass of superficial causes that can be observed.

In some ways, this view actually permits simplification in social research. In accounting for a given outcome, at present we usually look for a large number of causes. And it is true that there are lots of causal forces thrusting forward in a given society; for all purposes, virtually an infinite number of causal principles will exist that have ramifications of some sort or another for the variable under consideration. This would seem to be compatible with multivariate research of the conventional sort which leads to finding many different causes that appear to be playing some role in affecting the outcome. But I believe this to be wrong and to be symptomatic of the misdirection in sociology generally and nonexperimental social research in particular. The key step is to draw a distinction between the consequence of a given causal principle (or hypothesis or theory) and the manner in which that consequence unfolds in a given context. In most cases, a given end product is generated by probably one significant basic causal principle; the form through which that basic cause is channeled may well be highly variable and affected by other causal principles that operate, as well as modified by the idiosyncratic history of that setting. Focusing on the channeling process will lead us to think we are finding many causes, but these are what I have called the superficial causes. If this is correct, then our task is not so bad—we need to know what the underlying causal principle is. Chasing after the unique ramifications of that principle is harmless enough, just as long as we do not think that the superficial causal patterns are a substitute for a causal explanation in the basic sense used earlier.

We have to visualize a hierarchical set of basic causes working out their ramifications in a given context. The causal principles are not unique to that setting, but what may well be idiosyncratic or distinctive is the context in which their ramifications are worked out (because of such features as the historical context, demography, technology, etc.). Insofar as causal principles have compatible consequences, there is no difficulty. Insofar as they are not entirely compatible, the societal outcome in that context will be modified in the direction of minimizing the conflicting outcomes. If such harmony is not possible, certain forces will win out over other forces—albeit not inevitably because the amount of "bend" required for each outcome is variable, depending on the existing combination of specific circumstances.

A special problem remains: What would cause the outcomes to change over time? For all practical purposes, essentially no equilibrium is really possible between the different causal forces; there are so many causal forces and it is virtually impossible for exogenous forces to remain steady long enough for an equilibrium to occur between them all. Consider the wide impact of new developments in science and technology. Directly and indirectly, these touch on virtually every realm of social life. If only because of this, a constant flux would occur in the impact and ramifications of different basic causes. (In both advanced and less advanced societies, fluctuations in nature would have a similar consequence in that food supplies, the physical environment, and living conditions would be altered.) Because it would take many decades for such a large array of causal principles to work out a new equilibrium, there would be a continuous flux in: (1) the ability of a given causal force to attain sufficient consequence in the setting to materialize into an observable end product; (2) the extent to which the causal principle would reach its full consequences; and (3) the pathways through which the forces would operate. It is rather difficult to visualize such a span occurring without the conditions being altered through science, technology, and nature *or* through the continuous change due to the ramifications of internal features (for example, intrinsic population change).

An Example

Returning to the illustration involving a racial gap in income, let us assume the investigator finds that Q percent of the racial gap in income is caused by educational differences between whites and blacks. The notion here—and this is quite independent of the statistics used—is that the gap would decline just that much if racial differences in educational attainment were eliminated. Is that correct? (We will ignore the question of symmetry since there is nothing more to add to the earlier comments, although in practice there is probably a good chance that the causal linkages are asymmetrical. However, for the sake of argument, let us assume that a symmetrical relationship is in operation such that a decrease in the educational gap over time would in turn generate a decrease in income.) A conventional researcher would say that such a conclusion about a decline in the income gap is correct if four conditions are met: (1) black-white characteristics with respect to all other relevant attributes remain unchanged; (2) the influence of other factors on income is unchanged; (3) the forces leading to the shift in educational differences had no direct or indirect bearing on black-white income differences; and (4) the causal linkage between education and income is constant over time.

How reasonable a conclusion is this? All of these assumptions are really rather questionable, if one follows out the implications of the causal thesis presented here. Suppose we start with a radically different perspective on this question and see where it leads us. Let us hypothesize that racial or other interest groups will tend to take as much as they can for themselves and will give as little as is necessary to maintain the system and avoid having it overturned. In this case, whites will give blacks as little as they can. Under such circumstances, one would assume that the observed interrelations between income gaps and such features as education, discrimination, occupation, and family background all describe in a given case the current pathways leading from a specific causal force to the outcome of that force. If so, a complicated causal analysis of the factors contributing to the racial gaps in income has not the causal value that one might have assumed. It describes the given set of events at a given time; it describes what a black person might well follow as a get-ahead strategy if he or she can assume that not many other blacks will follow the same strategy and hence the basic matrix will remain unaltered. But there is no assurance that this matrix will continue to operate—indeed, there is virtual certainty that the matrix will not continue to operate if some superficial factor that *appears* to cause the income gap is no longer relevant (for example, if the groups end up with the same educational distribution). In which case, new rules and regulations will operate; the other regression coefficents will change in value in order to maintain the existing system.

If we think of this in regression terms, we normally view a given outcome as the effect of a given causal linkage (the partial regression coefficient, $^b yx_1.x_2x_3 . . . .x_n$) applied to a given compositional situation. Let us at least consider the possibility of viewing the regression coefficient not as a given causal force but as nothing more or less than a function of the composition. Thus composition combines with the regression coefficient to yield a constant outcome that is harmonious with a given causal principle. If we view the observed pattern of linkages in this light, a very interesting reversal occurs in the possible meaning of a given linkage between the independent and dependent variables. In the case of the apparent influence of education on income for whites and for blacks, we might instead think of the observed regressions as a function of the educational composition of blacks and whites combined with the broader force of whites endeavoring to maximize their income at the expense of blacks. At present, we view the process as black income being a function of: the black educational distribution ($Black_{x1}$) converted to income ($Black_y$) via the regression coefficient for blacks ($^{Black} b_{yx_1.x_2x_3. . . x_n}$); and white income is viewed in an analogous fashion as a function of the white educational distribution ($White_{x1}$) converted to income ($White_y$) via their distinctive regression coefficient ($^{White} b_{yx_1.x_2x_3. . . x_n}$) conversions.

The alternative is to view the observed set of causal forces that appear to generate lower black incomes as a misleading statement of what is really causing this income gap. The observed pattern should be viewed as a set of linkages that mediate some basic cause (such as the one suggested) that is pushing toward lower black incomes *and* other basic causes pushing toward other outcomes. The latter might include existing influences and powers of various occupational and industrial groups, some societal needs for a certain reward structure (a variant perhaps of the Davis-Moore theory), the ideology of the society, the incentive structure directed toward whites, and so forth. If the force generating the racial income gap was the dominant one in the marketplace, then essentially all other kinds of changes would not matter; the same outcome would occur with respect to black-white incomes. If the force generating lower black incomes was one of several roughly equal forces, then the influence of changes in educational composition on the income gap would be, at the very least, massively reduced from what the cross-sectional linkages at an earlier time would imply. The potential impact of educational changes between times 1 and 2 implied by the apparent causal influence of education on income gaps at t_1 would be modified at t_2. If the efforts of whites to control black incomes was an insignificant force in the system, then we would know it only because the racial income gap might well decline at t_2 even more rapidly than is implied by the observed causal linkages at t_1.

One suspects that this basic cause—if it operated to its full limit—would still be altered by the thrust generated by other basic causal forces. This would mean that in most instances the dependent variable will indeed change as composition changes; in other words, the influence of a basic causal factor will not be boundless. Even if the overpowering cause of the black-white income gap was the ability of whites to gain their maximum return, other basic social forces operating in the context would place restraints on the ability of these coefficients to shift over time if the composition called for such changes in order to maintain the same gap. If this theory about the basic cause of income differences were to be correct, one would expect to find an outcome in which: (1) the coefficient of income on education shifts substantially in the direction of nullifying the income consequences of black gains in education; and/or (2) there is a shift in the influence on income of other factors so as to increase their contribution to the income gap; and (3) there is a modest decline in the racial gap, far less than what would have been expected if the array of observed surface linkages found in the earlier time were still operating.

Let us visualize a situation in which investigators at different times look at black-white differences in the proportion who are physicians. At the time when slaves were initially brought over, there would be no evidence of discrimination in the marketplace; differences in formal education could account for the fact that all of the physicians were white. At the time of Emancipation, the conclusion would still not be that different; since such a large percentage of blacks were illiterate, a substantial part of the racial gap is accounted for once education is taken into consideration. During the decades since then, as blacks made educational progress, the relative influence of education on the racial gap would have declined and one would have to deal directly with discrimination. (This ignores the role various discriminatory forces played in keeping blacks from achieving educational parity. In that regard, this is really part of the Ceteris Paribus Error discussed in chapter 4.) For a given gap to remain fixed over time, as a general rule, we can say that the role of discrimination will go up as the differences between the groups on universalistic criteria decrease. Insofar as such a pattern occurs, there is evidence that the causal linkages observed at a given time of the sort described earlier are nothing more than the superficial outcomes of a given underlying causal thrust. This is perhaps self-evident, but how different our conclusions would be if the researcher persisted in working just with the superficial causes apparent at each point in time.

Measurement Issues

This distinction between basic and superficial causes looks not only to a different interpretation of the observed association but also makes one aware of the need to work with causes that are not necessarily measured. This does not mean the casual use of data without rigorous and carefully constructed research. Far from it! It means just the opposite—the careful use of data not for the purposes of simulating in simple-minded fashion that which is undoable, but rather for the purposes of evaluating hypotheses and theories about the causes underlying certain outcomes. This is done through examining the changing or constant linkages of superficial causal patterns observed for the dependent variable of interest over time. In many cases, the statistics currently being used are not appropriate for simulating the experiment, but they could be used to learn about the causes underlying a certain outcome. This can be done if there are measurements over time to see the magnitude of the dependent variable's change in relation to changes in the composition of the populations and in the superficial causal linkages observed at each point in time. Again, we are reminded that most questions of causality require longitudinal data.

CHOOSING BETWEEN CAUSAL MODELS

Let us visualize an almost infinite number of causal principles that *could*, under one circumstance or another, affect societal life. If my position is correct, we would normally expect to find that only a small number of these are the basic causes that account for the outcome found in a given setting. Under such circumstances, there would be no point in trying to decide if these various theories are inherently true or false—it would be a complete waste of energy. The data can help us decide only if a given theory is operating in the observed context.[8] If it is not a basic cause, the theory might operate as one under other more constrained conditions. As a consequence, the usual role of empirical research should not be to test the truth of a causal theory (unless the theory is an extremely restricted nongeneralizable proposition meant to apply to a specific context).[9] Rather, the role of research is to determine the breadth and applicability and relative power of a theory. By "power" is meant the ability of a given force to win out over other causal principles that would generate contradictory consequences. The impact of research on pure theory is to help us decide if theoretically derived causal propositions are useful in understanding a specific societal phenomenon of interest or, more generally, a wide spectrum of societal phenomena. Research can also tell us when the theories do not work and where none of the ones that we have appear to be adequate. It is also critical insofar as it raises questions about when a given proposition is a basic cause and when it is not. Research can be of great value too in determining the boundaries of a given theory or causal proposition—that is, seeing how many different circumstances and situations it holds in cases where the proposition runs into theories that would generate different consequences. But research cannot tell us whether different theories are *right*. If Theory A operates in a given setting and B does not, one cannot conclude that B is false. What it does mean is that B is not applicable in a certain class of settings!

It is futile to try to test the validity of a theory. First of all, no matter what we do and say, we are dealing with only a restricted subset of all possible societal conditions (after all, we would have to wait until the end of history before we could say that we have a random sample of all societies). So a given proposition may not be useful in the case at hand but it could be useful in a different context. (On the one hand, this assumes that theories are not universally applicable in time and space; on the other hand, it also rejects the notion that generalizations are impossible. Rather, the causal propositions have limits to where and when they will operate.) Second, we have enough of a task trying to learn what basic causes are operating in a given setting or range of settings. As a consequence, we are happy simply to ignore theories that do not help us, rather than attempting to show that they are false. Third, it is an open question whether abstract causal principles can be shown to be false. Where several theories could account for the same events, it does not mean that the researcher can blithely choose one over the other on the grounds that it is all arbitrary. Rather, it is necessary to think about settings where they would generate contradictory consequences. We would tend to favor the principles that had the widest consequences.

Thus, if propositions A, B, and C would all lead to the same consequence in Setting #1, but A does not help us in Settings 2, 3, 4 . . . N and B helps us in only a few of them and C does the trick in all cases, then we should favor C not because A and B are false, but because of the criterion of parsimony. The principle of parsimony is well known to social scientists but it appears to be ignored when we behave as if one theory is about to disprove another. What we can do, and must do, is attempt to deal with conflicting theories not in terms of deciding whether one is true and the other is not, but whether one seems to be more helpful in the sense of being applicable to a wider set of events. If all three causal principles (A,B,C) can account for only some of the other situations, but in a mutually exclusive way such that A helps to explain certain other settings that B cannot and B can explain certain other settings that A cannot, and so on, then it is not possible to distinguish between them in their utility for the setting in which all three satisfactorily account for the event in question. In that context, one would either conclude that the event in question is "overdetermined," in the sense that several propositions would lead to the observed consequence, or that it is necessary to state a new theory that would incorporate all of the narrower causal principles, or that an understanding is necessary of the counterbalancing forces that nullify principles A, B, and C in different contexts. Until one of these outcomes is achieved, it is necessary to conclude simply that we cannot fully choose between the different possible causal principles generating a certain outcome in the specific setting.

Although there is almost an infinite number of causal forces, this perspective actually makes life simpler than it is with the present multivariate approach. Rather than looking for a variety of causes to account for a given outcome, we would seek a causal principle that leads to a certain outcome, pure and simple. We can visualize a basic cause that is driving events to a particular end. A by-product is the particular set of superficial causal pathways (or surface causes) that lead to this end. It is possible that the surface causes will be of interest, but at best only secondarily and after the underlying cause is known. (We will not be able to judge until we know more about the underlying causes.)

Differences between Basic Causes

Although there are many causal principles, some are hardy in the sense that their ramifications occur under a wide variety of different conditions, whereas others are weak because their outcome will be operable only under certain very narrow conditions. Central Place Theory is an example of the latter; *it is a causal principle that is present in all settings, but its ramifications are greatly diminished or entirely muted in many of them.* This does not make the theory any less true than some other theory about urban location and distribution. It just makes it less applicable for a given context. Gresham's Law in economics (bad money driving out good money) or the Iron Law of Oligarchy (Michels, 1958) are examples of hardy propositions. Since exceptions are relatively rare, at least in the contexts that have been observed, it means that each of these generates a certain consequence regardless of the degree to which the setting may favor other and possibly conflicting causal principles.

In order to evaluate the utility of a given causal proposition, it is important that there be a clear-cut statement of the conditions under which it will operate. An example of this (from Lieberson 1971: 575−579) is the *hypothesis of compensating strategies.* This hypothesis attempts to show that political decisions would not invariably reflect the direct interests of the majority even if interest groups were alike in organization, wealth, and other competitive resources. If the population is atomized into a highly diverse set of interest groups that are neither fully harmonious with one another nor fully competitive and, if interest groups therefore differ not only in whether they are for or against an issue but also in the degree to which they benefit or lose, then this will lead to a certain kind of outcome. To wit, groups will pursue those issues that lead to the greatest net gain to their interests. In order to form coalitions to achieve such gains, they may well support other policies that they would otherwise be against.

> Four conditions are necessary for a "compensating" power situation to operate. First, power must be an exhaustible commodity such that each interest group has limited political influence. Second, the interests of the population must be diverse enough so that a given proposal will not have an equal impact on all segments. Third, governmental actions that favor a particular interest group must not eliminate the disadvantaged majority's potential for other gains. . . . Fourth, legislation beneficial to a specific interest must not at the same time create too great a loss for the majority of other interests. . . .
>
> When these conditions are met, it follows that a given group will not attempt to exert its influence on all issues to the same degree, but rather will concentrate

on those that generate the greatest net gain. To obtain passage of particularly beneficial legislation, an interest group may in turn support other proposals that, by themselves, create small losses (see Coleman 1964). (Lieberson 1971: 577−578)

This hypothesis is used to explain the existence of a massive military budget in the United States even though most industries actually would benefit if government expenditures were for nonmilitary items.

In all circumstances, we want principles of causation, but we would like as few of them as possible. Hardy principles that account for outcomes in a wide variety of settings are, of course, more desirable than notions that operate in a more narrowly confined context. The principles should not necessarily be of a concrete nature; a theory that said bankers will always win out over workers in any situation where they are in conflict would be less desirable than one that said, more abstractly, here is who will win and why in economic conflicts between different groups. If the latter could be applied to worker-banker conflicts successfully and to other conflicts, we would appreciate it more. Also, such a theory could allow for circumstances in which the workers do not lose out to the bankers. So it would mean a hardier and more useful causal principle. One problem among social researchers is the tendency to view specificity and concreteness as equal to Science and Rigorous Thinking, whereas broad and less precise generalizations are seen as more humanistic and mushy. Certainly there are many instances where some vague and broad notion turns out to be nothing more than the product of poorly conceived thinking. But this "precision" is often achieved only by analyzing surface causes because some of them are readily measured and operationalized. This is hardly sufficient reason for turning away from broad generalizations and causal principles.

CHAPTER TEN

From Controls
to Outcomes

A DIFFERENT WAY OF THINKING ABOUT
CONTROL VARIABLES

Social researchers operate as if they have actually created an experiment in which the possible influence of certain variables is "controlled." It is as if the researcher has used some sort of random assignment procedure or, if nonrandom, then at least one that is not selective on attributes that affect the processes under consideration. Our statistical analyses are in effect saying: *here is what the influence of each variable is, had such results been found under conditions of random assignment.* In point of fact, our social science knowledge is often telling us that there are no grounds for assuming that the observed pattern simulates what might have occurred had there been a true experiment. Conditions are usually not randomly assigned, and hence we cannot casually assume that the outcome is what would have occurred had there been random assignment. The issues to be faced are clear enough: When can control variables be used? What should be done when the application of the control variable approach is inappropriate?

Appropriate Use of Controls

Controls are appropriate in four different situations: (1) if the control approach is used merely as a descriptive device and not intended for analytical purposes; (2) if nonrandom assignment is irrelevant; (3) if there are grounds for assuming that some sort of random assignment model is operating or closely approximated because all of the selective processes have been taken into account; or (4) if there is a way of using controls to deal fully with selectivity.

The first situation can be disposed of rather quickly. Suppose the researcher finds evidence suggesting that variable X_{15} affects Y and is also associated with X_2, which likewise appears to affect Y. Looking at the influence of X_2 net of X_{15}, the researcher can simply and openly say here is what an experiment would show *if* we can pretend that there was no selectivity operating such that those subjects (nations, groups, individuals, or whatever) with high X_{15} assigned to different levels of X_2 (and in different degrees, hence the association) are identical to one another except for their level of X_2. Even if there is reason to think that a sorting process did operate which affects the relationships observed in unmeasured ways, we will just pretend that it did not exist. In that sense, the experimental control model is used to describe some data, using a certain stylized form.

Such a step is probably not useful for causal understanding or theoretical purposes or applied concerns. But it might be all right for a kind of simplistic verbal description of events. In a certain sense, it is no different from a population projection in which the researcher says, "If the current rates of age-specific mortality, fertility, and international migration continue into the future, here is what the population of the nation will be one hundred years from now." The researcher knows full well that it is extraordinarily unlikely that current rates will continue for such a long span. But the projection, if not taken as a serious prediction, does provide a way of describing the ramifications of a set of observed rates. In the matter of control variables, this is currently what most social research is about! Certainly we try to control for as many selective processes as possible and as many influences as possible; essentially we then assume that the model used duplicates of what would have been obtained had a true experiment occurred, even though we know that it is unlikely. Under such circumstances, we have a pretend experiment in the sense that we are saying, here is what the

output would mean if it were an experiment even though we think
that this is not the output we would have found.

The second situation is even simpler, but it provides circumstances when the control model is perfectly appropriate—namely, if
there is indication that selectivity is operating, but that the selectivity is irrelevant for the process under consideration. In such a
case, the researcher has every justification for using the control
variable approach *for the problem under consideration.*

A third situation that permits the use of the control variable
model is when there are grounds for assuming that some sort of
random assignment model is either operating or closely approximated. ("Random assignment" does not mean that associations are
absent, but rather that there is no unmeasured selectivity remaining
that affects the dependent variable under consideration.) There are
instances where the random assignment assumption is true or is
sufficiently close that the researcher can indeed apply normal statistical procedures. I believe this is particularly the case for a number of
basic demographic variables such as age, sex, race, ethnic origin
(assuming no measurement error), educational attainment, marital
status, and the like. For example, if we want to look at racial
differences in mortality, we must take into account age and sex.
Thus the operation will be radically different from what is done
when, say, SES and religion are taken into account in studying the
private-public school influence on test performance.

Suppose we match up blacks and whites of a given age and sex to
see what their differences are in mortality. Let Y represent mortality, X_1 = race, X_2 = age, and X_3 = sex. One can look at the
influence of X_1 on Y net of these two controls and be reasonably
confident that there is not an unmeasured selectivity problem. By
contrast, suppose private and public school children of a given SES
and religious background are matched up to see what their differences are in some standard school performance measure. Let Y
represent test performance, X_1 = type of school, X_2 = SES, and X_3
= religion. As indicated in chapter 2, if we consider the influence of
X_1 on Y net of these two controls, we can be reasonably confident
that severe selectivities are operating. In this case, in controlling for
X_2, we cannot be confident that a simple random assignment

mechanism was operating to put some children of a given SES into private schools whereas other children go to public schools. The same is true for religion. In the example involving racial differences in mortality, we can be reasonably confident that there are not the same selective assignment mechanisms operating.

Experience with this problem in a variety of contexts is needed before some generalizations can be made about the conditions when nonselectivity can be assumed or closely approximated without too much harm. For example, demographic variables are by no means always amenable to control procedures; a linkage between marital status and mortality would force us to ask whether entering marriage and remaining married were conditions that were somehow related to health. However, SES could probably be employed as a control variable in the mortality question without too much worry. The key issue, and this needs considerable attention, centers on the conditions under which the simulation assumption of random assignment can be reasonably made. It is not a matter of simply classifying some variables as appropriate and others as not—it will also depend on the relationship under consideration. At the moment, all that I can suggest is that the researcher be obliged to make the case for controls before going forward in using them. The case for controls has to involve more than saying that we have reason to think that X_1 affects Y and this is confounding our understanding of how X_2 is influencing Y. That is insufficient. The case also has to include grounds for thinking that we are closer to the true relationships after X_1 is taken into account than before. As chapter 2 has shown, it is not to be automatically assumed that the control procedure moves us toward a closer approximation of the "true" relationship, that is, the relationship that would have been found had an experiment taken place.

For those wanting to use control procedures in a serious way, it is vital to develop a model that explains why the control problem exists to begin with. That is, the researcher or the underlying theory should tell us why there is a *need* to control. Why are these variables correlated anyway? Models will be needed which go back far enough in the causal chain so that we reach branching points that involve either random assignment or nonrandom assignment in which the

selective factors do not influence the dependent variable and hence
there would be no need for additional controls. The latter situation
is the circumstance when nonrandom controls are irrelevant to the
problem.

This raises the fourth condition under which control variables can
be used successfully—namely, when a model can be developed that
directly tackles self-selectivity and correctly estimates its effect on
the relationship under consideration. At the present time, there are
interesting and promising efforts in this direction. If they suc-
ceed—and it is not yet clear how useful these new methods will
be—then a radical shift in the control variable approach might be
possible. At the moment, however, the picture is not clear. Let us
consider once more the private-public school problem. An important issue raised by critics of the Coleman, Hoffer, and Kilgore
study (1981, 1982a) is this matter of self-selectivity and its impact
on the school comparisons. Murnane (1981), Bryk (1981), and
Goldberger and Cain (1982) are among those who have criticized
the private-public school comparison on the grounds that the customary control variable approach applied in the comparison between school types did not really rule out the strong possibility that
the differences were generated by self-selective factors in terms of
who goes to these schools.

It is not my goal to draw any conclusions about the controversial
study or its policy implications, but rather to consider it in terms of
the general methodological issues. Both the critics and the authors
of this study seem not at all convinced that it is possible to use either
the standard procedures or some of the new methods to handle the
unmeasured self-selectivity issue. Murnane (1981: 485), for example, cites Barnow, Cain, and Goldberger (1980) to show that the
effects of self-selection cannot be controlled by simply including a
large number of background characteristics. He then goes on to
consider whether techniques more sophisticated than those employed by Coleman, Hoffer, and Kilgore could possibly provide a
way of dealing with the issue:

Would the use of other methods of analysis, more sophisticated than those
employed by Coleman et al., have eliminated the problem of bias due to the

effects of self-selection? Social scientists will disagree on this point. However, I believe that the answer is no. Eliminating selection bias requires the identification and measurement of at least one variable that influences a family's choice of public or private school and does not influence a child's achievement. If such a variable were found, it would be possible to use instrumental variable methods to estimate and control selection bias (Olsen, 1980). I believe, however, that all observable variables that influence choice of school—parents' education levels, for example—also influence achievement.

In principle, there is an alternative method for controlling selection bias that does not require fulfillment of these conditions. However, as Olsen (1980) has explained, when this alternative method, the Mills' ratio method, is applied in situations in which the conditions described above are not fulfilled, the estimated coefficients become unstable. Consequently, it may not be possible, even using more sophisticated methods of analysis than those employed by Coleman and his colleagues, to determine accurately the extent to which differences in achievement are due to differences in the children, or to differences in the schools. . . .

I believe that the conventional methodology is inappropriate for evaluating the relative effectiveness of public and private schools because selection mechanisms, the factors that influence which children attend which schools, and educational programs are not analytically distinct. (Murnane 1981: 485−486)

Bryk (1981: 502) is also dubious about the ability of conventional techniques to deal suitably with these selectivity issues. He notes that, "recent research (see, for example, Bryk and Weisberg 1977; Cronbach, Ragosa, Floden, and Price 1977; Weisberg, 1979) has clearly demonstrated that statistical adjustments may result in either over- or underadjustment of preexisting differences between groups. Since no empirical procedure exists for determining whether a data set has been adjusted correctly, we cannot be certain that Coleman, Hoffer, and Kilgore's estimations of school effects are correct." Bryk goes on to provide some strong evidence to suggest that the children attending these different types of high schools were different prior to starting high school in ways that the control variables do not come close to eliminating.[1]

Several critics of the private-public school study do recommend some of these new procedures for dealing with the selectivity issue: Bryk (1981: 503) suggests the analysis of covariance structures described in Jöreskog 1970 and Jöreskog and Sorbom 1978, as well as procedures developed by economists in which the selection process is directly modeled (Barnow, Cain, and Goldberger 1980; Heckman 1979). Goldberger and Cain (1982: 112−113) likewise

suggest trying the probit regression approach developed in econo-
metrics to deal with this problem. However, they recognize that it
is by no means certain that there will be a suitable variable that
affects school choice but does not affect the dependent variable (a
problem noted by Olsen). If not, then a collinearity problem will
prevent an adequate application of the Heckman approach. These
reservations are also shared by Coleman, Hoffer, and Kilgore, who
add some of their own to the applicability of the Heckman approach
(1982b: 171–172). They did, however, use this technique and
obtained radically different results with the two different specifica-
tions employed. In one case, there appeared to be no selection bias;
in the other, selection bias was significant but in the opposite
direction from expectations—to wit, selectivity was actually working to generate *higher* test scores for children attending public
schools (Coleman, Hoffer, and Kilgore 1981: 529–530).

In short, such procedures do not at present provide a handy
panacea for dealing with these issues of selectivity. If they develop
into an approach with widely applicable ramifications, then the
control variable approach could prove promising again. At the
moment, however, we should not use controls so freely and
thoughtlessly, always assuming that they move us closer to the
truth—or at least not further from it—than the results obtained
without applying controls. It is probably only under the conditions
specified earlier that they will meet the goals first visualized in the
experimental analogy with the physical sciences.

When Controls Are Inappropriate

The application of controls will decline radically if scholars consider
the conditions under which variables are taken into account. Because of selective processes that cannot be ruled out by the control
approach, controls are as likely as not actually to worsen the approximation of the true influence of the causal variable of interest. The
problems stemming from unmeasured variables are not new (see,
e.g., a book review by Wildavsky 1982), but implicitly there has
been the assumption that controlling helps reduce the influence of
selective processes. Further, the distinction between basic and

superficial types of causal factors should help us understand that our very reasons for wanting to control are often reasons for suspecting the outcome of such exercises. Namely, it is not by chance that certain patterns of association exist, and it is unlikely that other patterns will be found. The control exercise is all right for describing what would be approximated if all of the variables were free to vary with one another. But as an approximation to understanding what is really going on, such controls fail because the researcher is often controlling for superficial causes that have nothing to do with the outcome in the sense that they are merely intermediaries.

In the case of black-white income differences, for example, blacks are generally concentrated in positions within the society that would lead to lower incomes and, additionally, they earn less than whites in the same niches. The control logic of social research would normally lead us to ask for the relative contributions of each factor—decomposing the gap into two sources means controlling for each. But is it just chance that it turns out that blacks lose both in terms of the positions that they occupy as well as how they make out within these positions? It is almost certain that the same force leading to less desirable positions is also responsible for the lower incomes within these positions. If blacks were to reach equity with whites in niches, it is almost certain that the magnitude of the improvements would *not* be of the magnitude implied by the control analysis. It would be either much closer to equality or much farther away. It would be much less if the black improvement in occupations were caused as a secondary consequence to some other basic force—in other words, if the niche changes were a by-product enabling some other basic causal force to work out its consequences. However, if the black improvement in occupations represented a change in the forces working to undermine blacks, it is almost certain that other features of black disadvantages would also decline sharply.

If the control variable approach is valid, it has to be tested by the researcher to see if the assumptions underlying such an analysis are actually being met. Let us suppose that we control for everything and it works out that we know all the factors leading children to go to private as opposed to public schools. For the sake of argument, let us say that it is owing to the ambitions of parents and the SES of parents. For hypothetical purposes, the percentage going to private school within each cell is as follows:

		SES of Parents	
		High	Low
Ambition of Parents	High	86	14
	Low	21	4

How would we know that all controls were appropriately introduced? The traditional response is to propose testing if there is unmeasured selectivity hidden within the control variables. In this case, presumably the examination of any other characteristic would find no influence on the percentage going to private school within each subset. If child's personality type had no influence, then within the HH subset, for example, 86 percent of those with each personality type would go to private school. In similar fashion, for each personality characteristic, we would expect that 21 percent of the LH subset would be going to private schools and 79 percent would go to public schools (for simplicity of presentation, sampling errors will be ignored). Had it turned out that children with certain personality characteristics were especially likely to go to private schools, net of the aforementioned controls, researchers would normally include this factor into the equation as well.

Let us suppose that personality types A, B, and C are related to both how the child performs in school and whether or not the child ends up going to a private institution. Under such circumstances, the cross-tabulations might look like the following:

		Child's Personality	SES of Parents	
			High	Low
Ambition of Parents	High	A		
		B		
		C		
	Low	A		
		B		
		C		

Within each cell, we would be given the percentage attending private school. This is the classic process of elaboration, in which the researcher tries to apply as many controls as possible. Two fundamental assumptions seem to operate: (1) if private schools differ from public schools in their effect on test performances, the school effect should show up after all other possibly relevant factors are taken into account; and (2) we would feel more secure about having suitably taken into account all relevant factors if the researcher finds a massive part of the variation accounted for by the combined influence of the test variable and the control characteristics under consideration.

This approach to the control variable issue is no longer acceptable. If controls are to be used appropriately, one must be confident that the dependent variable's apparent linkage with the hypothesized causal factor(s) is not an artifact of unmeasured self-selective processes. Using the tabulations shown, can we be confident that it is just by chance (or selective on irrelevant characteristics) that some "LBH" children (children whose parents are of low SES, and who have personality characteristics B, and whose parents are highly ambitious) go to private schools and other LBH children go to public schools? The usual approach does not allow us to question the matter further. Since typically every available variable is considered that might influence Y, the normal control procedure will never let us know—in empirical terms—if we have done an adequate job. If we find anything else affecting the dependent variable, that too is thrown into the tabulation. Thus, if there is a factor for which unmeasured selectivity is operating, we will not know about it.

For those determined to use controls under these circumstances, when there is no confidence about the unmeasured influence of self-selectivity, the only alternative that I can suggest is to ask the following question: Does the observed set of tabulations appear to affect other variables that themselves have no apparent bearing on Y? In the case at hand, do LBH children attending private school differ on *any* attributes from LBH children who go to public schools? If they do not, then this would make us a little more confident that it is purely chance that determines which LBH children attend each type of school. If the children do differ on other attributes—even though these are not attributes that affect the dependent variable in which we are interested—there is less reason to think that we are dealing with random sorting into the control categories.[2] This will give us somewhat greater confidence about whether or not the sorting process is sufficiently random to justify the use of these controls. In effect, the researcher favoring control procedures is obliged to determine not only whether all possible controls are being used—as is the conventional expectation—but also whether pockets of heterogeneity can be generated within the subcells of the control variable combinations.

WHY USE CONTROL VARIABLES ANYWAY?

The control variable approach is really not a happy one—it promises much more than it can deliver. Ideally, it ought to be a simple way of simulating an experiment. In practice, there is usually dissatisfaction on the theoretical grounds that a factor believed to be important has either been omitted or inadequately measured. Likewise, there is usually empirical evidence from other studies that would suggest a significant omission in the case at hand. This leads to four typical steps in the contemporary approach to control variables:

1. The researcher can think of an almost infinite number of possible influences.

2. The researcher develops a very complicated causal model simply as a consequence of trying to incorporate all of these influences.

3. There remains the possibility of unmeasured selectivity with which the researcher cannot fully cope in quasi-experimental research.

4. The researcher can cope with the danger of unmeasured selectivity only by assuming that it is reduced by throwing in as many controls as possible until there appears to be less and less that is unexplained (using variance explained or chi square or the like).

But where does this leave us? A very complicated model is generated simply because the researcher has to have so many causes operating. It is an unhappy model because, almost certainly, all of the controls are still not taken into account. It is easy to resist the findings and hard to have anything even closely approximating a definitive result because the study is open to question on the grounds that all would be different if only X_{973} had been introduced. There is no justification for the assumption that more and more controls mean a closer approximation to what would have been found in a true experiment. The underlying assumption in the use of controls—that they are at least innocuous in approximating the truth—is not justified.

In short, the control variable approach rarely succeeds as an adequate simulation of an experiment, but it does leave us with incredibly complicated causal models. On top of that, it tends to lump together both superficial and basic causes in an indistinguishable, helter-skelter manner. If researchers still want to use this approach, it means using the criteria suggested earlier (and other criteria that can be developed) in order to take a much harder look at unmeasured selectivity. It also means trying to understand why the structure of control variables exists. This means a shift in focus from the dependent variable to the independent variables. In effect, one needs a theory or model that accounts for the nonrandom assignment of the control variables themselves. *It may well be that much can be learned about the basic causal force by simply examining the nature of the nonrandom combinations of variables for which we normally control.*

An alternative to the control variable mentality in quasi-experimental social research is simply to ask ourselves what is the outcome and worry less about the complicated maze of factors that *appear* to be contributing to the outcome. It is not necessary for social research to simulate experiments in order for social science to be a *science*. It is certainly highly desirable in those circumstances when it can be done. Actual experiments should be encouraged wherever possible, and the simulation of experiments through control variables is to be applauded whenever it is appropriate. Nevertheless, as noted early in this book, there is no point in trying to do the undoable. If most of our knowledge comes from nonexperimental data sets, and if such data cannot be treated through statistical analysis as if they are simulations of experiment, it does not follow that social science is not possible. The issue is false; a rigorous and falsifiable knowledge of society is not dependent on simulation of the experiment. Astronomers, to my knowledge, do not generally conduct experiments. They are hardly to be pitied.

The key point is that the social process itself, in many instances, makes the simulated control variable approach inappropriate. Since this is a vital feature of social processes, to simulate under such circumstances is often to fight the very process with which one is dealing. It is incorrect, for any society, to make the ceteris paribus assumption about the freedom of characteristics to vary and take every possible combination. Control processes lead to conclusions about the consequences of shifts in different variables that either will not occur or, if they do occur, will represent such fundamental changes in the society as to make it certain that the observed linkages will not remain unchanged with these new distributions of the variables.

OUTCOME ANALYSIS

I am suggesting that the application of controls through statistical procedures is, for the most part, unproductive. This does not mean that the *idea* of taking controls into account is bad. We are interested in controls because we recognize that many different forces are potentially causal factors in a given context. We want to know which ones are responsible for a given outcome or how powerful a given causal force is. In either case, there is a desire to net out the consequences of other causal forces. If empirical research, for the most part, cannot duplicate the control procedures that we think occur in the natural science experiment, this does not mean that controls should not be considered. However, they have to be thought of in theoretical terms rather than inferred from the data. This idea may be difficult for many researchers to accept. After all, a central goal of empirical research is to get at the relative role of different causal factors—certainly a *quantitative* question rather than one subject to armchair contemplation. But such an objection goes back to the use of superficial causes and the failure to consider the gross outcome.

Let us take the well-worked topic of intergenerational occupational mobility as an example. It seems impossible to think about outcomes here without dealing with many causal forces; after all, many factors affect occupational outcome. But is that right? Thinking of parent(P)—child(C) occupational linkages, we can visualize several extreme possibilities. One is that there is no P—C linkage at all. The occupational composition of children is unaffected by parental occupation. Another possibility is a caste system such that C = P. Still another is a partial relationship between P and C such that P affects C but not entirely. Two possible situations could be operable in the latter case. One is that P's effect is unfavorable on C such that children of high P tend to end up with occupations inferior to those attained by the children of low P. The other is, of course, what we find in out society, to wit, that high P have offspring who end up with higher occupations than do the offspring of the low P.

What should we do with this fact? It is perfectly appropriate to use every available statistical device to describe the occupational linkage between the two generations. How close is the linkage? What does it look like for particular subsets of the population? These and other *descriptive* questions are appropriate; indeed, they are to be encouraged. As indicated at the outset, one of the really valuable functions of empirical social research is a descriptive one. Social scientists who criticize activities simply because they are not theoretically driven are using warped and convoluted reasoning. In the stereotyped world of contemporary social science, there is a tendency to view such work not as a brick contributing to the construction of a great temple, but rather as a symbolic statement about one's disposition toward being a stark naked logical positivist. In point of fact, nobody is better prepared than contemporary social researchers to measure, describe, and summarize such features of the society. Is there really something to be gained by deprecating such an activity? Is the society better off if such questions are either left to speculation or addressed by less competent researchers? All too often, there is a propensity for those unsympathetic to empirical research to respond to solid empirical fact-finding not for what it is, but as if the researcher had implicitly said, "Here is what all social scientists ought do."

The control variable is a perfectly appropriate *descriptive* device; the problem occurs when control variables are viewed as an *analytical* procedure. It is one thing to ask, what is the occupational attainment of blacks and whites of a given educational level? It is another to ask, taking into account or controlling for the influence of education on attainment, what is the influence of race on attainment? In the private-public school example, it is appropriate to compare the test results of rich Protestant children attending private schools with the results of rich Protestant children who attend public schools. It is another matter to think that by controlling for religion and parental income, we have a true comparison of how public and private schools affect children's school performances. As a rule of thumb, one can ask the following question: Given the controls that I have applied, do I think that the results obtained are what would have been obtained if the subjects were randomly assigned to the attributes under consideration?

Where does this leave us? The first and foremost goal is to know the actual outcome for the question raised. In this case, we want to know what the linkage is between parental SES and offspring's SES. There is a partial positive linkage. Why this linkage exists and the reason for its magnitude cannot usually be determined through the conventional analyses of the various observed pathways. First, such an analysis would almost certainly become enmeshed in superficial causes (as described in chapter 9). Second, such an analysis would involve applications of all sorts of inappropriate controls.

What, then, would be the next step? Before considering this, we should keep in mind that all is trivial compared to this fundamental first step: namely, the decision to view the outcome as determined not by the superficial causal patterns observed, but rather as due to a causal force that will take a wide variety of paths. It is the outcome that counts, and it is finding the crucial cause of that outcome that is at issue. Right now we tend to view an outcome as net of a variety of small causal forces that are pulling in a variety of ways. This is dubious and unreal. If we have an outcome, it is the researcher's and theorist's job to determine the critical force whose presence or absence in the given context determines that outcome. After that, variation in the outcome can be studied, but that is a less fundamental issue. This, of course, is totally different from much of contemporary social research where it is variation that is the central question. Why does Y vary? I would say that this is a minor matter, one that should take second billing to the question, why is Y what it is?

In many cases, researchers believe that accounting for the variation is a way of verifying the validity of the basic causal forces under consideration. For that to work, the logical step has to be the following: If X_i is causing Y, then variation in X_i should be causing variation in Y. That is a questionable assumption. Going back to the gravity example in chapter 5, we may use such variables as density, surface, and shape to account for variation in the speed at which objects fall when placed in a container that is not a perfect vacuum. But that will never tell us anything about gravity and why objects fall to begin with. In the case of intergenerational occupational mobility, why do we have a partial positive system? That question cannot be answered, in my estimation, by finding out why the partial positive system fluctuates from setting to setting.

Dealing with Outcomes

There are many causal principles that would generate a certain outcome, and others that would generate a different outcome. One cannot conclude that the latter are false causal principles; all that can be said is that there is a more powerful causal principle operating in this context which makes them irrelevant. If there are several causal principles in a given context which are compatible with the outcome—and that is almost certain to be the case—then we cannot choose between them. What we then need are situations where they would generate different consequences. This is not so easy, and it means trying to decide if the data are good enough (here a good case study is extremely valuable) and getting appropriate situations. For example, one might encounter a situation where there is some superior causal force operating which is too powerful and which wipes out the effects of any of the competing forces from the first case. This view requires a lot more work of a different sort than would occur in either highly technical quantitative empirical research or in theoretical treatise. It involves a painstaking effort not unlike the game of "Clue," where different combinations of answers given to other players lead to the elimination of certain possibilities.

Similarly, in social research there is a need to combine certain causal combinations and consequences to determine a hierarchy of causal conditions such that causal proposition C will generate consequence Y_1, except under some specific condition where causal proposition D will operate in contradiction to C and generate Y_2. It is more complicated than this because we may have a hierarchy of causes, conditions, circumstances, and the like. Research of this nature calls for imagination and flare and intuition, but it also involves the ability to take every case seriously. That, of course, requires very good data. Great attention must be given to evaluating the quality of the data—and this does appear to be developing at present in social research.

All of this gives a different perspective on the role of historical events and/or situations outside of the United States. Currently we seem to have forgotten that sociology is not intrinsically a study of the contemporary United States. To be sure, there is at present some interest in dramatic earlier events in Europe and elsewhere in the world, as well as in events related to Marxist-generated theories. But a quick look at the leading sociological journals will show a relatively modest interest in other times and places. And such studies tend to deal with specially formulated problems, rarely seen as relevant to issues addressed in the present. From the perspective advanced here, such studies become extremely relevant in the sense that they may supply key situations in which a test is provided for contradictory data and evidence, or where there is some hope of resolution of different causal systems. At present, an event such as contemporary occupational mobility in the United States tends to be viewed as a process to be explained within, that is, as an entity itself rather than as a case of some form or another of a theory of mobility or the like.

What is being proposed here is, rather than a multivariate set of causes, the development of a hierarchy of causal principles and a set of propositions to relate them to one another in some structure. For example: Causal Principle A will generate certain consequences, except that it will be secondary to the outcomes generated by Causal Principle B. Hence, under certain specified conditions, the outcome expected from Causal Principle A will not occur. In turn, the outcome generated by Cause B will be secondary to C, and so on. This proposal will give us a body of theory with a set of hierarchies. Revision is always possible as new evidence comes into play such that earlier theories become special cases of a larger theory that incorporates these events. The Marxist approach is of special interest in this regard. On the one hand, it has an appealing feature—not unlike earlier Freudianism. Its zealots seem inclined to use it everywhere as a causal proposition that can explain everything. This is extremely attractive in a certain narrow sense—to wit, it represents an effort to generate theoretical explanations of various outcomes. On the other hand, it is extremely unattractive insofar as other causal propositions are relegated automatically to a secondary role without the kind of analysis required to justify such a step. If we have a causal proposition M, then researchers and theorists have to look for its limits and bounds, just as they would for any other causal proposition. The problem probably lies less with Marxist theory and more with Marxist practitioners. But if the Marxist approach was viewed as one of many possible causal forces, layered in a hierarchy of causal forces, this would be a good example of a desirable way of thinking about outcomes.

CHAPTER ELEVEN

Further Suggestions

At the outset of a paper criticizing the use of cross-sectional methods (in terms not unrelated to the points made in chapter 9 of this volume), Carlsson describes the unavoidable linkage between the nature of what one wants to understand and the appropriate tools for reaching that understanding.

> Research is a game against nature in which nature counters with a strategy of concealment, another name for the laws or dynamic principles holding in the area under study. Obviously, the effectiveness of a given strategy of discovery will depend on nature's strategy of concealment, and conversely, the effectiveness of the laws of nature as a strategy of concealment will depend on the strategy chosen by research workers. In due course it will be shown that a rather simple strategy of concealment may be quite effective given a certain strategy of discovery. As a first step we may ask, what *is* the favorite strategy of sociologists? (Carlsson 1972:323)

Carlsson was worried about a narrower set of problems in his paper, but the point is well taken. If a model of scientific discovery is inappropriately used in social research—in the sense that it does not conform to the nature of societal processes—then it is the model that has to be revised. Societal processes are not about to change just to make the discoveries possible.

In this respect, the quasi-experimental model makes assumptions that often are not met by the reality of social conditions. There is everything to be gained with the development of a disciplined and empirically based form of inquiry, but it has to be done within the limits posed by the nature of the beast. There is every reason to think that societal regularities and laws operate, but there are no grounds for assuming that they can be discovered and/or evaluated through an unthinking application of the reasoning that we *think* is employed in the experimental natural sciences. With this sermon in mind, this chapter provides additional suggestions for an alternative way of studying societal processes.

One should not get too discouraged, for the problem lies in the procedures, not in the subject matter itself. Society is far too orderly and regular for there not to be some strong social principles in operation. We encounter a high degree of regularity in everyday life; we know what to expect in most settings and situations. To be sure, the sun shows up and disappears each day with more order than what is encountered in social life. But the latter is still remarkably orderly—indeed, the disorders are noteworthy because they are not all that common. This means that there are powerful causal principles operating. We need to figure them out, formalize them, and bring data to bear.

FUNCTIONS OF RESEARCH

Empirical data can tell us what is happening far more readily than they can tell us why it is happening. "What is happening" can include all of the cross-tabulations, interactions, controls, modeling, and the like, that one might desire. There is nothing wrong with contemporary social research in that regard. Thus many of the time-honored functions of research should remain. As noted in chapter 7, the use of social research to describe or examine a set of events is perfectly appropriate. The social sciences are better equipped to do such work, and it is tragic to look down on these skills and the desirable function of describing the state of the society. It is no easy task to describe adequately the state of affairs, as can be seen in such issues as sampling, validity, and nonresponse. But it is potentially doable; in varying degrees we can deal with questionnaire construction, sampling biases, underenumeration, and the like.

Of course, other research functions also exist. Empirical research can examine the consequences hypothesized by a given theory. If a given theory leads one to expect certain events—or even correlations—to be present under the conditions specified, it is appropriate to ask researchers to see if indeed this holds. This is largely a descriptive matter, not a simulated experiment. It is one thing to ask if an association exists, as predicted by the theory; it is radically different to ask if the association is indicative of the cause. Learning if the correlations predicted by a theory occur is not the same as learning the causes of an event from the presence or absence of a correlation. One must draw a sharp distinction.

Another function of research can be discussed rather briefly, since it is easy to see its utility. This is to help demonstrate the *existence* of apparent forces hitherto not appreciated by showing simply that some possibility does indeed exist. Two classic studies in social psychology illustrate this function rather nicely. The experiment by Asch (1958: 174–183) demonstrated the influence of social conditions on judgments in a provocative and stimulating way. The Klineberg (1935) study of black IQ scores showed that such scores were not fixed but were directly altered by environmental factors. (Following the test scores of black children who had been moved to New York City from the South after World War I, Klineberg showed that their scores increased progressively with residence in the North.) The Klineberg study does not tell us the relative role of heredity vs. environment, and the Asch study does not provide us with specific limits to the influence of groups on judgments. But the studies do present evidence that such events can occur, that IQ is at least affected by environment, and that judgments on a rather clear-cut matter can be altered by the influence of a social group.

Obviously, there are other positive consequences of social research, not the least being the possibility of a serendipitous finding that stimulates new thinking and new issues. But the key point is to avoid the widespread assumption that these empirical procedures can explain the causal pattern. It is one thing to say that these patterns are found—it is a totally different matter to say why they are found. It will rarely be possible to use such data to indicate the reason. Only under exceptional circumstances can one make this step, and that calls for special considerations as to when the statistical manipulation of variables will give us some notion of causality. My objections here are not the conventional ones that there may be a spurious association and/or that all of the controls were not adequately applied. To be sure, these issues are not to be sneezed at. The causal models that are usually constructed cannot, in most cases, adequately provide an experimental analogue in which the researcher has created different combinations of conditions to examine the outcome. We are delighted when it can be done in social research, and certainly should take advantage of it whenever possible, but more often than not we cannot avoid some or all of the conditions that were discussed in Part I: unmeasured nonrandom selectivity, the existence of associations intimately related to the outcome and the causal force, contamination, and the like.

If it is true that the data cannot generally help us find the causal forces that operate, then we can understand why the linkage between theory and research is so weak. As a consequence, they are often misused in that regard since they come up with superficial causes. Empirical research can help us decide whether or not the results predicted by a theory occurred. This is particularly the case if the researcher deals with the gross outcome rather than the net outcome after a million and one controls are applied (see chap. 10). But rarely can research be used to provide the causes of an event in a manner analogous to what might be achieved if it were possible to experiment systematically with one potential cause after another. To be sure, it is impossible for any description to be void of theoretical dimensions (in the sense of how the measurements are made and what attributes are seen as relevant). So descriptive research is often implicitly generated by certain notions of what has causal relevance. But the key step is to avoid using the patterns of observed linkages as the evidence for generating a causal model. Otherwise, in most instances, one is asking something from the data that they cannot do.

Beyond that, the control variable approach is of little utility for problems involving prediction or social planning simply because it is almost certain that a change in the true causal force will not occur without the linkages between it and the dependent variable also changing. However, the control variable simulation of experiments is likely to create a superficial type of causal analysis in which the dependent variable remains relatively constant when these superficial causal factors are shifted. The control variable approach to prediction and/or social action is predicated on the assumptions that: (1) non-random sorting is taken into account through controls (or that this sorting remains constant over time); (2) the relationships between independent and dependent variables are invariant. Thus, on the one hand, if some superficial independent variable is altered, it is almost certain that the linkages will shift to maintain stability. On the other hand, if the basic causal variable changes, it is rather likely that the linkage with the dependent variable will also shift.

An example is in order. Suppose there is an election and we ask what are the characteristics of those either not voting or voting for a particular candidate. For the purely descriptive research function, we would have a careful report on the characteristics that might be linked with various voting behaviors, for example, age, sex, attitudes, ethnic group, residence, education, and occupation. The characteristics picked for cross-tabulation with voting would almost certainly be selected because they were thought to be relevant or "of interest." For the most part, a simple description of the results is in order. If age or sex or SES is found linked to voting behavior, it would be appropriate for the descriptive study to say that younger people or women or higher SES people were more likely to vote one way than another. (It would be trickier to do with an attitudinal variable since cause-and-effect would not be so clearly established. If people who hold certain attitudes voted for candidate X, it may well be that candidate X influenced their attitudes—not solely the other way around. Likewise, apathetic voters may well be less likely to vote because of who the candidates are—not simply because they have an "inherently" apathetic disposition, as witness the ability of the Reverend Jesse Jackson to get out hitherto unregistered black voters in the 1984 Democratic party primaries.) But, overall, there would be many voter characteristics that could be linked with one or another voting outcome in a relatively "clean" way.

What causes these linkages to exist in the way that they do? This is not answered by the linkages themselves. Nor can we find the answer by looking at a bunch of cross-tabulations such that we consider the influence of race, say, on voting net of education, occupation, income, and so on. Aside from all the other factors that have been mentioned throughout this book, there is yet another that has only been touched on so far. That is the propensity to restrict the causal variables to ones that are *observable* and *measurable*. This tendency in empirical research has been noted many times before and often leads to the criticism that social research tends to deal only with questions that can be measured. The point here is somewhat different—namely there is no reason to think that all causal principles are even *potentially* measurable. Let us return to this question after we have dispensed with the issue at hand.

It is also the case, as the analysis in chapter 5 demonstrated, that nonexperimental empirical research usually cannot be used to evaluate the relative importance of one theory vs. another. Empirical research can tell us whether the conclusions by one or another theory hold, but it tells us nothing about the relative *power* or *importance* of one theory vs. another. We can learn only whether or not the consequences of causal propositions occur, not whether one is more important than another.

ASKING BETTER QUESTIONS

Since so much of our research is at present oriented around variation issues, some of these issues need reconsideration if there is to be improvement in the research enterprise.

Variation Explained Is Not Existence Explained

Explanations of variation are not substitutes for explanations of the existence of the phenomenon itself. This statement runs counter to an almost uniform propensity in social research. Social scientists are variation-loving people who want to test out the cause of something by determining whether variation in the dependent variable is accounted for by variation in the hypothesized cause. They are uncomfortable with causal principles that do not imply variation in

outcome. Without variation in outcome, it does not seem possible
to test empirically the validity of the causal principle. Alas, such an
approach usually does not help us evaluate a causal principle—all
that it offers is the possibility of accounting for modifications in the
impact of the causal principle. As noted in the gravity example in
chapter 5, this can generate seriously distorted causal interpretations. Variance explained—in any one of its many statistical
forms—does not tell us why something exists to begin with. Why
do the bodies fall to the ground? This is not dealt with by the answer
to why the speed at which the bodies fall varies in a nonvacuum.
Likewise, the existence of intergenerational SES inheritance is not
answered by variations between parental SES groups.

   In a nutshell, the principle behind the existence of some
phenomenon cannot be discovered by examining quantitative variation in the phenomenon. First, we need to know why the phenomenon exists before we worry about variation in it. The variation
question is trivial if we do not know the answer to the first question.
One cannot go backward and take explanations for that variation to
find the key to understanding the phenomenon itself.

   Another example is suggested by a walk along an ocean beach.
One observes tides, which are apparently caused "by the earth's
turning beneath great bulges of water raised by the combined
gravitational fields of the moon and the sun" (Bascom 1964: 3—4).
There are some nice quantitative examples of tides that can be
related to the motion of the moon (see Bascom, 1964, chap. 5), but
one must bear in mind the key role of gravity in this. We can do
quantitative studies that deal with the consequences of a given
causal principle as applied to the problem at hand, but the variation
in the events will not inductively lead us to the cause. The variation
will lead us to an interesting problem and some clues, but we would
be sadly mistaken to think that explanation of the variance in tides is
explanation of tides.

   Those researchers who are convinced that there is only a problem
when variance exists should consider the extreme of such a position.
Suppose there was a uniform effect in social life such that a certain
outcome was inevitable. Would this be uninteresting? It might be,
from a variance perspective, since a certain outcome always came
out. It might be difficult to distinguish one theory from another

that implied the same outcome. But it certainly would not be unimportant for us to know what the underlying causal principle was. And, just as the tides are consequences of gravitational forces, it should be possible to examine the theory accounting for this uniformity in contexts where some variation in impact might be expected. It would be grossly improper and blindly ritualistic to neglect an event because it is uniform.

Limits to Variation

Obviously there is a great danger in trying to explain more variation than is appropriate. This was illustrated in chapter 1 when we talked about questions that are nullified because our theoretical and empirical knowledge has moved us beyond them. The example used was the question of why the assassination of President John F. Kennedy took place in Dallas. Because of a probabilistic approach involving very small probabilities, we know that there is no answer to the question if it is put in terms of why it should have happened in Dallas. At best, a probabilistic statement is all that we could hope for.

This issue is far more widespread than might otherwise appear. Let us start with the conventional coin toss example. If a number of unbiased coins are each tossed five consecutive times, we would get a wide variety of outcomes for each coin. There would be many coins with two or three heads resulting from the five tosses, fewer with one or four heads, and a small number with five or no heads (for each extreme, $p = .5^5$). We know that it would be a mistake to try to explain why each coin generated the particular number of heads and tails that it did. If the coins are unbiased, we could say that there was no specific reason for any given coin to have the combination of heads and tails that it did. Our statistical theory would handle the *distribution* of results and also tell us why we could expect to go no further than this. We could act on this theory by subjecting the coins to a second round of tosses. For each coin, we would find no consistency between the pattern of heads obtained in the two rounds, other than that suggested by the theory as due to chance.

This is very interesting because it illustrates an appropriate goal that social theory should fulfill—to wit, working out the limits of how exact the theory should be in accounting for events. There is reason to think that many social processes have a strong "chance" dimension to them, just as in the case of the assassination and the coin tosses. A theory that develops such limits makes a positive contribution. Among other things, it helps us avoid trying to do the undoable. This is a particularly important and difficult goal because, in social research, we rarely have opportunities—such as the coin toss illustrates—of repeating the events and seeing if there are chance dimensions. But the moral is very simple. Just because society does not give us many examples of this to show empirically, it does not make it any less likely that such chance forces are operating. And, when they do operate to some degree in carving out events, pursuit of overly precise explanations is nothing more than pursuit of the undoable.

Relevant here is the "amplification effect" described by Weisskopf (1981: 15–16), which "implies that very small causes sometimes have very large effects." The examples Weisskopf provides are widespread in physical and biological nature—and I think they must apply to social events as well.

Consider the fate of a single molecule in a gas, say, in the atmosphere. Can we predict the fate of the molecule in the course of time? The answer is definitely in the negative. Very small changes in the initial conditions are quickly amplified at each collision with other molecules. Even if we knew its initial condition with great accuracy, its final position would be practically impossible to determine. Furthermore, quantum mechanics puts a limit to the accuracy of initial conditions. . . .

Similar examples are found in the development of star systems. The laws of gravity require the formation of clusters in the primal hot gas of the early universe. Small density fluctuations grow by attracting neighboring gas molecules. The larger clots are even more powerful to attract more material. By this typical amplification process, the originally uniform gas separates in ever increasing groups which, at a later time, develop into galaxies and galaxy-clusters. It is impossible to predict the exact nature of cluster formation, although one can predict that some clusters must be formed due to gravitational amplification of small density fluctuations. Again we are not particularly interested in which star is in what cluster.

Geology presents many instances of amplification effects. One example is the shape of mountain ranges. We comprehend the formation of such ranges by tectonic activities of the earth crust, but we cannot explain why Mr. Blanc has the specific shape that we see today, nor can we predict what side of Mt. St. Helens will cave in at the next eruption. In these examples the effects of amplification are already of greater relevance to us. It should be added that the geological sciences allow a good deal of retrodiction. Many hypotheses on the development of our planet can be verified or falsified by searching for evidence concerning past events. . . .

Biological evolution is a prime example of relevant amplification processes. Small events on the atomic scale that are either in principle or practically unpredictable are amplified into large effects on the structure of the resulting phenotype. These effects are important and relevant because they are retained and multiplied by replication and natural selection. Here again, we comprehend the general trend but we cannot explain the specific events, e.g., why a certain species evolved with its typical properties. Just as in geology, bio-evolution admits a certain amount of retrodiction. Indeed, much of the supporting evidence rests on predictions of what necessarily would have to be found in fossils, and what kinds of biochemical processes could or could not evolve by natural selection. (Weisskopf 1981: 16–17)

Given these descriptions about molecules of gas, stars, mountains, biological evolution: can we really take it seriously when someone tells us why some specific historical event *had* to happen when it did? Should we not be saddened when researchers are urged to explain more and more of the variance with the thoughtless and counterproductive notion that more explained is better?

Policy Questions

Data needs and theoretical needs are not necessarily the same for all questions. This is particularly the case when dealing with policy questions. If a given outcome is desired, the researcher has not only to determine what is going on at present but also to develop some notion of the basic causes of the outcome—as opposed to the superficial causal factors that now maintain the system. If the outcome is to be changed in a certain direction, it will not be accomplished by tinkering with the superficial causal variables— such changes will have only modest influences at best. Rather, there is a need for knowledge about a basic cause that is sufficiently strong to overcome the existing entropy and, of course, that will change the outcome in the direction desired. Since asymmetrical causal patterns are probably commonly found, there is a strong chance that reversing the initial basic cause of the dependent variable of concern will not reverse the dependent variable and hence will not accomplish the goals of the policymakers involved. This is, admittedly, not a quick and ready solution, but at least it points us away from efforts that are likely to fail even though they appear to be so reasonable when the apparent causes are analyzed in the conventional manner.

Counterfactuals

Given our discussion of counterfactuals in chapter 3, it is safe to say that we are damned without them and damned with them. At the moment, I do not believe that we can go far with the simulated experiment. If any progress can be made in this area, however, it will be through the development of a body of maximally plausible counterfactuals upon which one can build and expand into other counterfactuals.

Now this does not mean that we just start with the most "obvious" notions about what is what. Rather, one pathway to take is to develop propositions about what will happen under a variety of conditions so that when a new condition is introduced, we will "know" what would have happened had it not been introduced. Of course, we do not know what would have happened—strictly speaking, that is a counterfactual statement. But there are stronger and weaker counterfactuals. The natural scientist, in an experiment involving a test drug and a placebo does not actually know what would have happened had the randomly assigned subjects been reversed in terms of the placebo vs. the test drug. But the technique is so powerful and the conditions so controlled that a high level of confidence exists which justifies the making of a counterfactual conclusion.

The experimental simulation fails at present in social research because we are continuously making counterfactual conditional statements that have outrageously weak grounds. In our eagerness to answer a question, we must not allow the introduction of such poorly based assumptions. In the long run, it would probably be better if we try to figure out what would be the normal outcome of the event without even thinking about introducing the cause of interest. Only then can we have confidence in deciding what the impact is, if any, of the new causal force. This is precisely why the study of Swedish fertility during World War II works as well as it does (discussed in chapter 3). In that case, the counterfactual statement appears to be well justified. As a consequence, we are confident that the sharp drop or increase in fertility observed nine months after a given political event is due to the political event. That is, we have strong confidence that we know *what would have been* the fertility pattern in Sweden if a given political event had not occurred. The simulated experiment has limited utility in social research, but its potential will at least be fully reached if the scholar pays as much attention to justifying the counterfactual assumption as to any other part of the research.

For example, if we want to know what the impact of school desegregation is on whites living in the central cities, a serious study of the movements of whites from central city to suburbs is absolutely mandatory *before* we can even think of trying to say how that pattern was altered by the introduction of school desegregation. As I tried to show in chapter 3, this cannot be done in that case (and probably in many other social research settings) by a comparison between desegregating and segregated cities in their levels of white outmovement. There would be many other issues, such as contamination and the nonrandom assignment problem. But the first step in dealing with all of this is to gain some grounds for making a well-justified counterfactual statement.

Theories and/or data that create strong counterfactuals, or disprove counterfactuals that we think are strong, are major advances to knowledge. An important function of theory is to suggest, or actually provide, new counterfactuals or to disprove old counterfactuals.

A SOCIAL THEORY OF DATA

We need a theory of data, not merely in the conventional epistemological sense, but one that applies to the specific issues in our daily work on a specific problem. If comparisons are made, we cannot assume that it is mere chance that some comparative possibilities exist and others do not. If X varies from one place to another in its level, it is just as necessary to ask why it varies as to ask what its apparent influence on Y is. For it is almost certain that the level of X found in each setting is not due to chance. It is part of the phenomenon under study—every bit as much as the apparent dependent variable. This goes back to the false analogy with experiments. If the researcher had randomly manipulated X's level from setting to setting, that would be one matter. But, of course, whatever led X to vary from setting to setting is not the experiment. Rather it is the operation of social principles that could easily be relevant to the dependent variable under study.

Likewise, if measurements are made, we cannot assume that it is by chance that certain times and places allow for such measurements and others do not. If we want to study the influence of a new force, we cannot assume that it is by chance that it operates now and not at some other time. For example, only when the sexual mores are looser is it likely that one can do a survey of sexual mores. In a period of highly repressive sexuality, it would not be easy to do such a survey—especially one that involved official approval, access to certain types of people, funding, the ability to take a random sample, and so on. (It would not be impossible, but much less likely.) Now this too means that the social conditions of interest are also determining the data available as much as anything else does. There is always the possibility of unobtrusive measures and indirect tests, but clearly the researcher would have to ask, "What does it mean, for the problem at hand, that I have such data available? Are there other circumstances for which such data cannot be obtained?"

Basically, this is also the issue raised by the discussion of contamination problems in chapter 3. The issue there too calls for not merely a theoretical explanation of what is going on substantively but also one that takes into account the kind of data that are found and what the data will say. Now, it is standard to expect the theory to predict the data—if the data are relevant and the theory valid. What is novel here is the notion that the theory be expected to help us understand not only the pattern found but also the presence of the data and the distribution and nature of the causal variables and conditions that can be studied.

The False Dichotomy between Theory and Data

This discussion suggests that it is incorrect to link data with theory in the way it is normally done. It is incorrect because in practice the two are manifestations of the same principles. A theory of data is needed as part of any theory about anything. In some sense, we need a theory that tells us what causes the data to be there as well as what causes them to be associated in a particular way. Such a theory of data would also entail an understanding of the processes so that we can see why the data do not superficially appear to work in the direction expected. This may be bothersome—and certainly it permits all sorts of slippery operations—but the issue is to fit the nature of the beast. And there is every reason to expect that the data will—because of the social forces that operate—sometimes appear to be different from what the substantive dimension of the theory would seem to predict.

An illustration is in order. The great Merton paper (1949), which showed the strong possibility that attitudes and behavior were not linked, is a data paper as much as it is a substantive paper. It tells us what to expect, not only in the imperfect linkage between prejudice and discrimination but also has implications for the connections between prejudice (viewed as an unmeasured attitude) and the measurements of that attitude. Just as we expect astronomy to tell us why we see what we see (as a way of tossing out irrelevant and misleading images), in similar fashion our knowledge about a given problem must include—on the theoretical level—a knowledge about the data that will be found. At present, we view the data as merely confirming or not confirming some theory. We never ask the theory to account for why the data appear in the form that they do. For a given phenomenon, the theory should not only tell us outcome and association but should also answer the following questions:

1. Under what circumstances can the phenomenon appear as a measurable event?

2. How does this subset of measurements differ from the universe of events in which the phenomenon occurs?

3. Under what circumstances will it be possible to have variation in the independent variables of interest?

4. How will the causal forces alter the "control test" comparisons?

IF IT'S RIGHT, AT LEAST JUSTIFY IT

As Kuhn observes (1962: 77), it is very difficult to deal with paradigm vacuums. If the control variable approach is largely off the mark, it will still be hard for us to give up this mode of thinking because we are only in the early stages of generating a more appropriate approach. I suggest to those who continue to deal in the usual way with controls that they employ a fair test to determine if there are grounds for thinking that the controls have suitably dealt with the selectivity issue. (Even if the test is favorable, however, this does not eliminate other criticisms, such as the failure to distinguish between superficial and basic causes.)

If selectivity has been fully taken into account in a situation where a large number of control variables are employed, a researcher should then be asked to determine if the association between some "neutral variable" and all of the control variables is the same for the different levels of the test variable. Let us go back to the private-public school example: If the study has adequately taken into account the different selective forces that operate to lead some children to attend one type of school as opposed to the other, what would one expect? It is reasonable to expect that the cross-tabulated controls in the private schools have the same influence on some neutral variable as the cross-tabulated controls do in the public schools. By a "neutral variable" I mean a variable that is not influenced by the test variable itself—in this case, the type of school.

Suppose children attending private schools are found to differ from public school children with respect to two parental characteristics, SES and the ambitions they have for offspring. If there is no unmeasured selectivity operating beyond these factors, it would mean that taking these two features into account will enable one to decide what the private-public school effect is. How can we decide if there are no other selective forces operating? If there is no difference between private and public school children whose parents are of a given combination of SES and ambition then the joint influence of parental SES and parental ambition on some variable not affected by school should be identical in each type of school. The association between these controls should be the same in private schools as in public schools, *if* there is no unmeasured selective process operating with respect to school attendance. This is a reasonable question for researchers conducting such studies to ask themselves and, at the very least, editors of journals should insist that they consider such an issue. To be sure, a satisfactory result here does not mean that other objections to the control approach are also eliminated. (A suitable control procedure allows for differences between test populations in the frequency of certain characteristics, but requires that the assignment be random within these categories. If not random, more controls have to be introduced.)

TRANSFORMATIONAL PRINCIPLES

In trying to work out appropriate solutions, I suggest that there is a type of causal principle that has the especially attractive quality of being relatively immune to the control variable issue. For lack of a better term, one might call these causal principles "transformational," that is, they bend a variety of inputs, regardless of their nature, into the same output. A wide range of initial conditions are changed, as it were, to reach a certain end. Controlling or otherwise dealing with the various inputs is a futile act when dealing with a transformational causal principle. Insofar as the nature of the inputs has no impact on the outcome, the control variable issue is trivial. Learning the transformational causal principle is what counts. Indeed, as we saw earlier, the shifting regression values leading to the same output is evidence that a transformational causal principle is operating. The bounds of a transformational principle are not limitless; hence when the values of the controls reach certain extremes, then indeed the outcome does not get pulled back to a common point. But this is a different matter from now, where we act as if a wide variety of observed low-level linkages are invariant. If inputs vary between time-one and time-two, right now we operate as if the linkages observed at time one are expected to operate at later periods even if—during the interim—there is a radical shift in the input values. Instead of considering invariances in the nature of the linkages between observed causal and dependent variables (and hence fluctuations in the outcome), I am suggesting that we ought consider invariances in the outcomes and view linkages that generate the observed outcomes as variant.

These transformational principles are especially desirable since they provide us with a way of distinguishing superficial from basic causes. The ideal causal principles for which we should be searching are, in my estimation, those that transform a large number of different conditions into the same outcome.

IN CONCLUSION

Empirical research in the social sciences is based on a belief about the way natural scientists conduct experiments in the laboratory. Social scientists go to great lengths to follow this model as far as possible—indeed, to the point where statistical procedures are used to simulate experiments with naturally occurring events. Did the experimental model we implicitly follow ever really exist in the hard sciences? Was it as simple as we visualize it? Do natural scientists currently follow this model? These are irrelevant questions. A central theme of this book is simply that the model we employ cannot, for the most part, be followed in the social sciences. This does not mean turning away from a systematic and rigorous effort to construct social science. Certainly, experimentation is perfectly reasonable in some of the social sciences; assuredly, there are occasions when statistical simulation can lead to an appropriate approximation of one. The conclusion remains that neither experiments nor quasi-experiments can be used to address satisfactorily many of the most important empirical problems in such fields as sociology, political science, anthropology, history, and economics (and, to a lesser extent, psychology and demography). The same applies to theories that assume the possibility of such a quasi-experimental model, even if the theorist would not actually conduct such empirical projects. What is needed is an approach to theory and social research that is realistic and productive. What goals *should* there be for theory and research? To answer this, a more prosaic and less lofty question must first be considered: What *can* these goals be?

Although the quasi-experimental model has limited applications in social science at the moment, it should be pursued whenever possible. As has been shown in Part One of this book, in many cases it cannot be executed because of such factors as the nonrandom nature of control variables or the existence of asymmetric causality. Is an alternative perhaps provided by the nonexperimental natural sciences? This is a reasonable question to ask, but a certain amount of caution is in order. I suspect that such disciplines still have it easier than social science on two dimensions. First, the nonexperimental natural sciences can more readily obtain repeated observations so that erroneous ones can be caught more easily and either corrected or tossed out. Second, many of these disciplines can rely on experimental research in other sciences that are directly and closely relevant. For example, research on optics and light can be used in astronomy, or research in chemistry can be applied to geology. Hence, although not experimental, such disciplines are closer to having an experimental underpinning than would otherwise appear to be the case. Certainly, these nonexperimental natural sciences are more closely linked to experimental evidence than is presently the case for much of social science.

Tempting as it is, one must avoid distinguishing natural from social science on the grounds that the latter has to face a far greater multiplicity of causes. The multiplicity exists not because of any intrinsic reasons, but because of three failures in our way of thinking. First, we have failed to distinguish between basic and superficial causes, thereby massively overestimating the number of causal forces that *appear* to be operating. Second, because of the emphasis on maximizing the statistical variance (or reducing chi-square, or whatever), we are driven toward introducing a large number of independent variables and therefore having theories that incorporate a large number of such causes. Third, our dependent variables are too complicated because we have not suitably abstracted out what the explanandum is. In many fields, one confronts a massive amount of "noise" and "random events." Consider evolution and the enormous amount of variation that exists. What occurs in such cases, however, is not an initial effort to account for every last bit of variation, but an attempt to develop a theory of variation and change. In social science, we have to develop a better grasp of what we want to explain and what is potentially explicable at a given point of knowledge. Among other things, this involves drawing distinctions between the noise and the signal, between the static and the message. What is it that we want to explain? But first, what is it that *can* be explained?

Notes

1: Introduction

1. Actually, there are all sorts of factors that keep Boyle's law from working exactly. For example, apparently PV declines somewhat when gas pressure is raised sufficiently.

2. To be sure, another approach would be possible if there was collective violence as opposed to the act of an individual. But again, one would face analogous questions about the probabilities of collective violence occurring in a specific locale.

2: Selectivity

1. The examples used in this chapter refer largely to the way in which selectivity among individuals can affect quasi-experimental studies that attempt to determine the effect of an institution on individuals. This is a matter of convenience and helpful in making the points clear. But the reader should keep in mind that the same points would apply on the macro level as well. If the dependent variable was an institution and if the independent variable was some major societal characteristic, the selectivity issue would still remain.

2. Among children whose families are in the highest income category ($38,000 or more), 19 percent attend private school. By contrast, 3 percent of those with incomes below $7,000 attend private school. (This is derived from the data shown in Table 3.5 of Coleman, Hoffer, and Kilgore, 1982a. The actual figures in each category were determined by applying the relevant percentage distributions to the numbers indicated for the sum of each column.)

3. Two outstanding exceptions—even to this day—are: the effort by Deutsch and Collins (1951: Chapter 4, Appendix B) to deal with selectivity as a possible influence in their evaluation of the impact of interracial housing on white attitudes toward blacks; and the discussion by Hyman (1955: 211–226) of self-selection in that and other studies.

4. Of course, selectivity could be operating on other dimensions as well, but that is another matter. We are interested here just in selectivity on factors influencing test scores.

3: Comparisons, Counterfactual Conditionals, and Contamination

1. The term "contamination" has a meaning here that is different from its usage in the pioneering methodological work by Hyman (1955), where he describes the errors generated by built-in design linkages between different independent variables or between an independent and dependent variable (pp. 179 ff.).

2. Note here how strong the evidence is on the linkage between Swedish fertility and these various political events. This is because of the exact timing that can be determined, with appropriate lags, in the case of fertility. Nevertheless, the general point about comparison is illustrated here. In this case, the timing of shifts in fertility is compared with both the timing of political events and with "normal" fertility fluctuations, that is, rates in previous years.

3. There is, incidentally, another issue—namely, the question of whether it is simply chance that the tax initiatives began when they did. Hence, there is the question of why the event to be studied occurred and whether that force might explain the consequent budget developments. In other words, to what degree is the initiative an "intervening variable" to begin with, with the causal thrust to be considered further back in the temporal order? To what degree is the theory too close to the specific events?

4. At the time of this writing, it is not yet possible to examine this matter in greater detail because of the lag between such events and the time involved before new budgets are prepared, go into effect, and are reported in some systematic fashion for each state.

5. Indeed, if they were organized and aware of the experiment, there would be an incentive to reduce outmigration in order to make the desegregated cities look "bad."

6. The years of the second and third largest annual immigration to the United States were respectively 1914 and 1913 (United States Bureau of the Census 1975: 105).

4: Asymmetrical Forms of Causation

1. The term "causal process" will be used here but, as the reader will see, this is not crucial. There is no need to get into the question of whether the current antipathy toward "causality" in physics needs to be imitated in the social sciences. Rather, let us simply follow Braithwaite (1968: 320): "When a person asks for a cause of a particular event (e.g., the fall of this picture to the floor at noon yesterday), what he is requesting is the specification of a preceding or simultaneous event which, in conjunction with certain unspecified cause factors of the nature of permanent conditions, is nomically sufficient to determine the occurrence of the event to be explained (the explicandum-event) in accordance with a causal law." Observe that there is reference here to simultaneous events as

well as chronological sequences. Invariant relationships in which there is no temporal sequence, such as Ohm's law or the principle of the lever, are certainly uniformities that are especially attractive to science (Cohen and Nagel 1934: 247–248). As we shall see, they are also found in the social sciences and are a type of irreversible causal process.

2. Another dimension to the symmetrical-asymmetrical distinction pertains to the *time* that it takes for the dependent variable to shift—for example, if the lag between changes in X_1 and changes in Y depends on the direction of the change in X_1. Under such circumstances, the influence of an increase in X_1 on Y may be different from the influence of a decrease in X_1 not in terms of the ultimate value of Y, but in terms of the time it takes to be reached. In other words, Y might move up faster than it moves down. However, for present purposes, it is sufficient to assume that changes are instantaneous. Likewise note that the discussion is also pertinent to nonrecursive causal relationships as well as the recursive relationships addressed here. There is no assurance in the nonrecursive case, for example, that the influence of Y on X_1 is truly reversible such that the upward movement of Y generates changes in X_1 comparable to the downward movement in Y across the same range of Y values.

3. After all, the assumption that the narrow range of events covered in any study will necessarily represent the full impact of one independent variable vs. another is highly questionable. In a certain sense, it entails the projection of a given relationship well beyond the range observed (whether that be linear or not) within the bounds covered.

4. This does not address the separate question of whether the gap can be removed. One must keep in mind the distinction between process and event. An irreversible process does not mean an irreversible event—rather, an irreversible process refers to a state of affairs that cannot be removed or changed simply by reversing the force that caused its initial occurrence. The historical origins of an ethnic or racial stratification system may be causally linked to certain basic characteristics of the economic system that existed at the time. These earlier needs may dissolve at a later point, but the ethnic hierarchy will tend to go on anyway. In the United States, for example, the decline in the need for blacks in the cotton fields did not reverse the changes that occurred earlier as a consequence of that need (Lieberson 1970: 179).

5. A set of programs that proved at best to be only partially successful.

6. A great deal of damage is done when social scientists act as if the validity of a constant force is determined by the inevitability of the outcome—a matter we shall consider in chapter 5, when variance is discussed.

7. This, of course, makes a counterfactual conditional assumption; in point of fact, there is no way of knowing since conditions are indeed not the same. It is even conceivable that the relationship would not have been reversible even if all other conditions were the same. The point is that other conditions change in the interim such that the initial causal variable reverses itself in noncomparable circumstances. Hence the reversibility of the relationship is prevented regardless of whether or not it is potentially so under conditions where everything else remains constant.

8. This is compatible with Ogburn's classic thesis about cultural lag (1950: 200—213) in the sense that events continue after their initial causes or functions disappear.

5: Variation, Level of Analysis, and the Research Question

1. Unless specified to the contrary, the terms "variation," "variance," and "variability" will be used interchangeably here to denote nonuniformity of values with respect to a given characteristic of interest to the researcher.

2. Winch (1958: 43) argues that, "the central problem of sociology, that of giving an account of the nature of social phenomena in general, itself belongs to philosophy. In fact . . . this part of sociology is really misbegotten epistemology . . . because its problems have been largely misconstrued, and therefore mishandled, as a species of scientific problem." See also the review of the ethnomethodological position presented in Coser 1975: 696—698.

3. To be sure, there is some recognition of a possible trade-off between goodness-of-fit and simplicity. See Fienberg 1977: 47.

4. So long as the values of X are at least minutely different from one another if they are associated with different values of Y.

5. All four clusters, taken together, accounted for an additional 4.5 percent of the variance (Spilerman 1970: 645).

6. The coin-tossing experiment has certain advantages over most social research situations simply because it is an experiment; hence it would be possible to determine whether the coins with apparent head-producing tendencies on the initial round maintained such tendencies on the second round. We often cannot do that in social research settings, although it is not unknown. In the nonexperimental social science research situation, we usually do not have anything analogous to a second round of observations—or, when we do, the conditions are sufficiently different to keep us from being as confident as we can be with the coins.

7. Just to make the analogy even closer to the typical nonexperimental social research situation, visualize a setting in which not all of the objects are dropped from the same height or necessarily with the same wind conditions. The situation will therefore become even more complicated and fitting; it all will be even more demanding. Yet all of the time there will be no concern with gravity per se.

8. There are procedures for estimating the conditions under which cross-level inference is more or less appropriate. See the approach suggested by Firebaugh 1982, as well as his review of earlier efforts.

9. Since the original examination, we have learned that higher-level inferences about lower-level processes are likely to magnify the effect of specification errors in the lower-level models (Hannan and Burstein 1974: 391) and the regression coefficient may be affected under some circumstances (Hammond 1973: 773).

10. This brief statement does not do justice to the Blaus' theoretical reasoning, but it is sufficient for the level of analysis issue under consideration here.

11. This ignores the technical issue involving that part of a nation's population not living in one of the metropolitan areas covered in the intercity analysis.

Let us just assume, for heuristic purposes, that all of the population in the nation lives in one or another of the metropolitan areas under study.

6: Control Variables

1. They also make it possible to determine the combined influence of a variety of causal factors on the dependent variable in situations where the different independent variables are themselves associated with one another. This feature will not be discussed here, but obviously points made about the net influence of a given independent variable are relevant to this too.

2. The controversy over black-white differences in IQ scores is not a topic that I want to debate in this book (see, however, Lieberson 1980: 135). But it is a great example of just this point about controls. To wit, much of the argument centers around controls that were omitted and the consequences of their inclusion for the influence of race on the test scores net of all sorts of other influences associated with race (e.g., SES, parental education, school opportunities, and cultural bias in the test).

3. This discussion, of course, ignores measurement errors and other problems of execution. It also ignores the possibility of other unmeasured differences operating (Situations VI and IX in Chart 2.1). But such a result does at least support the assumption that an analogue exists to the true experimental model.

4. When I say "affects," I do not necessarily mean that the X_1-Y relationship either disappears or is reversed, but simply that it changes to a statistically significant degree.

5. Strictly speaking, the study contrasted those children born when their mother and/or father was an adolescent with those children born when both parents were older. The latter category can include children born to parents who had another child earlier when they were adolescents. So the data refer to parental age at the time the specific child was born.

6. There could be a variety of combined effects in which both forces operate— for example, the two might pull on the dependent variable in opposite directions or they might both operate in the same direction.

7. This shift is due to the increased chance of a low SES destination among those in the P_h population who become pregnant as teenagers.

8. As was noted earlier, there would normally be no need to control for the independent variables if they were uncorrelated with the independent variable of interest.

9. In most multivariate approaches, even if the research is focused on the influence of a specific variable, an understanding is required of all associations that exist between any of the independent variables and/or between the specific dependent variable of interest and the controls.

10. If there is no association between X_1 and X_2, it is unnecessary to worry about the involvement of X_3 in the linkage. Of course, one would still remain concerned in the conventional control variable approach about the possibility of some unmeasured antecedent causal characteristic influencing the apparent linkage between X_1 and Y.

11. For convenience and to avoid needless detail, only comparisons between

means are discussed here. In point of fact, the careful researcher would consider the entire distribution of X_3 in each cell. But the comments made about means would apply to the total distributions as well.

12. This assumes that there are no other conditional factors differentiating within the parental educational categories and/or that they too do not affect the dependent variable of interest.

13. The basic source of Hauser's data is the Reiss and Rhodes 1957 study (see Hauser 1970: 646) which took place before there was widespread racial integration in Davidson County.

14. It is possible that school differences on these controls are substantially greater than those due to these forces. This is not trivial, but the researcher has to decide whether it is worth looking into.

15. Certain exceptions might exist to this general statement if we go into complicated interactive functions, but let us not worry about that here.

7: More about Current Practices

1. Accordingly, certain pernicious practices will be ignored here simply because they are errors in execution and do not represent an inherently erroneous conception of what social research can and should be.

2. It is not uncommon for researchers to pursue both of these goals, that is, obtain information about the state of affairs and then attempt to account for that state of affairs.

3. An interesting exchange exists between Hans Zeisel (1982a,b), on one side, and Rossi, Berk, and Lenihan (1982), on the other, with respect to the latter's 1980 book. I am in no position to evaluate the correctness of the charges and counterargument about the book; such an effort is beyond the purview of this volume. But regardless of whether the Zeisel claim is valid in this instance, he certainly illustrates how easy it is to misuse completely the control procedure. Prisoners about to be released from jail are randomly selected to receive or not receive a monthly monetary allowance. At issue is the question of whether ex-cons return to crime because they lack income in the first few months after their release. According to Zeisel, the recidivism rate is identical for the experimental and control groups. This seems to indicate clearly that financial help at the time of release—at least of the magnitude used in the experiment—will not lower the rearrest rate of ex-cons. In this case, Zeisel claims that the experimenters go on to a different conclusion. They observe that the test group is less likely to be employed than the control group and, in either group, those without work are more likely to return to crime. Hence, when one controls for differences between the two groups in their work rates—that is, cross-tabulates work experience by recidivism for each group—it turns out that the recidivism rates are slightly lower for those receiving payments. Thus, when one controls for work experience after release, as it were, it would look as if the introduction of payments reduces the recidivism rate when, in point of fact, the aggregate rates are identical for the two groups, and the differentials in work rates—which is what is being controlled in order to generate a favorable conclusion about the experimental group—are clearly due to the introduction of payments!

4. If strong conclusions cannot be drawn about the validity of one theory vs.

another in almost all social research situations, this is further support for my contention that there are grossly erroneous assumptions underlying contemporary social research. At one and the same time, researchers act as if their data ought to help evaluate the relative merits of different theories while recognizing the general inability to do so in most circumstances.

5. This is analogous in social research to the explanation of racial differences in income as opposed to the applied issue of increasing the relative income position of blacks.

6. Even if X_{28} were to be approached as an endogenous variable with its variation to be accounted for, ultimately one gets to exogenous variables in which their presence or levels are taken as givens. A moment's reflection will show that this is a sticky piece of business. On the one hand, obviously we cannot expect any researcher to go back infinitely in the causal chain; on the other hand, the point of origin should not be an arbitrary one, dictated by either the researcher's whims or the availability of data.

7. In more complicated cases, where there are biases in the situation, the testing materials may themselves also be dependent on the outcomes received by certain subsets of the population, that is, the tests used can be such as to generate a certain favorable outcome for some subsets of the population. This claim is often made in the area of race and ethnic relations with respect to the use of irrelevant tests for certain jobs.

8. This does not mean that no change is possible—far from it. But it will not be brought about by attempting to manipulate the superficial causal variables. See chapter 10 for a discussion of this matter.

8: And Now What?

1. Indeed, in some cases existing knowledge will generate work that will lead to its own eventual destruction or at least substantial revision. Moreover, as Sica (1983: 209) points out, it is hardly possible for a grand scheme of things to anticipate all of the intellectual turns and developments that might prove of value. It is pretentious even to think of formalizing the extraordinarily complicated and vital thought process that, out of ignorance, we are forced to label "intuition."

9: Rethinking Causality

1. Or, in the less than perfect case of asymmetry, changes in one direction for X will produce much smaller changes in Y than occur when X changes in the opposite direction. This takes place even over the same range of X values; it is not simply a case where Y is a nonlinear function of X such that unit shifts in X have varying effects on the changes in Y. If a nonlinear function was purely symmetrical, then Y would return to its initial value as X moved in the opposite direction back to its initial level. This would not occur in an asymmetrical relationship. Hence the symmetry of a relationship is not to be confused with the linearity of the form.

2. In that case, some other independent variable would have to operate for the changes in Y to be reversed when X is shifting in its nonresponsive direction.

Again, an asymmetrical causal relationship does not mean that the dependent variable cannot be changed or reversed. Rather, it means that a specific independent variable will change the dependent variable in only one direction. Some other independent variable will have to operate for the changes in Y to be reversed.

3. By "probabilistic" I mean theories formulated or tested such that the presence of a given condition increases or decreases the probability of some consequence, but not in an all-or-nothing absolute way. Exceptions are not per se taken as disproof but rather as indications that the theory does not (for whatever reason) account for all of the observed variation in the dependent variable.

4. These criticisms do not apply to cross-sectional data when the conditions have been randomly introduced, such as would occur under true experimental situations.

5. To be sure, these great changes would not always be visible at an early stage of their development or even distinguishable from other developments that prove to be of a minor nature.

6. If the dependent variable is nominal, in similar fashion its presence or absence in a given category will not be affected.

7. In the case of a basic causal relationship that is asymmetrical, changes in one direction in X will lead to no changes in Y and this will not be distinguishable from what would occur if it was a superficial causal linkage. But changes in the opposite direction would lead to true changes in Y if a basic cause was operating, whereas changes in direction would have no impact on Y if the apparent causal linkage was superficial.

8. Note here that it is a different matter to question the logic of a proposed principle. Issues involving redundancy, circularity, meaning, consistency, and the like, are always appropriate.

9. And then we would have the question of whether indeed it is a theory.

10: From Controls to Outcomes

1. Coleman, Hoffer, and Kilgore (1981b: 529) deal with this issue directly and observe that the results are changed when their full set of seventeen controls is applied. However, as they themselves note, these include seven that are not clearly prior variables. At any rate, we are told that the differences are then reduced, but the authors do not specify by how much or whether there is still any significant gap remaining. Rather, they do note that gaps for sixth-grade expectations are almost entirely eliminated after these controls are applied. That is interesting, but it still does not answer the question at hand about eighth-grade expectations.

2. If these other attributes had been found to affect the dependent variable, they would have been considered as relevant controls.

References

Allen, Roy George Douglas. *Mathematical Analysis for Economists*. London: Macmillan, 1956.

Asch, Solomon E. "Effects of Group Pressure upon the Modification and Distortion of Judgments." In *Readings in Social Psychology*, 3d ed., edited by Eleanor E. Maccoby, Theodore M. Newcomb, and Eugene L. Hartley, pp. 174–183. New York: Rinehart and Winston, 1958.

Barbour, Ian G. "Science and Religion Today." In *Science and Religion*, edited by Ian G. Barbour, pp. 3–17. New York: Harper & Row, 1968.

Barnow, Burt S., and Glen G. Cain. "A Reanalysis of the Effect of Head Start on Cognitive Development: Methodology and Empirical Findings." *Journal of Human Resources* 12 (1977): 177–197.

Barnow, Burt S., Glen G. Cain, and Arthur S. Goldberger. "Issues in the Analysis of Selectivity Bias." In *Evaluation Studies Review Annual*, vol. 5, edited by E. W. Stromsdorfer and G. Farkas, pp. 43–59. Beverly Hills, Calif.: Sage Publications, 1980.

Bascom, Willard. *Waves and Beaches*. Garden City, N.Y.: Anchor Books, 1964.

Blalock, Hubert M., Jr. *Causal Inferences in Nonexperimental Research*. Chapel Hill: University of North Carolina Press, 1961.

Blau, Judith R., and Peter M. Blau. "The Cost of Inequality: Metropolitan Structure and Violent Crime." *American Sociological Review* 47 (1982): 114–129.

Blau, Peter M. *Inequality and Heterogeneity*. New York: Free Press, 1977.

Bottomore, T. B. *Critics of Society: Radical Thought in North America*. New York: Pantheon, 1968.

Braithwaite, Richard Bevan. *Scientific Explanation*. London: Cambridge University Press, 1968.

Brown, Julia S., and Brian G. Gilmartin. "Sociology Today: Lacunae, Emphases, and Surfeits." *American Sociologist* 4 (1969): 283–291.

Bryk, Anthony S. "Disciplined Inquiry or Policy Argument?" *Harvard Educational Review* 51 (1981): 497–509.

Bryk, Anthony S., and H. I. Weisberg. "Use of the Nonequivalent Control Group Design When Subjects are Growing." *Psychological Bulletin* 84 (1977): 950–962.

Burgess, Ernest W. "Basic Social Data." In *Chicago: An Experiment in Social Science Research*, edited by T. V. Smith and Leonard D. White, pp. 47–66. Chicago: University of Chicago Press, 1929.

Burtt, Edwin A. *Metaphysical Foundations of Modern Physical Science*. Garden City, N.Y.: Doubleday, 1954.

Campbell, Donald T., and Albert Erlebacher. "How Regression Artifacts in Quasi-Experimental Evaluations Can Mistakenly Make Compensatory Education Look Harmful." In *Disadvantaged Child, vol. 3*, edited by Jerome Hellmuth, pp. 185–210. New York: Brunner/Mazel, 1970.

Campbell, Donald T., and Julian Stanley. *Experimental and Quasi-Experimental Designs for Research*. Chicago: Rand McNally, 1966.

Card, Josefina J. "Long-Term Consequences for Children of Teenage Parents." *Demography* 18 (1981): 137–156.

Carlsson, G. "Social Trends and Human Decision: Discretionary Change As a Field of Research." In *Theory and Methods in Behavioral Sciences*, edited by Paul Lindblom, pp. 129–146. Stockholm: Scandinavian University Books, 1970.

———. "Lagged Structures and Cross-Sectional Methods." *Acta Sociologica* 15 (1972): 323–341.

Cohen, Jacob, and Patricia Cohen. *Applied Multiple Regression/Correlation Analysis for the Behavioral Sciences*. Hillsdale, N.J.: Lawrence Erlbaum Associates, 1975.

Cohen, Morris R., and Ernest Nagel. *An Introduction to Logic and Scientific Method*. New York: Harcourt, Brace and Co., 1934.

Coleman, James S. "Collective Decisions." *Sociological Inquiry* 34 (1964): 166–181.

———. "Liberty and Equality in School Desegregation." *Social Policy* 6 (1976): 9–13.

———. "Population Stability and Equal Rights." *Society* 14 (1977): 34–35.

Coleman, James S., Ernest Q. Campbell, Carol J. Hobson, James McPartland, Alexander M. Mood, Frederic D. Weinfeld, and Robert L. York. *Equality of Educational Opportunity*. Washington, D.C.: U.S. Government Printing Office, 1966.

Coleman, James S., Thomas Hoffer, and Sally Kilgore. "Questions and Answers: Our Response." *Harvard Educational Review* 51 (1981): 526–545.

———. *High School Achievement: Public, Catholic and Other Private Schools Compared*. New York: Basic Books, 1982a.

———. "Achievement and Segregation in Secondary Schools: A Further Look at Public and Private School Differences." *Sociology of Education* 55 (1982b): 162–182.

Coleman, James S., Sara D. Kelly, and John A. Moore. *Trends in School Segregation, 1968–73*. Washington, D.C.: Urban Institute, 1975.

Committee on Research. "Report." *American Sociological Review* 23 (1958): 704–711.

Cook, Thomas D., Hilary Appleton, Ross Conner, Ann Shaffer, Gary Tamkin, and Stephen J. Weber. *"Sesame Street" Revisited.* New York: Russell Sage Foundation, 1975.

Cook, Thomas D., and Donald T. Campbell. *Quasi-Experimentation: Design and Analysis Issues for Field Settings.* Chicago: Rand McNally, 1979.

Cootner, Paul H., ed. *The Random Character of Stock Market Prices,* rev. ed. Cambridge, Mass.: M.I.T. Press, 1964.

Coser, Lewis. "Two Methods in Search of Substance." *American Sociological Review* 40 (1975): 691−700.

———. "Reply to my Critics." *American Sociologist* 11 (1976): 33−38.

Costner, Herbert L. "Prologue." In *Sociological Methodology, 1971,* edited by Herbert L. Costner, pp. ix−xvi. San Francisco: Jossey-Bass, 1971.

Cronback, L. J., D. R. Ragosa, R. E. Floden, and G. G. Price. *Analysis of Covariance in Nonrandomized Experiments: Parameters Affecting Bias.* Stanford, Calif.: Stanford Evaluation Consortium, 1977.

Croxton, Frederick E., and Dudley J. Cowden. *Applied General Statistics.* New York: Prentice-Hall, 1939.

Deutsch, Morton, and Mary Evans Collins. *Interracial Housing.* Minneapolis: University of Minnesota Press, 1951.

Duncan, Otis Dudley. *Introduction to Structural Equation Models.* New York: Academic Press, 1975.

Durkheim, Emile. *The Rules of Sociological Method.* Glencoe, Ill.: Free Press, 1950.

Ewbank, Douglas C. *Age Misreporting and Age-Selective Underenumeration: Sources, Patterns, and Consequences for Demographic Analysis.* Washington, D.C.: National Academy Press, 1981.

Farley, Reynolds. "Is Coleman Right?" *Social Policy* 6 (1976): 14−23.

Featherman, David L. "Coser's '. . . In Search of Substance.' " *American Sociologist* 11 (1976): 21−27.

Fienberg, Stephen E. *The Analysis of Cross-Classified Categorical Data.* Cambridge, Mass.: MIT Press, 1977.

Firebaugh, Glenn. "Cross-National Versus Historical Regression Models: Conditions of Equivalence in Comparative Analysis." *Comparative Social Research* 3 (1980): 333−344.

Fishman, Joshua A., Robert L. Cooper, and Andrew W. Conrad. *The Spread of English.* Rowley, Mass.: Newbury House, 1977.

Galtung, Johan. *Theory and Methods of Social Research.* Oslo, Norway: Universitetsforlaget, 1967.

Goldberger, Arthur S. "Selection Bias in Evaluating Treatment Effects: The Case of Interaction." *Discussion Papers,* Institute for Research on Poverty, University of Wisconsin, 1972.

Goldberger, Arthur S., and Glen G. Cain. "The Causal Analysis of Cognitive Outcomes in the Coleman, Hoffer, and Kilgore Report." *Sociology of Education* 55 (1982): 103−122.

Greeley, Andrew M. *Catholic High Schools and Minority Students.* New Brunswick, N.J.: Transaction Books, 1982.

Griliches, Zvi, and William M. Mason. "Education, Income, and Ability." In *Structural Equation Models in the Social Sciences,* edited by Arthur S. Goldberger and Otis Dudley Duncan, pp. 285−316. New York: Seminar Press, 1973.

Grüner, Rolf. *Theory and Power: On the Character of Modern Science.* Amsterdam: B. R. Grüner Publishing Co., 1977.

Hagood, Margaret Jarman. *Statistics for Sociologists.* New York: Reynal and Hitchcock, 1941.

Hamblin, Robert L., R. Brooke Jacobsen, and Jerry L. L. Miller. *A Mathematical Theory of Social Change.* New York: Wiley, 1973.

Hammond, John L. "Two Sources of Error in Ecological Correlations." *American Sociological Review* 38 (1973): 764—777.

Hannan, Michael T., and Leigh Burstein. "Estimation from Grouped Observations." *American Sociological Review* 39 (1974): 374—392.

Hanushek, Eric A., and John E. Jackson. *Statistical Methods for Social Scientists.* New York: Academic Press, 1977.

Harris, Marlys. "Why Private Schools Can Pay Off." *Money* 10 (1981): 92—98.

Hauser, Robert M. "Context and Consex: A Cautionary Tale." *American Journal of Sociology* 75 (1970): 645—664.

Heckman, James J. "Sample Selection Bias As a Specification Error." *Econometrica* 47 (1979): 153—161.

Hirschi, Travis, and Hanan C. Selvin. *Principles of Survey Analysis.* New York: Free Press, 1973.

Homans, George C. *The Human Groups.* New York: Harcourt, Brace & World, 1950.

Hope, Keith. "A Counterfactual Theory of Comparative Mobility Analysis." Unpublished manuscript, Nuffield College, Oxford, 1980.

Hovland, Carl I. "Reconciling Conflicting Results Derived from Experimental and Survey Studies of Attitude Change." In *Continuities in the Language of Social Research,* edited by Paul F. Lazarsfeld, Ann K. Pasanella, and Morris Rosenberg, pp. 439—462. New York: Free Press, 1972.

Hyman, Herbert. *Survey Design and Analysis: Principles, Cases and Procedures.* Glencoe, Ill.: Free Press, 1955.

Jensen, Gary F., and Dean G. Rojek. *Delinquency: A Sociological View.* Lexington, Mass.: D. C. Heath, 1980.

Jöreskog, K. G. "A General Method for Analysis of Covariance Structures." *Biometrika* 57 (1970): 239—251.

Jöreskog, K. G., and D. Sorbom. *LISREL IV: Analysis of Linear Structural Relationships by the Method of Maximum Likelihood: Users Guide.* Chicago: International Educational Services, 1978.

Kaplan, Abraham. *The Conduct of Inquiry: Methodology for Behavioral Science.* San Francisco: Chandler Publishing Co., 1964.

Kenny, David A., and Steven H. Cohen. "A Reexamination of Selection and Growth Processes in the Nonequivalent Control Group Design." In *Sociological Methodology, 1980,* edited by Karl F. Schuessler, pp. 290—313. San Francisco: Jossey-Bass, 1979.

Kleck, Gary. "Racial Discrimination in Criminal Sentencing: A Critical Evaluation of the Evidence with Additional Evidence on the Death Penalty." *American Sociological Review* 46 (1981): 783—805.

Klineberg, Otto. *Negro Intelligence and Selective Migration.* New York: Columbia University Press, 1935.

Kuhn, Thomas S. *The Structure of Scientific Revolutions*. Chicago: University of Chicago Press, 1962.

Lasker, Gabriel W., and Robert N. Tyzzer. *Physical Anthropology*. 3d ed. New York: Holt, Rinehart and Winston, 1982.

Lazarsfeld, Paul F., Ann K. Pasanella, and Morris Rosenberg, eds. *Continuities in the Language of Social Research*. New York: Free Press, 1972.

Lewis, David K. *Counterfactuals*. Cambridge, Mass.: Harvard University Press, 1973.

Lieberson, Stanley. "Stratification and Ethnic Groups." *Sociological Inquiry* 40 (1970): 172−181.

————. "An Empirical Study of Military-Industrial Linkages." *American Journal of Sociology* 76 (1971): 562−584.

————. "A Reconsideration of the Income Differences Found between Migrants and Northern-born Blacks." *American Journal of Sociology* 83 (1978):940−966.

————. *A Piece of the Pie: Blacks and White Immigrants Since 1880*. Berkeley: University of California Press, 1980.

————. *Language Diversity and Language Contact*. Stanford, Calif.: Stanford University Press, 1981.

Lieberson, Stanley, Guy Dalto, and Mary Ellen Marsden. "The Course of Mother Tongue Diversity in Nations." *American Journal of Sociology* 81 (1975):34−61.

Lieberson, Stanley, and Lynn K. Hansen. "National Development, Mother Tongue Diversity, and the Comparative Study of Nations." *American Sociological Review* 39 (1974): 523−541.

Lieberson, Stanley, and Arnold R. Silverman. "The Precipitants and Underlying Conditions of Race Riots." *American Sociological Review* 30 (1965): 887−898.

Lord, Frederich M. "Statistical Adjustment When Comparing Preexisting Groups." *Psychological Bulletin* 72 (1969): 336−337.

Lösch, August. *The Economics of Location*. New Haven, Conn.: Yale University Press, 1954.

Lysander, A. "Krigshändelser och födelsefrekvens." *Svenska Läkartidningen* 38 (1941): 1045−1050.

Mason, William M. "On the Socioeconomic Effects of Military Service." Unpublished doctoral dissertation, Department of Sociology, University of Chicago, 1970.

Merton, Robert K. "Discrimination and the American Creed." In *Discrimination and National Welfare*, edited by Robert M. MacIver, pp. 99−126. New York: Harper & Row, 1949.

————. *Social Theory and Social Structure*. rev. ed. Glencoe, Ill.: Free Press, 1957.

Michels, Robert. *Political Parties: A Sociological Study of the Oligarchical Tendencies of Modern Democracy*. Glencoe, Ill.: Free Press, 1958.

Mosteller, Frederick, and Daniel P. Moynihan, eds. *On Equality of Educational Opportunity*. New York: Random House, 1972.

Mueller, John H., Karl Schuessler, and Herbert Costner. *Statistical Reasoning in Sociology*. 3d ed. Boston: Houghton Mifflin, 1977.

Murnane, Richard J. "Evidence, Analysis, and Unanswered Questions." *Harvard Educational Review* 51 (1981): 483−489.

Nagel, Ernest. *The Structure of Science: Problems in the Logic of Scientific Explanation.* New York: Harcourt, Brace & World, 1961.

Nagel, Ernest, ed. *John Stuart Mill's Philosophy of Scientific Method.* New York: Hafner, 1950.

Nordtvedt, Kenneth L., Jr., James E. Faller, and Jesse W. Beams. "Gravitation." In *Encyclopaedia Britannica, Macropaedia, vol. 8.* Chicago: Encyclopaedia Britannica, 1974.

Nowak, Stefan. *Methodology of Sociological Research: General Problems.* Dordrecht, Holland: D. Reidel, 1977.

Nute, Donald. *Topics in Conditional Logic.* Dordrecht, Holland: D. Reidel, 1980.

Ogburn, William F. *Social Change: With Respect to Culture and Original Nature.* New York: Viking Press, 1950.

Olsen, R. J. "A Least Squares Correction for Selectivity Bias." *Econometrica* 8 (1980): 1815–1820.

Petersen, William. *Population.* 3d ed. New York: Macmillan, 1975.

Pollock, John L. *Subjunctive Reasoning.* Dordrecht, Holland: D. Reidel, 1976.

Popper, Karl R. *The Poverty of Historicism.* New York: Harper, 1964.

Prigogine, Ilya. *From Being To Becoming.* San Francisco: W. H. Freeman, 1980.

Radelet, Michael L. "Racial Characteristics and the Imposition of the Death Penalty." *American Sociological Review* 46 (1981): 918–927.

Reid, Sue Titus. *Crime and Criminology.* New York: Holt, Rinehart and Winston, 1979.

Reiss, Albert J., Jr., and Albert Lewis Rhodes. "A Sociopsychological Study of Adolescent Conformity and Deviation." Summary of report of completed research, U.S. Office of Education, project # 507, 1959. [Cited in Hauser, 1970.]

Reitz, Jeffrey G. *The Survival of Ethnic Groups.* Toronto, Canada: McGraw-Hill Ryerson, 1980.

Rindfuss, Ronald R., John Shelton Reed, and Craig St. John. "A Fertility Reaction to a Historical Event: Southern White Birthrates and the 1954 Desegregation Ruling." In *Demography of Racial and Ethnic Groups,* edited by Frank D. Bean and W. Parker Frisbie, pp. 213–220. New York: Academic Press, 1978.

Robinson, William S. "Ecological Correlations and the Behavior of Individuals." *American Sociological Review* 15 (1950): 351–357.

Rosenberg, Morris. "Dispositional Concepts in Behavioral Science." In *Qualitative and Quantitative Social Research: Papers in Honor of Paul F. Lazarsfeld,* edited by Robert K. Merton, James S. Coleman, and Peter H. Rossi, pp. 245–260. New York: Free Press, 1979.

Rossi, Peter H., Richard A. Berk, and Kenneth J. Lenihan. *Money, Work, and Crime: Experimental Evidence.* New York: Academic Press, 1980.

―――. "Saying It Wrong with Figures: A Comment on Zeisel." *American Journal of Sociology* 88 (1982): 390–393.

Salmon, Wesley C. *Statistical Explanation and Statistical Relevance.* Pittsburgh: University of Pittsburgh Press, 1971.

Sellitz, Claire, Lawrence S. Wrightsman, and Stuart W. Cook. *Research Methods in Social Relations.* 3d ed. New York: Holt, Rinehart and Winston, 1976.

Shenton, Herbert Newhard. *Cosmopolitan Conversation*. New York: Columbia University Press, 1933.

Sica, Alan. "Parsons, Jr." *American Journal of Sociology* 89 (1983): 200–219.

Simmel, Georg. *The Sociology of Georg Simmel*. Glencoe, Ill.: Free Press, 1950.

Smith, H. W. *Strategies of Social Research: The Methodological Imagination*. 2d ed. Englewood Cliffs, N.J.: Prentice-Hall, 1981.

Smith, Marshall S. "*Equality of Educational Opportunity*: The Basic Findings Reconsidered." In *On Equality of Educational Opportunity*, edited by Frederick Mosteller and Daniel P. Moynihan, pp. 230–342. New York: Random House, 1972.

Smith, T. V., and Leonard D. White, eds. *Chicago: An Experiment in Social Science Research*. Chicago: University of Chicago Press, 1929.

Spilerman, Seymour. "The Causes of Racial Disturbances: A Comparison of Alternative Explanations." *American Sociological Review* 35 (1970): 627–649.

———. "The Causes of Racial Disturbances: Tests of an Explanation." *American Sociological Review* 36 (1971): 427–442.

Stalnaker, Robert. "A Theory of Conditionals." *American Philosophical Quarterly*, monograph series 2 (1968): 98–112.

Treiman, Donald J. *Occupational Prestige in Comparative Perspective*. New York: Academic Press, 1977.

U.S. News & World Report. "Taxpayer Revolt: Where It's Spreading Now." *U.S. News & World Report* (June 26, 1978), pp. 16–19.

United States Bureau of the Census. *Historical Statistics of the United States, Colonial Times to 1970, Bicentennial Edition, Part 1*. Washington, D.C.: U.S. Government Printing Office, 1975.

Waite, Linda J., and Kristin A. Moore. "The Impact of an Early First Birth on Young Women's Educational Attainment." *Social Forces* 56 (1978): 845–865.

Wallace, T. Dudley. "Pretest Estimation in Regression: A Survey." *American Journal of Agricultural Economics* 59 (1977): 431–443.

Weber, Max. *The Protestant Ethic and the Spirit of Capitalism*. New York: Scribner's, 1958.

Weisberg, H. I. "Statistical Adjustments and Uncontrolled Studies." *Psychological Bulletin* 86 (1979): 1149–1164.

Weisskopf, Victor F. "Frontiers and Limits of Physical Science." *Bulletin of the American Academy of Arts and Sciences* 35 (1981): 4–23.

Wildavsky, Aaron. "What Would One Have to Believe to Believe in Multiple Regression?" *Contemporary Psychology* 27 (1982): 903–904.

Winch, Peter. *The Idea of a Social Science and Its Relation to Philosophy*. London: Routledge and Kegan Paul, 1958.

Yule, G. Udny, and M. G. Kendall. *An Introduction to the Theory of Statistics*. 14th ed. London: Charles Griffin, 1950.

Zeisel, Hans. "Disagreement over the Evaluation of a Controlled Experiment." *American Journal of Sociology* 88 (1982a): 378–389.

———. "Hans Zeisel Concludes the Debate." *American Journal of Sociology* 88 (1982b): 394–396.

Index

Designer: UC Press Staff
Compositor: Trend-Western
Printer: Edwards Bros., Inc.
Binder: Edwards Bros., Inc.
Text: 11/13 Garamond
Display: Garamond